Drawing the Line

Art Therapy with the Difficult Client

Lisa B. Moschini

WILEY

John Wiley & Sons, Inc.

Library of Congress Cataloging-in-Publication Data

Moschini, Lisa B.
    Drawing the line : art therapy with the difficult client / Lisa B. Moschini
        p. cm.
    ISBN 0-471-68773-1 (pbk./CD-ROM)
        1. Art therapy. 2. Drawing—Therapeutic use. 3. Psychotherapist and patient. I. Title.
RC489.A7M675 2005
615.9'5156—dc22
                                                                                    2004049161

Printed in the United States of America

10 9 8 7 6 5 4 3 2 1

*This book is dedicated to the treasures of my youth:
to my father, the late Giuliano P. Moschini, for you held my hand;
and to my mother, Josephine, for you taught me to be myself.
Together you provided a precious balance of wisdom, love, and compassion.*

Contents

Contents

Tables

Illustrations

Preface

Who is the difficult client? Often, therapists classify these clients according to groupings:

- Children
- Adults
- Criminals
- Psychotics
- Borderlines

Or perhaps just subcategories of these groups:

- Children who refuse to talk
- Adults who don't accept responsibility
- Criminals who rape
- Psychotics who regress
- Borderlines who both love and reject

The difficult client is frequently defined on the basis of the therapist's beliefs, morals, prejudices, fears, and worries: a self-concept of the therapist projected onto the client or a label that protects the therapist's feelings of helplessness when he or she is faced with a client who is resistant to the process of therapy. As people, we want to be liked and well regarded; as therapists, we want to be effective. Yet the difficult client does not engender those feelings. Instead the interaction is often distant, demanding, and frustrating.

Drawing the Line: Art Therapy with the Difficult Client is an examination of how the blending of expressive arts and psychotherapy can both support and enhance the professional in his or her clinical practice.

I have endeavored to write this book with both the mental health professional and the novice in mind. Therefore, I explain not only the fundamental principles and techniques of art therapy but also how to effectively merge the tradition of art psychotherapy with that of conventional verbal therapy.

Designed as a look from within as well as without, this book offers practical and theoretical information on defense mechanisms; developmental stage theories; projective testing and drawing analysis; art therapy directives; and case histories from individual, group, and family art therapy. Additionally, it is filled with voices and artwork taken directly from my fourteen years of experience as a licensed marriage family therapist with a master's degree in clinical art therapy.

The difficult client requires a specialized approach, and it is my hope that the methods offered herein will benefit both the therapist and the client in the therapeutic process.

Lisa B. Moschini, MA, LMFT

Acknowledgments

I would like to extend my deepest appreciation to the following people for their gracious assistance, support, and patience.

Lisa Sedgwick
Ann Miller
Devra Brewer
Tina Posey
JoAnn Smulick
Dr. David Fennell
Bob and Martha Brewer
Brynn Barge
Lance Daur
Alicia Golchuck
Jennifer Long
Mark McGonigle

Kevin Wilson
Soojin Kim
Tanner Barge
Dayle Dempsey
Frankie Dugan
Madison Long
Stephen G. Moschini
Trent Posey
Eden Sedgwick
Mandy Womble
Richard Maynard
Wanda Newton

A Difficult Client Defined

Drawing the Line: Art Therapy with the Difficult Client is intended for all who have felt frustration when faced with a resistant or difficult client. In my experience as a practicing therapist, supervisor, and lecturer I have had the opportunity to listen to a myriad of clinicians discuss this very topic. What defines the difficult client? Is there a set of criteria that can be applied to the whole of the population? One common definition that fits each individual?

In fourteen years of clinical practice that singular definition has remained elusive. Instead, what I have found is a common reaction or affect-laden response centered on the therapist's exasperation. A feeling of helplessness sometimes embedded in anger, at other times couched in pleas for assistance. A threat to the clinician's own confidence. At this point, we have become not only the transference object but also an object of countertransference: A response to the patient-therapist interaction based on emotional feelings.

So now the question takes on further complexity. How can we as clinicians provide opportunities of growth for both our clients and ourselves?

One answer is art psychotherapy.

As a psychodynamic therapist I believe development is epigenetic and take note of the unconscious processes that drive the individual as he or she maneuvers through his or her environment. As an art psychotherapist, I have learned to interpret these unconscious and repetitious symbols. Thus, the visual experience takes the place of language as a nonverbal means of communication. A picture always speaks the truth. Regardless of age or

1

ability, art never lies. It may reveal only one side, one moment within the here and now, one facet, but that facet is the truth.

To that end I invite each reader to participate in a brief and very personal expression, for without looking within ourselves how are we to help others? Without understanding there can be no growth.

To begin you will need two sheets of white drawing paper preferably no smaller than 8" × 10", a set of markers, a sheet of lined paper, and at least 30 to 45 minutes of uninterrupted time. I now ask you to find a safe, quiet, and comfortable area where you can complete the following assignment.

1. On the first sheet of paper draw the best person that you can. Make certain that you draw the entire body, not just a floating head or a stick figure.
2. Once that is complete, name your person by writing the name on the paper.
3. On the second sheet of paper draw the best opposite-gendered person (i.e., if you drew a male, now draw a female) you can. Make certain that you draw the entire body, not just a floating head or a stick figure.
4. Once that is complete, name your person by writing the name on the paper.
5. On the lined paper answer the following questions about your drawings:
   a. Describe each figure; be as specific as possible. Include their likes, dislikes, pet peeves, interests, goals, vocation. Imagine you were talking to a friend about these people—what would you say?
   b. How did you feel while drawing? What were you thinking?
   c. Write something else about each person.
   d. Looking at the drawings, what do you think?

At this juncture, as awkward as it may seem, take your drawings and the lined sheet of paper and place them in a safe area. We will be discussing them in detail in Chapter 3, and you will retrieve them at that time. However, if you cannot wait, feel free to jump forward to Part 2 and join me in assessment procedures.

In this book I introduce the clinician to the power of art and its use with a difficult client. Consequently, I will focus on the theoretical constructs that form the basis of psychotherapy, practical solutions for assessment and treatment, and case history reviews (in all instances, identifying information has been changed to protect the clients). This book will offer the reader, regardless of your training or experience, a direction to take when verbal therapy has failed and will allow you to see through walls built over many years. I hope that it will also serve as an adjunct to your work with any number of clients, outside of those outlined in this book, and in so doing offer creative venues into the unconscious, where therapy can blossom.

In the end, how do I define the difficult client? The difficult client lies within each of us—our beliefs, morals, prejudices, fears, and worries—our self-concept.

Ultimately, the definition of a difficult client comes from a difficult source—from within each of us.

In the Beginning

Pictures, symbols, signs—that was the language of man. Long before words held meaning we communicated through art. On the walls of caves, images of animals were drawn one over the other. The Egyptians rendered living stories within their tombs and temples, while the Greeks depicted emotion on painted pottery. Even written language is based on the use of symbols. "Writing . . . was originally an independent language, as it has remained to this day in China. Writing seems to have consisted originally of pictures, which generally became conventionalized, coming in time to represent syllables, and finally letters" (Russell, 1921, words and meaning section, para. 5). On and on art symbolized an individual's thoughts, feelings, realities, and fantasies.

Art has always held a power over humans—the power to connect, to cleanse, and, lest we forget, to intensify. As an example, a drawing of a hand would be identified by all as a hand, even though the language might be different. Yet the spoken word can have numerous definitions. Chase (1956), using the above example, writes, "Take the word "hand." In 'his hand' it refers to a location on the human body, in 'hour hand' to a strikingly dissimilar object, in 'all hands on deck' to another reference, in 'a good hand at gardening' to another" (p. 260). Thus, over time language has become attached to what we have come to understand. It shifts, it changes, it's denied, it's distorted, and ultimately it can be exceedingly deceptive.

As we discuss the intellectualization of language, this is the point where art therapy flourishes. In a moment it breaks through our very human defenses and allows us to see within the recesses of our psyche. Let's take the phrase "A picture is worth a thousand words" and apply it to a self-portrait. Figure I.1 was rendered by a preteen who was instructed to paint a self-portrait using only shape and color (see disk to view in color).

One does not require words to feel this child's pain. A darkened, red figure, a floating headless body with open mouth, cries into the abyss. The

I.1 Self-Portrait

symbol overwhelms in its intensity. The product is permanent. Reviewed without distortion it is a memory recorded for all to see and revisit, a painting that allows us to feel and experience another's reality. This rendering was the child's symbol for a sexual assault. It rose from her need to express a traumatic experience. These thoughts, so very difficult to communicate verbally, were symbolized safely through the art.

As a therapist, think of the times you have expected your clients to discuss intimate, embarrassing, or traumatic secrets. Would you be willing to share one of yours with a professional? A stranger? In detail? Yet that is exactly what we request of every new client. The beauty of art therapy lies in its ability to break through the verbal defenses acquired over a lifetime. Art, being a less customary form of communication, allows the unconscious to break forward. Thus, material in any expressive or evocative therapy that is important will repeat.

> Symbols communicate inhibitions; they often evoke memories repressed in earlier life. At the same time they address a motif that points to the future. The symbol, as the focal point of psychic development, is the foundation of creative development in a therapeutic process. (Kast, 1989, p. 27)

In times past, man symbolized everything in order to make sense of the world. Lacking scientific knowledge, humans relied upon primeval beliefs. Fiske (1870) writes:

In the original conception the world is itself a gigantic tortoise swimming in a boundless ocean; the flat surface of the earth is the lower plate which covers the reptile's belly; the rounded shell which covers his back is the sky; and the human race lives and moves and has its being inside of the tortoise . . . they [Indians] regard the tortoise as the symbol of the world, and address it as the mother of mankind. (myths of the barbaric world section, para. 33)

These primeval beliefs stretched across continents and formed common legends in places where people had no contact with one another. Fiske has written extensively on this subject, and here I will outline one example. He notes that the legend of William Tell was found among those in Denmark, Norway, Finland, Russia, Persia, England, Iceland, and India. He further goes on to relate that the Turks and Mongolians, despite never having held a book, could recite the legend intact in relation to one of their own tribesmen. As though this were not enough, he outlines a poem of Farid-Uddin Attar, born in 1119, that revolves around a prince who shoots an apple from the head of his page. This phenomenon correlates to what Freud called "archaic remnants" and what Jung, taking one step further, identified with the term "archetypes" or "primordial images." In its most simplistic definition an archetype is made up of basic symbols or images without a known origin. These innate ideas may vary in content, but their basic pattern remains intact. Edward Carpenter (1920), in his book *Pagan and Christian Creeds: Their Origin and Meaning*, agrees wholeheartedly with Jung and states, "Deep, deep in the human mind there is that burning blazing light of the world-consciousness—so deep indeed that the vast majority of individuals are hardly aware of its existence" (rites of expiation and redemption section, para. 4).

The fundamental importance of these collective images will become all too clear when we discuss assessments and assessment procedures. However, at the present time suffice it to say that "symbols address our intellect much less than they do our universal perspective and our relatedness to the invisible reality that transcends us" (Kast, 1989, p. 13). They lie in our dreams and in our art. Symbolism is our guide to the truth.

Interaction Is the Key

Anna Freud (1946) writes, "The technique of translating symbols is a short cut to understanding, or, more correctly, a way of plunging from the highest strata of consciousness to the lowest strata of the unconscious without pausing" (p. 16). As such, the art production allows the therapist to respond to the covert, as well as the overt, aspects of a client's psyche.

An example is the mask completed by an adolescent male. This client's history included physical abuse as well as severe neglect before he was in preschool. In describing his home life he stated, "It was a hell hole." By the age of seven he had been removed from his home environment and placed into foster homes, group homes, and residential treatment settings. As a "multiple failure placement youth" he was grandiose, hostile, and impulsive. His mistrust, coupled with his intelligence, had only provided a forum for manipulation in verbal therapy. In an effort to break through these well-honed defenses he was given a papier maché mask and asked to paint on the outside "What I show the world."

The left side of Figure I.2, completed in the first session, had the client mixing a rust color carefully and meticulously. In our second session he stated he needed to "add" to the mask and proceeded to spray the front with red glitter spray (right side of Figure I.2) and add two strands of hair. Immersed in the process, he never spoke.

These additions took the entire session. Quite honestly, the red glitter spray added nothing to the final product. Yet this attention to a detail that produced no noticeable effects was an essential symbol. It stood for something exceedingly important; was it something he did not want others to see? Perhaps something he wanted to reveal? Or something he couldn't reason?

In any event, it was a personal symbol.

In the third session I requested that he turn the mask over and on the inside paint "What I hide from the world." His reaction was to fill the inside with black paint (left side of Figure I.3). Interestingly enough, it was in that session that I first noticed the client's wardrobe, even though I had seen

I.2 Outside Mask: Sessions 1 & 2

6

I.3 Inside Mask: Sessions 3 & 4

him every day for many months; like the mask, he too was layered in black. In a nonconfrontive and very curious manner I pointed this out to him, and a casual discussion ensued for the remainder of the session.

In the fourth session he arrived wearing black jeans, with a light-colored shirt. The right side of Figure I.3 depicts the mask completed at the session. Spontaneously, he began to discuss the striped colors, yet it must be noted that his explanation was detached and intellectual. He described the coating of red glitter as happiness (note that this continues to be a nonvisible color); the darkest portion (forehead) equaled his anger, and just below (eyebrows to pupils) a light stripe of rust was defined as a state between happiness and hurt, while the lower portion of the mask (eyes to chin) symbolized sadness. It must be kept in mind that even though the completed mask has striped colors to denote a myriad of feelings, the base color on the inside is black. Anger.

Even though the client's interpretation was intellectualized, from a symbolic and metaphorical standpoint every nuance has meaning. In this project not only do the colors symbolize emotions, but how the color is applied and where are equally important. The red "over-coating" of glitter (red equaling happiness) is not visible within the completed mask, nor is it visible within this client. The black anger, on the inside, not only pervades his "inside" but also is left in the forehead region, where we think and reason and where he carried his anger—the memories ever present.

Attempting to make sense of his life situation, wishing for the ideal childhood, yet faced with his identity as a "failure," he inevitably lashed out in aggressiveness. In addition, on the outside of the mask (Figure I.2) black triangles are placed around the eyes. Is all this client sees tainted with anger? The lower portion of the mask (right side of Figure I.3) represents his sadness and is found in the mouth area. An apt placement, for instead of experiencing the sadness he propelled it forward in a passive-aggressive manner so others were left to feel bewilderment and hurt. A comfortable holding environment so the client could escape meaningful interactions. The "in-between" feelings are inconsequential and difficult to find between these two overbearing forces.

All said, an individual can intellectualize verbally, but an art production opens the window to unconscious meaning. In this project no direct interpretation was made of the underlying process, yet this information was utilized to help the client produce work that expressed his emotionally laden material while reassuring and supporting his fragile sense of self. "Particularly useful are methods which encourage verbalization, or substitute acting-out of the anger. . . . His ego must have time to gradually abandon its dependent position and again take over full responsibility" (Sargent, 1974, p. 150). In Part 3 we will revisit this client as a case study utilizing art therapy coupled with the mutual storytelling techniques of Richard Gardner.

Beyond individual therapy lies group therapy, yet for many therapists residential, or inpatient, group therapy proves exceedingly challenging. As part of a larger system these groups are often lost within the institutionalized setting. Additionally, training for group inpatient therapy at the university level is often lacking, which leaves the clinician to rely on training that may not encompass a focus on interpersonal, here-and-now, interactional learning. Yalom (1983), a master of group process, outlined three major options with an inpatient population: to focus on (1) the here-and-now, (2) the then-and-there problem, or (3) a common theme. He advocates the here-and-now focus, which helps clients to observe their own process through group interaction. He further describes the problems encountered in a then-and-there group, which range from one person's monopolizing the hour (with little success in solving the issue) to a grousing session that wastes precious therapeutic opportunities. He defines a common theme discussion as an interesting personal or issue-oriented conversation that leaves members with a lack of mastery over their individual concerns.

In short, within a content-focused group the therapist has a tendency to neglect the process, and it is through these changes that therapy can move forward for both the individual and the group. Words, which can be denied and shaped into a favorable light by a manipulative client, are useless when faced with an art production.

One such example was an adult male with a history of auditory hallucinations that began when he was a teenager. With a below-average intelligence, he compensated through bravado. Extensive testing revealed that he showed himself in a positive light, while experiencing a great deal of paranoia, rumination, and perceptual disturbances. Results also suggested the presence of anxiety and poor emotional resources for coping. In groups he would sermonize to the other members and was either idolized or ignored. His verbal statements were a combination of grandiosity and nonsense, yet to an institutionalized client he appeared confident and worldly. At the time of this project he had less than one week left in the group, as he had been released. Until he completed this drawing (Figure I.4), the client's discussion on his discharge was focused on how he had achieved his freedom and how others could learn from his example.

The group was instructed to "Draw a feeling of your choosing" on the fourth side of premade boxes. Figure I.4 represents the client's completed image. Before I discuss the project, look at it. Does it appear calm? Anxious? How does it make you feel? Look closely at all the elements. What

I.4 Short-Timer's Box

9

does it say to you? All these questions need to be asked if the group members are going to learn to observe their own processes.

The steps that the client took to finish this drawing are as follows: He finished the hourglass quickly. As he sat and waited for the other members, he slowly added to the picture. The first addition was the broken glass in the upper portion; note the glass shards at the base. He then drew two birds (upper and lower right) that he called doves. As the drawing progressed, he added the anxious squiggles that border the box.

When it was his turn to speak, he proudly explained that this drawing represented his "short time" in the facility. The "doves" represented his upcoming freedom; rendered in the color black, these doves of peace appear more like seagulls, scavengers. He offered no further elaboration. The group fell silent as I asked for feelings on the drawing. It only took one individual to point out the broken glass shards and the brown border before all were agreeing that the image looked anxious and fearful. The client, thrown off guard, attempted to dismiss and minimize the group's input. However, by stepping back from his defensive position and observing his own art production, he eventually spoke of his fears—without sermonizing, without bravado—just as a person afraid of a community that had not embraced him for numerous years. Yalom (1983) states:

> One elementary but important goal of the inpatient group is that patients simply learn that talking helps. They learn that unburdening and discussing their problems not only offers immediate relief but also initiates the process of change. Through the therapeutic factor of universality . . . one may learn that others are very much like oneself, that one is not unique, either in the wretched feelings or thoughts that one has, or in terms of the events of one's own life. To learn, often for the first time, that one's experience is, after all, human and shared by many others is enormously reassuring and one of the most potent antidotes to a state of devastating isolation. (p. 56)

In this vein the art can prove to be a most tangible visual, where feelings can be explored and interactional styles discussed, a permanent record available for all to see.

Developing the Language of Metaphor

One cannot explore consciousness, or self-awareness, without asking how we arrive at such a state. It is widely believed that the portion of our personality that dictates our thoughts, memories, feelings, impulses, and desires is built upon a sequence of phases. As infants we respond on a primary level of consciousness, which mainly encompasses sensations, instincts, and movement. As adults we become increasingly free to experience memory, language, and symbolization. All told, as humans, we must master specific developmental tasks. Regardless of whether you subscribe to a psychosocial model, a psychosexual model, or a model that encompasses intellectual development, the stages of human life must be solved. Thus, the emerging personality forms our identity. Do we trust? Are we self-absorbed? Impulsive? Generous? Do we thrive in our daydreams? Have past humiliations produced shame and guilt? Each answer produces who we are, the sum of ourselves. It is in this manner that we experience our external world.

It is this personality that grapples with outside pressures, copes with crisis, interacts in social situations, and builds memories that can be accessed through the conscious and unconscious. Jay Haley (1976) states, "The psychodynamic therapist as well as the behavior therapist is interested in metaphors about the past because of an assumption that past traumas lead to present difficulties" (p. 98).

An adolescent male whose identity is overwhelmed by memories of sexual abuse spontaneously drew an image of flames (Figure I.5) after a visit with his family.

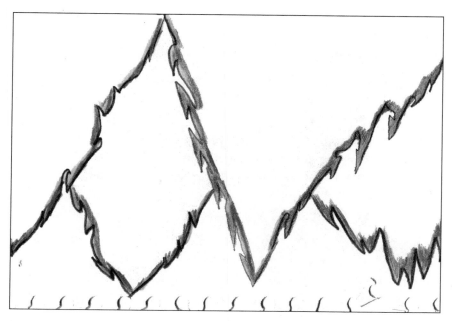

I.5 Flames of Passion

In an individual session he completed Figure I.6. In this drawing he retreats from the home where the abuse occurred while the sky looms dark and foreboding. The flames reappear underneath his feet, and, unlike the beacon of light he heads toward, these flames offer no illumination, only engulfment.

Figure I.7 is a self-portrait drawn by a middle-aged male. At the time of this rendering he had been hospitalized numerous times for schizophrenia.

Expression in the language of metaphor does not require that a client

I.6 *Memories of Sexual Abuse*

I.7 The Winds of the Sun

speak in logical or even rational ways. Of course, in reality, fire does not engulf from below the sidewalk, yet in Figure I.6 the flames occupy a third of the page with their force. How can someone describe schizophrenia when they themselves are schizophrenic? Figure I.7 clearly demonstrates the feeling behind the disease without the use of words. Jay Haley (1976) characterizes this type of communication as analogic. He states, "In an analogic language each message refers to a context of other messages. . . . Included in this style of communication are 'play' and 'ritual,' as well as all forms of art" (p. 92).

It is this process that the Mexican artist Frida Kahlo utilized. The traumatic experiences of her childhood and young womanhood were expressed through her self-portraits, masks, and paintings. Each image explored her pain and trauma. She is not alone: Numerous artists have utilized the safety of creativity to express their fears and thoughts. Things were felt before they were spoken, and it is through art that all manner of client can communicate.

From family mural drawings to polarities, art therapy directives offer an analogic portrait of an individual's life. These portraits become artistic metaphors, examples of the here-and-now.

When symptoms are seen as metaphors, the question is whether the metaphor has changed. One might use projective tests before and after therapy to determine changes in metaphors, but the reliability of these tests is doubtful. A clinician would not stake his or her reputation on the outcome of a projective test, partly because the influence of the tester enters into performance. . . . For example, a woman is likely to give a different response to an inkblot if she is talking to a tester than if her mother is administering the test. (Haley, 1976, pp. 104–105)

However, if a blank piece of paper is offered and the "tester" is removed from the process, much as in art projective testing, then the aforementioned concern is significantly diminished. This allows the clinician to look within the mind of the client without the test developers' preconceived ideas, theories, or beliefs coming into play.

The use of projective drawings, especially the House-Tree-Person assessment, has been in practice for many years. From Florence Goodenough's Draw-a-Man assessments to Leopold Caligor's sorely neglected Eight-Card Redrawing Test (8CRT), interpretation of artwork has been refined and evaluated and, as such, has become an established procedure for many practitioners in their assessment interviews. Camara, Nathan, and Puente (2000) have stated that projective testing assessments are some of the tests most frequently administered by clinical psychologists. Karen Machover (1949) states, "The figure is, in a way, an introduction to the individual who is drawing" (p. 35). She further states:

Again we repeat the basic assumption, verified repeatedly in clinical experience, that the human figure drawn by an individual who is directed to "draw a person" relates intimately to the impulses, anxieties, conflicts, and compensations characteristic of that individual. In some sense, the figure drawn *is* the person, and the paper corresponds to the environment. This may be a crude formulation, but serves well as a working hypothesis. The process of drawing the human figure is for the subject, whether he realizes it or not, a problem not only in graphic skill, but one of projecting himself in all of the body meanings and attitudes that have come to be represented in his body image. (p. 35)

In short, when we draw, we do not reproduce one particular characteristic (e.g., a body image or facial expression) but a composite derived from many occasions, impressions, and memories. Therefore, the focus of art therapy is first on the experience and then on the understanding. In this manner the discovery becomes less intellectual and increasingly personal. Children, unlike adults, have an innate ability to symbolize their problems through play. In time, their displaced symbols become regrouped into themes of mastery and provide relief. As adults, play is frowned upon, so our outlet is often dreams (both nocturnal and daydreams); however, these are not often remembered or easily discussed. So how can this vast store of knowledge, locked deep in the dungeons of our mind, be released?

Through art.

Art transcends all ages, all cultures, and all beliefs. All we have to do is listen to its message.

Things to Come

This book is divided into three parts: the first focusing on theory, the second on art assessment procedures, and the last on case histories. Each chapter utilizes art productions from group therapy, individual sessions, projective testing, children's free drawings, and family therapy to demonstrate the concepts discussed. In all cases, identifying information has been changed to protect the clients.

Part I explores and illustrates select defense mechanisms designed to protect the individual from anxiety as well as examining the norms of behavior through comparison of the theories of Piaget, Freud, and Erikson. Furthermore, it reviews the use of fairy tales, myths, and fables within a therapeutic context.

Part II focuses on the projective techniques of art therapy. Thus, it includes art therapy literature that has helped to systematize the analysis of drawings, a review of three art projective tests, exploration of assessment directives, a multipage listing of popular symbols, and case histories that illustrate how specific projective techniques are interpreted. Additionally, it offers a versatile listing of directives for use within an individual as well as a group setting framework.

As we turn from theory to practice, Part III walks the reader through four individual case histories of both adults and adolescents, four categories of interpersonal group therapy based on the theories of Yalom, and two highly effective family therapy directives.

As with all case histories within this book, the information concerning therapy and clinical matters is factual. However, the clients' personal information, including names (where applicable), dates, and places have been substituted to retain confidentiality.

The accompanying disk shows some art in color. When disk art duplicates figures shown in the book in black and white, the text callout notes this.

PART I

DEFENSE MECHANISMS AND THE NORMS OF BEHAVIOR

CHAPTER

1

In My Defense

I n art therapy one accepts as basic to treatment the psychoanalytic mechanisms of repression, projection, identification, and sublimation (Naumburg, 1953). These mechanisms, used unconsciously, are incorporated to
defend against feelings of anxiety that have become uncomfortable, humil-
iating, or shameful. Removed from the ego, experiences may be isolated,
but they are never forgotten. They creep into our relationships and have
the power to both protect and stifle. This repression, however, "will make
itself felt sooner or later in some manner if it is at all vital to . . . development" (Whitmont, 1969, p. 107).

It is to this end that the art experience offers its invaluable service. The
ability to vent emotions through the process of art allows for both distance
and perspective. As Judy Rubin (1984) points out, "in the doing part of art
therapy, patients do not talk about feelings or relationships from a distance,
but they get into them and feel them" (p. 140). Thus, art therapy allows the
therapist and the client to embrace these defensive measures by making
them part of the treatment plan.

An example is the utilization of directives that target specific defenses.
If we focus on repression, the withholding from consciousness ideas, impulses, or feelings, a perfect directive would be as follows: "Draw all the
things you think of that you don't want to think of." In the same vein, a directive for displacement, whereby an unacceptable emotion is transferred
from one object to a more acceptable substitute, could be "When something bad happens at (home), show how you handle it at (school/work)."
The ability to design directives around an individual's defense is endless
and is only hampered by a lack of imagination.

To state it simply, one must tailor the directives to match the patient's expression. The goal is to think and create in the client's language. Thus, if clients offer defenses, we reply with metaphor.

In this chapter I have chosen the most common defenses that I have encountered in my work and in the supervision of others. This list, however, is by no means exhaustive, nor have I adhered to a strict Freudian classification. Since Freud's initial theory of repression appeared in 1894, and since his reformulating of it in 1926, numerous clinicians have emerged with their own descriptions.

Currently, there is consensus among researchers regarding the following aspects of the defense mechanism construct.

1. An overall definition of a defense is that it is the individual's automatic psychological response to internal or external stressors or emotional conflict. . . .
2. Defenses generally act automatically, that is, without conscious effort. . . .
3. Character traits are in part made up of specific defenses which individuals use repetitively in diverse situations. . . .
4. A process of consensus has favored those defenses manifesting clear, nonoverlapping definitions, reliability, and demonstrated empirical findings.
5. Defenses affect adaptation. Each defense presumably is highly adaptive in certain situations. . . .
6. When defenses are least adaptive, they protect the individual from awareness or stressors and/or associated conflicts at the price of constricting awareness, freedom to choose, and flexibility in maximizing positive outcomes. . . .
7. Despite the use of developmental terms to describe groups of defenses, such as immature or mature, the question of whether defenses emerge in a certain normative developmental sequence represents an empirically open issue. (Perry, 1993, pp. 277–278)

In addition, Perry (1993) speaks of psychologists' attempts to include a sixth dynamic axis in the *Diagnostic and Statistic Manual of Mental Disorders*, fourth edition (*DSM-IV*): "An axis for defenses appeared to be the most clinically useful possibility with consistent scientific support" (p. 298). Of course, this has not occurred, but arguments for such an inclusion range from the ability to measure prognosis to a method of classification to guide treatment and treatment planning.

Just as defense mechanisms tend to be organized hierarchically, from maladaptive to adaptive, they are often associated with specific personality traits. Valliant and Drake (cited in Jacobson & Cooper, 1993) focused on

Axis II personality disorders and found that immature defenses were present in over 60 percent of the population studied, versus 10 percent who were not diagnosed with an Axis II disorder. With regard to Axis I disorders, studies point out that select defenses have shown correlation, both positive and negative (Jacobson & Cooper).

What does any of this have to do with art therapy? Everything. The use of art therapy allows clients to break through their well-honed defenses and provides an emotional release. If we look at symbolization, in which one object or idea is employed to represent another, the art product is the symbol. If we review projection, the client is able to project verbally unacknowledged feelings through his or her creations. With the neurotic defense of asceticism impulses are denied to such a point that masochistic pleasure can become a source of gratification. Thus, the prohibition of instinct can be safely expressed through the completion of directives, found tolerable, and, in the later stages of therapy, practiced without the media.

Before we discuss select defense mechanisms, I would like to state that the following drawings could be analyzed on many different levels (e.g., interpreted for their disparate elements and general characteristics, along developmental lines, as a complete body of work, as an aid in diagnosis, etc.). However, for the purposes of this chapter we will only be analyzing them as they relate to the client's defenses.

Intellectualization

Intellectualization is defined as an emotional response, or impulse, that is controlled by thinking instead of experiencing. The thoughts are a protection, or defense, against anxiety due to unacceptable impulses. "Intellectualization seeks to make a connection between drives and ideational content. In this way drives are perceived as more under ego control which can operate in the area of words and intellect as an active coping device to handle aggression" (Malmquist, 1985, p. 58). Simply stated, this defense is the discharge of aggression or other unacceptable emotions in response to signal anxiety. Often, intellectualization is noted in clients with obsessive traits.

If we return to Figure I.4, it can be said that this adult male employed intellectualization in his relationships with others. He would sermonize with a passion on any topic, especially those having to do with religion or philosophy, and confuse the lower-functioning patients to no end. By so doing he never had to face his own life failures, frustrations, or crises. Yet, when he was left without the ability of speech, alone, to quietly create, the affect escaped without his permission. Out of his comfort zone, faced with the artwork, no longer able to rationalize his neurotic defense, he momentarily allowed himself to experience the feelings of fear.

In another group therapy example the same patient created a clay bear standing before a construction paper home (Figure 1.1).

In the following group session the members were instructed to pass their creations to the member on their right, and that group member was to add to the original artwork. Figure 1.2 shows what this patient's neighbor added to his figure.

As I watched this project in progress, I could not help but notice that the once-orange home now looked like a prison, while the panda took on the role of jailor. Once the projects had been passed back to the original artists, they discussed what they thought of the additions (see Figure 1.2). This man stated, "I like it. It looks safe and secure." The rest of the group heartily agreed. When I pointed out that the house now looked like a prison, I received explanations from "that's how siding looks" to excuses that blamed the materials. Beyond the obvious ego regression that institutionalization had created (this is discussed later in the chapter) not one person saw the "bars" as foreboding or related them in any way to their situation. These rationalizations were obviously necessary to the patients, for, as Malmquist (1985) states, "rationalizations and displacements are often required to maintain the intellectual position, perhaps because the defense is being challenged in discussion" (p. 58).

Another example is taken from a mural drawing. Each of the five members of this group was instructed to draw an animal; they then passed the drawings, completing various tasks to promote interaction, until the sec-

1.1 At Home

1.2 Safe and Secure

ond-to-last person was instructed to make a friend for the animal. All the renderings were given back to the original artist, and the group had to fit all the different images into one cohesive mural. With this project I did not intervene or make any suggestions throughout the process. Figure 1.3 shows the completed project.

As we look along the bottom of the mural, we see a horse, multiple cats, two people, and an exceedingly small monkey hanging from a tree on the viewer's left. As we move to the viewer's right, a lion and lioness are poking out from behind foliage. In back we see two roaming dinosaurs, with seagulls flying above. Beyond what each animal implies symbolically about the creators, the mural has two definitive species—those of predator and prey. As the group had to problem solve and fit all these items into one purposefully very small area, the discussion mainly surrounded the dinosaurs and where to put them. The lion and lioness were largely ignored because they were not "in plain view." Some of the members wanted the dinosaurs on the baseline of the paper; this, however, was dismissed since they could hurt the people and domesticated animals.

They then argued over how to contain these predators. One member suggested a fence, but the other four members quickly rejected the idea. As a compromise, the group created a lake and added rocks to keep the ani-

1.3 Group Mural

mals at bay. Note how the rocks are drawn: gingerly placed as stepping stones instead of as a means of containment. In the end only one group member continued to assert the fact that the dinosaurs needed to be fenced or they would "destroy others." Just as with Figure 1.2, this group began to arrive at excuses and rationalizations of why the dinosaurs would not do anything so violent. Just as with intellectualization, in order to defend against their anxiety they employed this excess of thinking. The need to protect against unacceptable impulses, or situations, is so strong that even man-eating dinosaurs can be tamed if we think hard enough.

One of the few images to bring a consensus of affect was Figure 1.4. This group of eight adult males was given the directive "Create a free drawing to represent any feeling you choose."

This patient, an adult male, was diagnosed as a paranoid schizophrenic. At this juncture in his treatment he was stabilized on medications but had a tendency toward thought blocking and disorganized thinking. This patient's main defense was introjection.

In assessing this drawing we see an extremely powerful-looking and muscular male standing in his cell while the cinderblock wall both frames and encloses his body. Suffice it to say that this rendering was not well received. While the patient spoke of jail time, he spontaneously began to explore his feelings of loneliness and fright. The group, in a common voice, implored

1.4 Feelings of Loneliness

him to "put that away," adding, "that's awful. . . . I don't even want to think about that." Faced with the group's reaction, the patient laughed, apologized, and retreated into his pattern of self-punishing behaviors.

Conversion

This basic ego defense is popularly defined as an emotional conflict that has been transformed into a physical disability. However, the symbolic guise of conversion is not measured merely in terms of somatic complaints. Laughlin (1970) has offered the most comprehensive definition, which I will utilize for the purpose of this section.

> Conversion is the name for the unconscious process through which certain elements of intrapsychic conflicts, which would otherwise give rise to anxiety if they gained consciousness, instead secure a varying measure of symbolic external expression. The ideas or impulses, which are consciously disowned, plus elements of psychologic defenses against them, are changed, transmuted, or converted usually with a greater or lesser degree of symbolism, into a variety of physical, physiologic, behavioral, and psychologic manifestations. (p. 32)

He further delineates six types of conversion behavior. We shall be exploring the fifth and sixth: conversion delinquency and antisocial and criminal behavior. These classifications "result from unconscious impulses, seething resentment, and hatred being converted so as to erupt into external violence" (Laughlin, 1970, p. 38).

The case we will discuss revolves around a teenaged girl who found herself placed in a residential treatment center for two counts of assault, both against family members. The minor's parents had divorced by the time she was a toddler and her biological parents fought over guardianship for numerous years. Eventually, she was transitioned into her mother's home with her half-sister and stepfather, on a permanent basis. By late latency her stepfather began molesting her; she told no one for months. However, once she found the courage, her mother immediately reported the abuse and her stepfather turned himself in that day. Since then, the client has verbalized feelings of guilt for taking away her mother's husband and her sister's father. Prior to her arrest the client was involved in private counseling to address the molestation issues, which the client felt she had sufficiently discussed. Yet her behavior spoke to the contrary. She had adopted the role of the parentified child and not only mediated between her biological parents, but would act as caretaker to her younger half sibling. She possessed a warm and sunny disposition and was involved in numerous team sports. Overall, she was the perfect student, the perfect sister, and the devoted child. Yet she had repressed the traumatic experiences until they had been not only disguised, but also symbolized through the external expression of flawlessness. However, when faced with a failure, she lashed out toward the world all that had been unconsciously hidden. The shame and guilt once again tucked safely away she returned to the perfect student, the perfect sister, the devoted child.

This resistance to exploration (even though she was exceedingly verbal) and the abuse and ensuing conflicts proved an obstacle in therapy. So thoroughly had she repressed her anxiety that verbal therapy was ineffective. It was at this point that an art project was introduced. The client was given plasticene clay and told to make anything that she wished. Figure 1.5 shows what she created in the first session.

What do you see? What visceral feeling or thought comes to mind? When interpreting art, this is an important ability to develop. At this juncture the mortar and pestle were viewed as a symbolic penis and vagina. The function of a pestle is to grind, pound, or stamp; therefore not only its shape, but also its practical use was taken as a representation for this client's sexual abuse. It is important to note that this interpretation was not made to

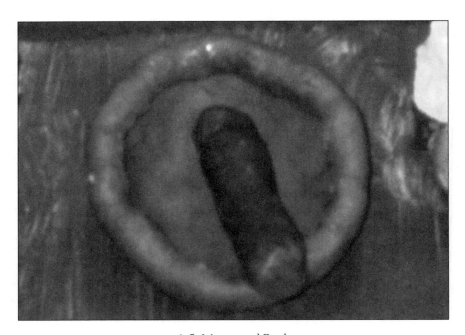

1.5 Mortar and Pestle

the client. Instead it was simply identified as one possibility and noted for future reference.

As outlined earlier, symbols cannot only be construed through a common understanding (i.e. the dove as a symbol of peace) but they are intensely personal. The image of the mortar and pestle is not one most teenagers gravitate toward. Thus, it was surmised that this represented a personal symbol that would need to be taken into account with the final art production. In the next session clay was once again offered and she created three items—the die, flower, and butterfly (Figure 1.6).

As with the first session, no interpretation was given; she was simply allowed to create as much or as little as she chose. These three items were then assessed next to the mortar and pestle figure. Was the die an attempt to convert into oppositional behavior due to the dislike of the art project? Were the flower and butterfly her attempt to rectify her angry emotions (reaction formation)? Was the die perhaps a symbol for her feelings? Note there is only one, not two. Was it a wish that her emotions could just "pass away?" As these were clearly personal symbols, there was no way of knowing without directly interpreting and exploring, and due to her level of repression this was not a prudent choice. Thus, a decision was made to provide her with containment. If she were truly converting the repressed memories of her sexual abuse, she would need something to surround the welling up of feelings. In other words she would require a symbolic boundary where she could safely place her anxiety and anxious thoughts. Thus, heavy cardboard and paint were introduced. The clay remained available, however, the focus was now placed on making a painting. Figure 1.7 is the painting that she created.

The tissue paper creations on the bottom half of the painting are trees.

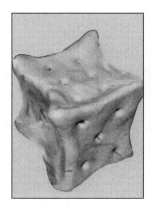  

1.6 Feelings in Clay

1.7 Converting Memories of Sexual Abuse

She then went on to make a clay figure (Figure 1.8). This, she stated, was a "man without a body." It is completed in a primitive style, a circular mass with eyes and mouth, devoid of detail it has the power to bring forth what one sees (remembers) and not what is actually present.

In the ensuing session (Figure 1.9) she placed all the disparate clay productions (i.e., the die, mortar and pestle, and now the bodiless man) into some order. A new addition was the "Hot and Spicy" wrapper that at first she placed below, changed her mind, and fixed under the sun.

As with Figure 1.5, examine the final art product. These items that she had made singularly have now been placed into a cohesive order. Thus, where she placed an item, where she chose not to, how she arranged the figures, both in proximity and distance, all take on significance. It is at this point that the whole must be taken into account.

What is your first impression?

Note the closeness of the "bodiless man" next to the symbolic genitalia. Note the feeling. Why place a candy wrapper into the picture? And if doing so is necessary, why place it under the sun?

After having looked the entire image over, take your hand and block the lower third. What a very different image this mixed media production

1.8 *Man without a Body*

1.9 *Hot and Spicy*

becomes. A rainbow bursting with color spreads across the page while three birds and a butterfly move freely. The only image out of context is the "Hot n' Spicy" wrapper glued into place under the oversized sun's rays. While making the image the client struggled with where to place this wrapper and initially wanted to place it on the lower third.

Now hold your hand over the upper two thirds of the page and notice the linear quality. Everything forms a straight line across the bottom of the boundary. Green tissue paper trees look like explosions, especially directly above the bodiless head. At the end of the line rests a single red flower.

There are numerous ways that this project could be interpreted. It could be taken apart, dissected, and assessed in a singular fashion (i.e., from a standpoint of general symbols and their understanding: the sun being representative of parental love and support, a source of warmth, butterflies being associated with the search for elusive love and beauty, flowers representing a need for love and beauty, color symbolism, etc.). Or it could be explored from a position of personal symbolism and the client's free associations with the mortar and pestle, the bodiless man, and the affect generated. Or, finally, it could be assessed from the point of view that the abuse, rather than having been explored and processed, was quietly and efficiently repressed, and any direct interpretation or questioning would produce a multiplicity of verbal statements, all designed to minimize the experience. In this way, the shame and guilt all converged into a host of defenses (i.e., conversion, intellectualization, reaction formation) that provided a safe forum where the traumatic memories were not relived.

Yet who but the client can decide the path of therapy? Therefore, utilizing the art as the product of transference, the therapist gently questioned her. Her response to how the mortar and pestle fit with the image was dismissal; she didn't know. This reply offered all that the therapist required. She was not ready to allow this intensely personal symbol to be explored—not directly, at any rate. It is interesting to note that the client sat quietly after the question for quite some time, after which she stated, "Can we now please not do this any more and go back to your office and talk?"

In the office she followed through on her statement and slowly began to discuss the molestation with less intellectualization and more process. Whether the art was the impetus for this is up to you to decide.

Condensation

As previously discussed, symbols are the cornerstone of art therapy. The nonverbal language of symbols speaks to us on a multiplicity of levels and incorporates not simply one memory, object, or feeling but many, which are united through the unconscious process of creation. This emotion and affect give the art its power. It is in this vein that we arrive at condensation, often classified as a minor ego defense. It is defined as a process by which "several concepts, ideas, or needs are condensed in their figurative representation so that a single symbol, object, or figure serves to stand for them. . . . Through the telescoping operation of Condensation one object, figure, or symbol can represent several" (Laughlin, 1970, p. 455).

In art therapy condensation takes on significance beyond its standing as an ego defense. The created symbols allow access into the unconscious, which frees the clinician to unearth the process instead of remaining tied to the content of a client's verbalizations or behavioral acting out. In this manner a singular clay object, multiplied, destroyed, and rebuilt does not merely become a symbol of the destructive path encountered by one youth; it also provides a safe forum in which to express his guilt, pain, and fears.

Figure 1.10 begins a case study of a late adolescent male who had spent the majority of his life in large institutions or group homes. In addition he was a shame-based, highly impulsive youth who preferred the role of victim in his social relationships. Often he would taunt and antagonize peers and adults until he was rejected. In this manner he recapitulated the familial dynamics of approach and avoidance. This chaos then projected onto his current "family" of peers and adults allowed him to control the ensuing rebuff, thus offering him a sense of power within his environment.

With each passing day, as he approached the age of majority, his fear increased. He made frantic efforts to avoid abandonment through regressive characteristics. He became hostile, rude, and belligerent, with rapid shifts that characterized emotional instability. He refused to attend group therapy and was withdrawn and resistant when seen individually. Unable to cope with impending adulthood, he had regressed to childhood. At this point the treatment team decided that he required less verbal and increasingly tactile interventions that would provide him with a sense of reparative mastery as well as meeting his developmental needs of separation and individuation. Thus, art therapy was introduced. Over the next nine sessions he was given plasticene clay and instructed: "make anything you want."

The client had a multiplicity of color choices but decided to work with blue and minimally added red to the microphone. He did not offer any information about his creations, and the therapist did not question him about them. These early art therapy sessions were simply utilized as a holding environment, while the clay figures were utilized as transitional objects.

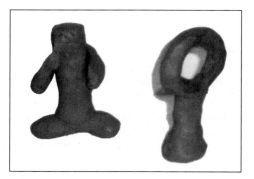

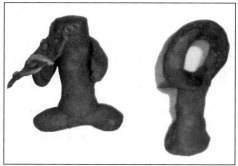

1.10 The Blue Man and the
Anger Microphone

1.11 The Blue Man and the
Butterfly

In the second session the client retrieved his art production and proceeded to smash the background figure. This was not an unexpected occurrence, as it was certainly in keeping with his identification with the victim as well as being an action related to his feelings of abandonment depression. Thus, each time he destroyed the figure, the therapist quietly remade it. The therapist made no verbal reproach and expressed only toleration for the ambivalent feelings. This cycle continued five times, until the therapist began work on a butterfly. Once this was completed the session ended.

In the third session the client was once again introduced to the clay productions. He spent his time fixing the figure the therapist had initially restored. This exchange was an important one in the relationship. The therapist, having lent her ego to the client symbolically, showed him that nothing was irreparable. The client, having been allowed to vent his anger and aggression without rejection, symbolically apologized through a sense of industry (repairing the damage) instead of assuming the inferior role. At the end of the session the client placed the butterfly on the now-repaired person (Figure 1.11).

At this point the client had not identified the figures, and due to his regressive features he was not pressed for clarification. However, in the fourth session he voluntarily offered an explanation. Figure 1.12 shows all the productions made to this point, with two new additions.

While the client worked on the white figure, the therapist made a second butterfly (found at the white figure's feet). The client stated that the "Blue man's sad." While the white man scolds the blue man for his indiscretions, "He tells him to do the right thing. They fight but they make up." The figure in the foreground he identified as a microphone. He simply stated, "This is the blue man's anger. He's sad when the anger comes out."

At the conclusion of the session the client placed the therapist's butterfly on the anger microphone. Needless to say, his description is replete with symbolism. His emotions and social relationships have been condensed into the clay figure representations. The therapist embodies the butterfly and the white man (superego figures), while the client resides in the blue figure as his anger is magnified through the microphone. Overall, these contradictory emotional states exist not only side by side but also within the client and, in this instance, his transitional objects. This splitting continues to be the cornerstone of his rage, fear, and guilt. The following two sessions (encompassed in Figure 1.13) show his continued compartmentalization.

In the background a blue home ("where everyone relaxes and plays") is placed in close proximity with the white home ("where they sleep and eat"). A red garage (center) protects the car so the "Blue man can fix it in safety."

In the fifth session the client had made a blue lake; however, after the therapist informed the client that she would be on vacation for a period of two weeks (in the sixth session) he destroyed the lake. It is interesting to note that water, in modern psychology, is frequently viewed as a symbol of the mother or the female side of the personality.

Upon the therapist's return, the project was resumed and Figure 1.14 was completed.

The client worked quietly, with a flat affect, and created a snowman (placed in the background on the viewer's right) and added black clay to the white home. He stated, "This is the place you can go and discuss your feelings." He then began to explore the art room and added a feather and plastic wheels to the car. However, as the session progressed, he became increasingly agitated. He then destroyed the therapist's butterfly and the anger microphone, saying, "I don't need them." This regression is typical

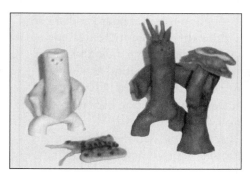
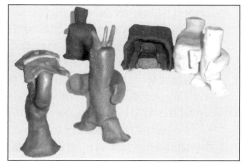

1.12 He Tells Him to Do the Right Thing   *1.13 Compartmentalizing His Emotions*

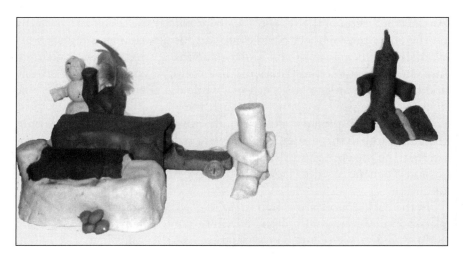

1.14 Abandonment Feelings Well

when abandonment feelings well from within, but the black roof added to the white building gave room for hope.

At this point the therapist remade the butterfly and stated, "The butterfly came back and now it's stronger." This use of metaphor was less intrusive than if the therapist had attempted to explore the client's feelings of loss and abandonment in a direct manner. After noting that the blue man was now completely separated from the other objects, the therapist placed the butterfly at the man's feet (object constancy), and this ended the session. Once again, no verbal discussion was imposed; only symbolic gestures and verbal metaphors would be utilized until the client felt safe and comfortable.

In the eighth art therapy session the client was once again presented with the clay objects, but he stated that he didn't want to work in clay any longer: he wanted to make a picture. He sought out poster board and chose pencils (a very controlled medium) and drew the image on the left side of Figure 1.15. The writing above the wavy-lined man says, "Talk about how you feel." He carefully placed the completed drawing behind the clay objects and spoke briefly about the picture. The client stated, "This is how anxious people draw." Note how similar this figure is to the blue man that represents the client (right side of Figure 1.15).

The initial on the wavy-lined man's chest (digitally changed) belongs to the client, and this reinforced the therapist's interpretation that the men that the client was making all symbolized aspects of him. It is also noteworthy that at this juncture the client wanted desperately to give up the

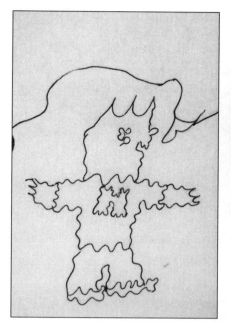

1.15 The Symbol Remains the Same

transitional object (clay men) yet was unable to, and thus utilizing a new medium (drawing) continued to yield the same symbol. He was, however, attempting to move toward autonomy, and therefore his assertive actions were met with approval and acceptance.

In the last art therapy session the client returned to the clay project and spent an inordinate amount of time on the car. He detailed it with headlights and moved it around the area in play. He then gave the white man (superego symbol) eyeglasses and stated, "Now he can see better." He then added a heart to the white man and snowman and positioned the blue home and man (negative aspects of the self) in the background. As we look over the completed project (Figure 1.16; see disk to view in color), the created symbols represent not only the client but also his emotions and the contrasting parts of his personality (id, ego, and superego). It is also noteworthy that through the defense mechanism of condensation he created figures to represent these aspects. The white man symbolized the superego (he scolds the blue man and tells him to do the right thing), and this superego was found not only within the client but also within the therapist. The blue man, with his anger microphone, as a representation of the id is a lone figure venting and acting in accordance only with its own desires. Yet as the project progressed he soon leaves the blue house (of fun), destroys the

1.16 Open Arms

anger microphone (and does not recreate it), and enters a house of safety (the white house) where he can discuss feelings. Finally, a snowman appears. Initially placed in the background (Figure 1.14), it takes center stage next to the white man and is given a heart. This figure, the antithesis of the others, has been given open arms with a less regressive trunk.

Figure 1.16 was the last art therapy project completed by the client. The defense mechanism of condensation, as well as this client's infantile regressive features, was rechanneled into a burning desire to plan for and discuss his future living arrangements in the community.

The release of this client's id drives, through the use of transitional objects in a structured environment, allowed the regressive process to run free without judgment. The abandonment depression, which he was able to experience and not just process intellectually, was successfully navigated through quiet listening and uninterrupted attention. In short, the client's fears were permitted liberation through symbolization, whereupon he was then able to find a satisfaction that was both ego supportive and stabilizing.

Regression

The last defense mechanism we will illustrate is regression. Regression is often equated with a fixation to earlier developmental points—specifically, infantile behavior patterns. The ego, to avoid anxiety or hostility, returns to a safe haven, a developmental point in the past, where it can rely upon a dependent position for comfort. The satisfaction that the individual achieves can be all encompassing, as with psychosis, or partial.

Laughlin (1970) classifies regression as either "minor," which he defines as transitory and tending to be secondary to the mental illness, or "major," which he associates with psychotic reactions and which is a prominent influence in the individual's life. It is these categories—minor regression and major regression—that we will illustrate through two different clients. Both are adult males who have a significant history of placement in both board and care homes and the forensic hospital setting. It is important to note that, especially with adult males, institutionalized regression is a common problem. The individual, removed from the community and often placed far from the familial support system, quickly adjusts to a dependent style of living. The cycle of release and return to prison, jail, or the hospital is all too familiar. In most situations these individuals have spent more time living with strangers than they have with family members or independently. They little understand the responsibilities of adulthood, and maturation has been fixated on a dependent level.

The confinement, therefore, is imposed both from without (rules, restrictions, and authority) and from within (fear of release, vulnerability to anxiety, and the ensuing ego regression). At this point I would like to refer to Figures 1.1 and 1.2. The neighbor in the project who placed bars on the once-orange home was an elderly, unmarried male. As previously outlined, the group was highly defensive in their response to my comments that the home now looked like a prison. Met with this resistance, I simply filed away the intellectualizations as the group continued work on the clay project. The following week this patient returned to his individual assignment (Figure 1.17) and finished earlier than the rest of the group.

As we sat quietly waiting for the others, he spontaneously stated, "the snail only knows the box." After inspecting his creation and recalling the bars he placed on the orange home I knew that his dependent position was purely unconscious. Wavering over whether to interpret or question, I decided to reply from a feeling affect; thus, I stated, "That must be extremely sad for him." The conversation abruptly stopped, and the client immediately set to work undoing the thought (see Figure 1.18). He quickly fashioned a youthful snail (how can one be sad with others around?) and the planet Saturn (the second-largest planet in the solar system, whose presence certainly undoes the closeness of confinement), all without saying a word.

One could not erase the regression any more completely than this patient did by symbolically enlarging the box to encompass the sky, moon, planet, and the continued future generation of snails. Yet the symbolism

1.17 The Snail Only Knows the Box   *1.18 Erasing the Regression*

reaches beyond that of regression and the defense mechanism of undoing: It encompasses the entire project. This patient had a multiplicity of choices, both in object and color, yet he chose the snail as his animal and a specific planet. These choices are not arbitrary; they arose from his unconscious in response to the directive ("create an animal" and "an environment for the animal to live [in]") and ultimately represented a response to an interpretation that was too confrontive for his fragile sense of self (Figure 1.18). If we explore each element separately, we find the snail to be a slow-moving animal (or person) that also possesses a protective shell (for safety, security, and shelter). Next, the representation of Saturn has been encased in the same colors as the snail, even though a wide range of colors was available. This planet, beyond the fact of its size, also possesses a protective "shell" in the form of its icy ring. In addition, "Saturn symbolizes time which, with its ravenous appetite for life, devours all its creations, whether they are beings, things, ideas or sentiments. . . . Hence, Saturn is symbolic of activity, of slow, implacable dynamism, of realization and communication" (Cirlot, 1971, p. 278).

The regression that this patient exhibited, no matter how hard he tried to hide it, had devoured him. He was an institutionalized career criminal with a mental illness who had been taken care of his entire life. His regression was total; the realization, frightening.

The second example, that of a major regression characteristic of the oral phase of development, was created by a young adult diagnosed with chronic schizophrenia. After prior releases into the community, he had been placed in board and care homes, but eventually he had run—only to live a transient lifestyle until he was re-arrested for a crime. At the time of these renderings he was again looking at placement in a board and care home. As you will note, his drawings tend to have shapes within shapes and excessive scribbling, which is indicative of a 3-year-old's rendering. However, the primitive detailing, disproportion, and disorganization found within these drawings is also representative of schizophrenic artwork and bespeaks of the fragmentation of personality.

At the time of his placement the patient was not experiencing hallucinations and was taking the most recent antipsychotic medication. However, the following series of drawings shows a progressive embracing of regressive behavior. The anxiety that the impending discharge date produced in this patient had created a deterioration in functioning. Ultimately, he was progressively retreating into primitive forms of perception, and within a month his drawings had regressed to form, shape, and simplistic lines.

Figure 1.19 typifies this patient's difficulty with language and communication. As we look at the individual components in the drawing, there are shapes within shapes, as well as scribbling over lines, and the incongruent quality all bespeak of a regressive and "loose" style.

Additionally, his impaired communication skills are evident in the writing found on the upper right. It reads, "When I am angry I carry my honor when there is a conflic a am suppose to be as when we eat patience." He explained that "honor" stood for remaining calm and brushing off perceived disdain. The definition of "eat patience" was holding the anger within. The disorganized speech noted in his writing has a tangential

1.19 When I Am Angry

39

quality when taken alone; however, in the context of his other drawings and explanations it pointed toward sexual issues related to abuse and inadequacies.

His next two renderings placed more pieces within the ensuing puzzle. In Figure 1.20 he drew his "experiences of hurt." This rendering is completely symbolic and appears aggressively sexual in nature. He titled the image "Love oasis ignorance." All marks with the exception of the linked circles are his experiences of hurt. The raindrop shape symbolized pain, while the word "ignorance" stood for lack of honor, which in turn stood for a lack of manhood. The linked circles were the love oasis. At the end of the session I asked the patient to place himself within the image; he is found as a small dot just inside the circled area.

By Figure 1.21 he was again utilizing shapes within shapes and continued to use sexualized symbols (note the sun). However, on this day he was also verbally fantasizing about how we would set up house and how I would take care of him. With each statement and drawing, it was clear he was regressing into a state of dependency. The disintegration, produced by anxiety, was finding outlet in the safety and comfort of the familiar and a familiar person to take care of his needs. Yet the schizophrenic patient, fearful of closeness, tends to distort feelings and thereby concretize his or her thoughts. As Arieti (1955) has said, "physical love is a concrete symbolization of what is really wanted: love and reassurance" (p. 477). As a final remark, in Figure 1.21 the patient is found on the far left with two

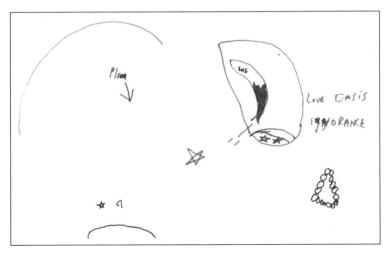

1.20 Love Oasis Ignorance

1.21 Sexualized Symbols

friends. He is the image without a face. This author is located in the center of the form page. However, the rain was not in the initial drawing; the
patient added this after I interpreted his desire to marry as a need for closeness. Once again, we see the defense of undoing come to light when
prompted by a translation that is too close to the basic need or thought.

As the sessions progressed, they focused both verbally and pictorially on
the board and care placement. This was the basis of his anxiety and needed
to be processed so that he would not retreat into complete infantile behavior. One such polarity directive was "Draw how you feel in the hospital
and how you think you will feel at the board and care home," which is outlined in Figure 1.22. He stated that his drawing (viewer's left) was the ward
dayroom and the dots were the people milling about.

An example of the patient's artwork prior to his disintegration is found
in Figure 1.23, whose directive was "Draw the good things in your life on
one side of the paper, and things you should stay away from on the other
side." This rendering is juxtaposed with an illustration of a later directive:
"What do you imagine the board and care home will look like, and what
will you be doing?" (Figure 1.24).

The car in Figure 1.23 is well formed, though phallic in nature, and is
identified as a Porsche. However, the cars in Figure 1.24 (lower left side)
are merely shapes and form, devoid of detail.

This patient's major regression occurred in response to the overwhelm-

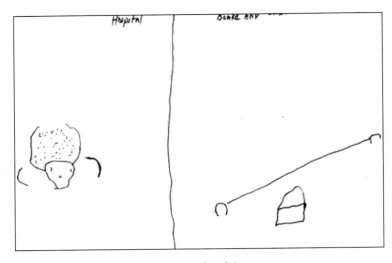

1.22 Board and Care

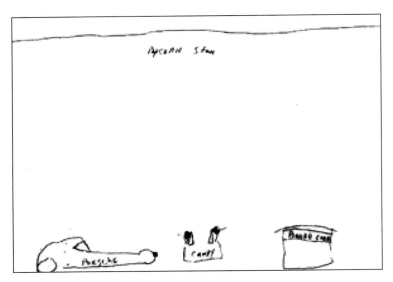

1.23 The Good Things in Life

ing anxiety produced by his impending board and care home placement. Furthermore, it was during the session in which Figure 1.24 was completed that the patient divulged that a resident at a board and care had sexually molested him, which precipitated his running away. In the end the patient remained in the hospital an additional three months to allow him an op-

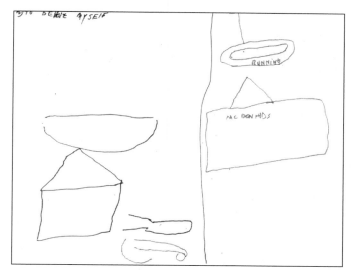

1.24 Life at the Board and Care

portunity to process his concerns with both clinicians and board and care home operators prior to reentry into the community.

Summary

Ultimately, identifying and understanding defense mechanisms are important skills that aid in the assessment of and intervention with a client's adaptive and maladaptive responses to the environment. The utility of art therapy was aptly described by Levick (1983) when she said that art therapy "also provides an opportunity to re-experience conflict and then to resolve and to integrate the resolution" (p. 9). The employment of art not only served to identify the defenses but also allowed a safe forum in which the disquiet, trauma, and fear could be expressed while providing ample boundaries so that the anxiety was not overwhelming. In other instances it served to underscore the unconscious conflict and allowed a partial ego regression, which ultimately proved beneficial. In time, what makes the art therapy experience so valuable is the ability to vent repressed material, experiences, and emotions through the process.

It is important to make a distinction between a coping mechanism and a defense mechanism. In the examples provided, the individuals employed a rigid, unconscious style of thinking to protect themselves from anxiety, whereas a coping mechanism implies a desire to meet the troubles and contend with them on a conscious or, at worst, a preconscious level. A maladaptive defense mechanism is never utilized deliberately or consciously, while a coping mechanism can be called upon to master the problem rather than masking it.

We are now ready to examine adaptive adjustment through a discussion of how behavior develops in typical and predictable sequences and how these stages apply both to art therapy and to defense mechanisms. Finally, I will offer practical suggestions to enhance treatment.

2

Adaptation and Integration

Numerous theorists (e.g., Kernberg, 1975; Greenspan, 1979; Anna Freud, 1946) have postulated that defenses occur at specific stages of development. For example, Wilhelm Reich (1949) found a relationship between character and defense formation, while Meissner, Mack, and Semrad (1975) have grouped select defenses according to developmental phases. Malerstein and Ahern (1982) in their discussion of character structure had this to say about defense mechanisms:

> The psyche of a person is not a disjunctive aggregate, but, over the years, has developed into an organized, integrated, abiding system of approaches. . . . He has at his disposal a certain array of defense mechanisms. These defense mechanisms tend to go together in clusters. Where we find one or two, we will usually find the other defenses of the cluster. These mechanisms will have certain coherence with each other as well as with the other functions of a person's psyche. (p. 27)

The importance of an accurate assessment and clinical diagnosis cannot be overstated. Thus, the whole of the individual must be taken into account, and this includes their nonverbal communication. To this end, art therapy allows the nonverbal expression of unconscious defense mechanisms. As an example, refer to Figures 1.5 through 1.9. These figures illustrate the defense mechanism conversion. However, if we now employ the use of developmental theory and couple this with the ensuing defense mechanism, we can arrive at a very accurate clinical picture and create a treatment plan that will benefit the whole person as he or she approaches the world. As stated in the example, the client's verbalizations, though abundant, were merely rationalizations about her sexual abuse. All of her feelings were located in the past, buried deep. She parented her mother and sister to make up for the guilt she felt over having taken away the husband and father. All the difficulties that this client exhibited were dealt with outside of herself. Thus, when the stress, humiliation, and shame mounted, she would act out (ultimately on the two people she was parenting—her sister and mother), purge herself of her shame through aggression, and then become the symbol of perfection. In addition, her artwork was created entirely of symbols. She formed a pestle and mortar (penis and vagina), exploding crowns on the trees, a bodiless person, and on and on. All of this points toward the intuitive stage of Piaget's cognitive development. This age—5 to 7—grasps surface qualities through the use of inductive reasoning.

In this client's case her inductive reasoning surrounded the belief that if bad things happen it is because you are bad. Overall, shame and humiliation are prominent as the child begins to struggle with complex problems. Thus, fixated as she was at the intuitive stage of development, rationalizing was her main verbal defense, which made traditional therapy ineffective. Yet with art therapy the thoughts and feelings she had hidden from consciousness were allowed symbolic expression, and the defense mechanisms of conversion and reaction formation were then articulated.

In the end it is the typical and predictable sequences of behavior that I utilize to guide my use of the art, choice of media, and the ensuing directives. For without a cornerstone to guide us we would be hard pressed to interpret the artwork in any manner other than a haphazard one.

The art of art therapy is less about how pleasingly the drawing is rendered and more about the elements that are either drawn or disregarded. I have often been asked by clinicians, "But I can't draw . . . doesn't that skew the assessment?" My response has always been a resounding no. It has been suggested in psychological as well as art literature that individuals project their personality into their drawings. Thus, it is not in the ability but in the manner that interpretation comes alive. That is why it is vital that the norms of drawing be understood. Lowenfeld and Brittain (1982) state, "The child draws only what is actively in his mind. Therefore the drawing gives us an excellent record of the things that are of importance to the child during the drawing process. A child knows a great deal more in a passive way than he ever uses" (p. 34). In the same manner any person, regardless of age, whether versed or not in the art of drawing, utilizes an unconscious process that allows for more freedom than verbalization affords.

As an example already offered, refer to Figures 1.19 through 1.24. Figure 1.24 (drawn by a schizophrenic) underscores how a remembered trauma triggered an ever-increasing regression. However, this figure does not indicate a developmental delay to infancy. Other drawings that this client produced showed he was capable of drawing people, places, and environments. Unfortunately, as he emotionally decompensated, his drawings increasingly worsened until they took on an infantile quality (which is often characteristic of coartated schizophrenics). Thus, Figure 1.24 becomes an example of infantile regression, while all of his drawings taken in total are an example of developmental delays fixated in early latency. In addition, it was noted in the example that Figure 1.23 was a dayroom with people milling in its center. This is an important distinction to make, as interpretation revolves around not only the completed art project but also the client's verbal statement regarding the rendering. This process (questioning the client) cannot and should not be left out. As Lowenfeld and Brittain (1982) aptly state,

> To examine the picture without understanding what the child's intention was, to make assumptions about personality from one example of artwork, or to assess competence in art on the basis of what is included or omitted from the product, does both the product and the child an injustice. (p. 30)

Thus, when assessing or interpreting the art the therapist must take an entire history into account. This includes the client's social and familial history (recent and remote), cultural identity, medical history (including medications), chronological age, presenting problem, substance abuse history, developmental history, mental status, and of course his or her verbalization about the completed project. All of these elements are necessary for a correct interpretation of the product and an accurate understanding of the client's mental health.

DiLeo (1973) states, "valid appraisal of a child's drawing is not possible without taking into account the age and developmental level. . . . The significance of omission and exaggeration depends upon the level at which the child is functioning. An enormous head at age four or five is quite usual" (p. 34).

In Figures 2.1 and 2.2 this occurrence will be illustrated. Figure 2.1 is a 5.9-year-old female's drawing of her family. Note the oversized head and the beginning of attentiveness to environmental detail (e.g., joints in the shoulders and elbows, high-heeled shoes on the mother, tongues lolling in anticipation, and obvious differences between the drawing of the eyes and the nose). All of this suggests the beginning of intuitive thought.

In comparison, Figure 2.2 (details from larger House-Tree-Person drawings) offers two examples that contain oversized heads, yet these drawings were completed by a middle-aged male (left) and an adolescent (right).

2.1 My Family

2.2 Examples of Oversized Heads

Both of these drawings (after an evaluation of the complete House-Tree-Person assessment, which will be further discussed in Chapter 3) indicate the possibility of organicity (the oversized head being simply one indicator) even though both of the clients spoke well for themselves on a purely verbal level. In addition, the drawn person on the left side of Figure 2.2 was the client's second attempt. In Figure 2.3 this patient slowly completed a rendering of a circular head with pinpoint eyes, a button nose, and smiley face. He then drew the figure's left arm, worked his way down to the left leg, and in drawing the right leg connected the line to the hand area of the right arm.

At this point he looked at the drawing quizzically, seeming to understand that something was wrong but not what or how to fix the problem. Then he drew in the dwarflike left foot and stated that he had messed up. At this point I gave him a second piece of paper and instructed him to begin over. Throughout the assessment the patient verbalized, "this is hard. . . . This is fun, I'm having a good time. . . . I like doing this."

2.3 Dwarf Foot

It is important to state that the left foot (which I call a dwarf foot due to folk belief that dwarfs were often depicted with feet shaped like a duck's) is seen frequently in schizophrenic drawings. It is also a frequent occurrence in the drawings of 5-year-olds. This could be due to the fact that children rely on primary processing until they move into a logical mode of reasoning at roughly the age of seven. Equally, schizophrenics operate on primary processing, which relies heavily on primitive, id-related experiences and also runs counter to a logical mode of reasoning.

Images showing organicity will be reviewed in detail in Chapter 3; however, I have chosen to illustrate one that clearly defines a general retardation in development.

An adult male drew Figure 2.4. A psychiatric evaluation dated one year prior to my assessment stated that the patient had been given drug injections, against his will, which resulted in toxic psychosis.

According to Piaget's theory of child development, during the preconceptual phase the child is able to hold mental representations of objects in his or her head. It is also during this phase that tadpole figures emerge. Howard Gardner (1980) says this about tadpole figures: "While they tend to have two protuberances at the bottom, which are usually seen as legs, and may (less frequently) have two extensions on the side, which are perhaps arms, they consist of but a single central circle" (p. 61). Thus, Figure

2.4 Organic Tadpole Drawing

2.4 shows an adult male drawing in much the same style as a 4-year-old. From the tadpole person playing golf in the foreground to the house, located on the viewer's left, and the tree on the right, each detail points toward an internal model rather than any degree of realism. The house has a garage in the lower right square with a car parked in it, yet the car is drawn from a worm's-eye view and is more a symbol than a representation. The tree has a baseline that wraps around the trunk, while the crown of the tree is drawn as a black ball; the branches extend from the trunk into the air instead of into the crown itself. This distorted and disorganized vision is certainly a trademark of schizophrenia with concomitant pervasive developmental delays, yet in a child's renderings it could designate a normal phase of development.

I cannot stress enough the importance of understanding the developmental stages when interpreting the artwork, yet when utilizing art one must also take into account the chosen medium. The use of media can enhance a client's functioning, frustrate the client, or offer an inaccurate picture of his or her personality and any developmental delays that may exist. By way of example, Figure 2.5 shows two paintings by an adult male. He prefers to paint, and the majority of his projects, when he utilizes acrylics, turn out like the examples in Figure 2.5. He is never satisfied with the result and tends to sulk when the vision in his head is not replicated on the paper. These drawings, with their emphasis on simplistic geometric forms, look as though a child in kindergarten created them, and if these were all we had

2.5 *Acrylic Paintings*

interpreted we would have arrived at an assessment that pointed toward significant developmental delays and emotional disturbances for this client.

However, other work created by the same client (Figure 2.6) provides a very different picture. These detailed and integrated renderings, done in marker, also point toward developmental delays, yet they look more like an 11-year-old's drawings—a gain of 5 years, which is considerable, developmentally speaking.

Many examples could be offered that demonstrate developmental delays through the use of artwork. However, at this point I would like to introduce an extremely useful tool on behavioral patterns and modes of growth. Tables 2.1 and 2.2 have been created from the written work of Gesell and Ilg (*The Child from Five to Ten*, 1940) and Gesell, Ilg, and Ames (*Youth: The Years From 10 To 16*, 1956). These books have identified repetitious patterns of growth. Table 2.1 identifies parallel patterns.

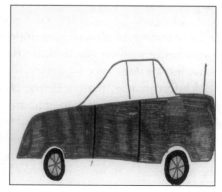

2.6 *Fine-Line Markers*

51

Table 2.1 Parallel Patterns of Growth

Age (in years)	Parallel Age	Characteristics
2.5	5.5–6.0	Worsening behavior; "no" and "mine" prominent vocabulary
3.0	6.5	Increased amicability; "yes" and "we" prominent vocabulary
3.5	7.0	Inward thrust; increased moodiness and anxieties
4.0	8.0	Outward thrust; expansive and boisterous behavior
4.5	9.0	Attempt to combine outward and inward thrusts; increased self-sufficiency
5.0	10.0	Achievement of balance, but merely temporarily

In contrast, Table 2.2 outlines how the growing adolescent's behavior reverts to that of earlier stages. It is at this juncture that clinicians often have difficulty in distinguishing the norms of development and instead believe a delay is occurring rather than a period of growth and change.

As these two tables indicate, the emerging adolescent not only proceeds forward on a predetermined growth pattern but reverts to preceding levels, much to the chagrin of parents and child therapists. Margaret Mahler (1975) also discussed this pattern in her review of the growing infant in the separation-individuation stage of development. Each subphase brings exploratory behaviors that first focus on the mother (differentiation), then branch outward toward the environment (practicing), only to return to the reassuring closeness and safety of the mother (rapprochement). In the end the child (on the road to object constancy) is able to internalize the mother through a mental representation and thus no longer requires strict physical closeness. These states of repetitious instability produce more than mere conflict, however: They help the individual grow into an independent being who is able to anticipate and weigh the consequences of behavioral choices.

Unfortunately, many clients, both adults and youths, exhibit a longstanding history of poor judgment. Couple this fact with the prevalence of institutionalized dependency, and frustration-based aggression can quickly become the norm. Just as the growing adolescent or grown adult will utilize manipulation, a child aged 3 has an instinctive understanding of what will be tolerated by those in his or her life. The problem for the clinician is deciphering the maze of the human psyche. Is the presenting problem a function of the personality? A developmental delay? A failure in the develop-

Table 2.2 Behavioral Reversion

Age (in years)	Reversion Age	Characteristics
11	2.5–5.5	Behavior once again worsens.
12	3.0–6.0	Increased amicability occurs.
13	3.5–7.0	Inward thrust is the focus.
14	4.0–8.0	Outward thrust is the focus.
15	4.5–9.0	Self-sufficiency increases.
16	5.0–10.0	Balance is achieved.

mental process? A normal repetition of the growth pattern? A product of an evolving identity? A fixation? A dependency reaction? Regression?

We can answer these questions by exploring those that have come before, and this chapter concentrates most on the theories of Piaget, Freud, and Erikson.

Jean Piaget

Piaget's stage theory of cognitive development in children outlined four major stages: (1) sensorimotor, (2) preoperational, (3) concrete operations, and (4) formal operations. However, for the purposes of this book I will break down the two phases within the Preoperational stage, as these phases are exceedingly important to the growing child's development. All of these stages not only occur in continuous progressions but allow the individual to interact with the environment with increasing levels of competency and skill. With each stage a broader range of thinking develops as the individual forms a larger understanding of the world. This focus on the intellectual growth of the child and the lack of attention to emotional and social influences have brought criticism upon Piaget's theory. However, at the same time, this focus on cognition parallels perfectly our understanding of a growing child's repertoire of artwork. "To accomplish a particular task, a comprehension of the task itself is necessary. Piaget and others have provided evidence that learning is tied to maturation—a physiological, biological functioning that is predetermined in each individual" (Lowenfeld & Brittain, 1982, p. 221). Thus, a child will not be able to draw a circle until age 3, a square until age 4, a triangle until age 5, and a diamond until the age of 6 or 7. Lowenfeld and Brittain describe why this is so:

> For example, trying to teach a three year old how to draw a cube would be a big waste of time. What would be needed are a lot of pre-cube experiences: a year of scribbling to establish visual-motor control, a year of manipulation

of objects to acquaint the youngster with two- and three-dimensionality, a year of two-dimensional drawing to establish drawing abilities, a year of physical expressiveness to perfect the understanding of left and right, up and down, front and back. Now, the youngster is ready to learn how to draw a cube. (p. 221)

In this manner children's drawings develop in predictable and sequential stages, and it is this fact that we will be weaving into Piaget's theory of cognitive development.

Piaget's first phase, the sensorimotor phase, lasts from birth to the age of 2. The infant is said to go through six definitive stages, each indicating a broader range of thinking as accommodation and assimilation form an ever-growing understanding of the larger world. From birth to 1 month the newborn possesses reflexes that lead them to grasp with their hands and suck with their mouths. However, these reflexes are purely spontaneous; the infants are reacting to the environment and their own organic demands. From the age of 1 to 4 months (primary circular reactions) they expand upon and combine what they have previously learned. They now bring their mouths to objects and grasp the objects they are sucking on. However, these actions are poorly integrated and have a large trial-and-error component. At the age of 4 to 8 months (secondary circular reactions) the child possesses coordination between vision and grasping; it is at this point that events can last and the child can act upon them. The term *circular* in the name for this phase is used to denote a repetitive cycle of events. "Grasping and holding a finger and repeatedly banging an object for noise production are typical infant activities in this period" (Maier, 1978, p. 34). As the child reaches 8 months to 12 months (secondary schemata) we see the "first actually intelligent behavior patterns" (Piaget, 1952, p. 210). The child, now able to experiment with objects, discovers new ways to obtain goals. "Adaptive behavior leads to random experimentation. In adaptation, the child fits new activities and objects of experience to previously acquired ways of conceiving" (Maier, p. 36). Thus, as the child now grasps for crayons, markers, and pens he or she has learned that with application certain effects will follow. In Figure 2.7, which was drawn by a female whom we will call Anna at the age of 12 months, we see a tangle of lines that have produced a colorful and somewhat subtle effect upon a previously blank piece of paper. This application of familiar means (grasping) to new situations (drawing) "permits a real accommodation of the schema to the object and no longer merely a global application as in the third stage" (Piaget, p. 262).

At 12 to 18 months (tertiary circular reactions), the child begins to ex-

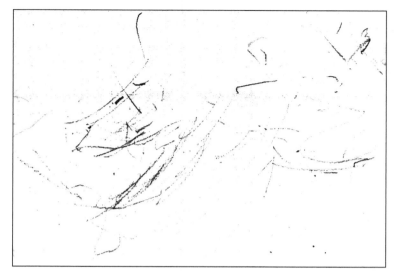

2.7 Anna at Age 12 Months

2.8 Anna at Age 17 Months

periment with and vary actions, mainly to see the effects. It is at this stage that scribbling becomes prominent. Far from being a waste of time, these random scribbles "are based upon the physical and psychological develop- ment of the child, not upon some representational intent. Making the haphazard array of lines, however, is extremely enjoyable" (Lowenfeld & Brittain, 1982, p. 172). In Figure 2.8, Anna, now 17 months, experiments with light and heavy strokes, dots, lines, and circles. This experimentation with the crayons yields a very different end product from what transpired 5 months earlier (Figure 2.7). The boldness of the lines in Figure 2.8 shows how Anna assimilates and accommodates the crayon, whereas in Figure 2.7 she lacked the motor control to produce an effective image.

The final stage of Piaget's phase one (invention of new means, age 18 to 24 months) is said to "represent a climax of previous acquisitions and constitutes a bridge to the next developmental phase" (Maier, 1978, p. 39). The child is now able to form mental combinations, and with this ability comes an increasing control over his or her scribbles. In Figure 2.9, three drawings completed by a 23-month-old boy illustrates continued pleasure in kinesthetic movement, with a controlled scribble as the end result. Notice how the final drawing is more tentative than the other two, as he has chosen to utilize a ballpoint pen rather than the familiar crayon.

The second phase in Piaget's theory revolves around what he terms the preconceptual phase. In this stage, which corresponds with ages 2 to 4 years old, the child is able to hold mental representations of objects within his or her head. Thus, the creation and use of symbols as a means of communication flourish. "Primarily, these symbols have a personal reference for the child" (Maier, 1978, p. 41). This is also a time when children begin to name their scribbles and attribute them to the surrounding environment. Thus, they have moved from kinesthetic thinking (Figures 2.7 through 2.9) to the first attempts at representation.

In Figure 2.10 we see how Anna, at age 3, begins to experiment and draw simple forms. She combined these forms into designs that she titled, "Dizzy,

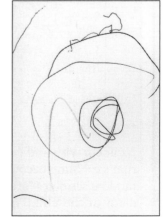

2.9 23-Month-Old Male

2.10 Dizzy, Mommy, Spinning Very Fast

Mommy, spinning very fast." Thus, we see how Anna's mental image of motion is communicated symbolically even though this drawing shows little difference from scribbles completed in earlier stages.

Figures 2.11 and 2.12 were drawn by a child I will call Molly. Figure 2.11 (age 2.3 years) was titled "Mommy and avocado." Once again, the completed drawing looks nothing like its label, yet in the children's minds these drawings (Figures 2.10 and 2.11) implied a wide range of representations; unfortunately, none are recognizable at this stage.

In Figure 2.12 (see disk to view in color), Molly, now aged 2.5 years, has not offered a title, yet color begins to dominate. At this stage the use of color is purely exploratory and does not factor into the image. The colors are placed boldly on the paper but merely in a random order.

It isn't until age 3.5 to 4 that the titled scribbles begin to take on a shape that is minimally recognizable. This form made up of circles and lines, often referred to as a *tadpole figure*, frequently represents the important people in the child's life.

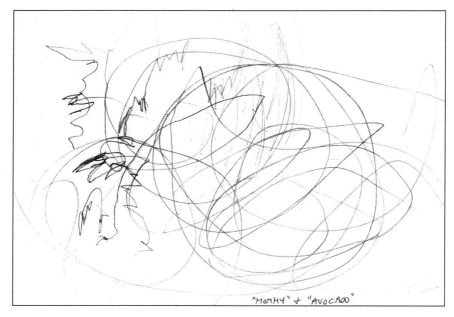

2.11 Mommy and Avocado

2.12 Molly at Age Two and a Half

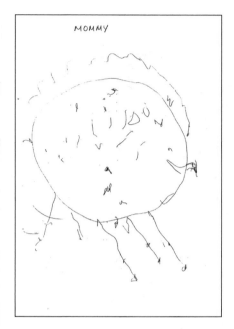
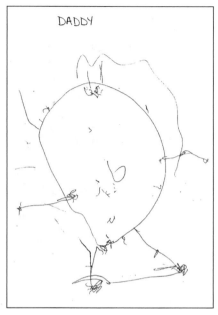

MOMMY

DADDY

2.13 Anna's Tadpole Figures

In Figure 2.13, Anna's incorporation of a circle becomes less of a scribble and more recognizable as a representation of her mother and father, although adults would be hard pressed to title this image accurately if asked to by the child. Piaget explains that the omission of body parts is due to the child's incomplete mental image. However, there is much debate as to why children leave out the body, with no definitive conclusion at this time.

As children develop, "they make less use of the idiosyncratic symbols and more of the conventional signs" (Siegler, 1978, p. 34). Therefore, this period is a time when concepts, language, and mental representations grow. This growth leads children into social awareness and participation, a shifting from egocentricity to more gregarious behavior.

By Piaget's stage of Intuitive Thought children begin to grapple with more complex problems. It is between these ages (4 to 7) that they coordinate their subjective and egocentric versions of the world with the real world (Maier, 1978). However, their drawings continue to be a symbolic representation of objects and things that surround them. They have a tendency to reason from the conclusion when making judgments. Therefore, rules tend to get lost, while the outcome becomes all important.

In Figure 2.14, Anna, who at age 4 years 11 months is just leaving the

2.14 Anna at Age 4 Years 11 Months

scribbling stage, has drawn a tricolored house. These colorful stripes, having no relationship to reality, are typical for children at this stage of development. "In drawings and paintings done by children of this age there is often little relationship between the color selected to paint an object and the object represented" (Lowenfeld & Brittain, 1982, p. 208).

This phenomenon is continued in other drawings completed between the ages of 4.5 and 5 years old. Figure 2.15 shows three houses drawn by a child I will call LeAnn. These homes (all drawn within a 1-month period) typify the beginning stages of a schema (an approximate figurative representation).

In these drawings LeAnn is just beginning to generalize the image of a house, yet the houses are rendered in very different styles. In one drawing the house has numerous windows and no door, while in another an oversized flower dwarfs the doorway, and still another drawing shows a definitive roof while a series of lines indicates the body of the house. It is not until roughly the age of 7, the end of the Intuitive Thought stage, that children's renderings are drawn in a consistent fashion.

2.15 LeAnn's Three Houses

2.16 One-Dimensional Drawings

Thus, at age 6 children are beginning to "compare the image of the object with its perception" (Piaget & Inhelder, 1971, p. 15). In addition, Piaget and Inhelder identify two stages of imagery: The first is static and one-dimensional, while the second is energetic and dynamic in nature. Figure 2.16 shows examples of one-dimensional images as drawn by Anna (a volcano) and LeAnn (flower people) between the ages of 5 and 6.5.

These images have few if any details and lack grounding lines, which would allow the viewer a sense of realism. It is believed that the amount of details found within a drawing offers insight into the child's awareness of the world around him or her (Goodenough, 1926). Therefore, in the early stages of Intuitive Thought the images tend to be bland. However, by the age of 7 these images are replete with information and energy.

In Figures 2.17 and 2.18 (ages 6.5 to 7) we see a beginning knowledge of

2.17 Anna at Age Six and a Half

operations. The children (Anna and LeAnn) are now capable of representing logical and integrated pictures.

In Figure 2.17, Anna has compartmentalized the goings-on in the house
within the frames of the windows. Her father is seen driving up with a bois-
terous "Hi" (note the attention to detail on the headlights), while the family cat is shown descending the stairs.

2.18 LeAnn at Age 6 Years 9 Months

In Figure 2.18, completed by LeAnn at age 6 years and 9 months, we see a growing attention to detail and a fluency of ideas. She has drawn a baseline where one figure stands, while a flying kite pulls "Curious George" away.

Thus, both girls not only have indicated pictorial sequencing through spontaneous drawings but have advanced from intuitive thought to Piaget's fourth phase: concrete operations. The concrete operations phase has been achieved when the child can think logically about physical objects and their relations. The child is now becoming aware of others' points of view and can incorporate this thinking through situational behavioral experiences (e.g., good versus bad, social rules and codes).

Figure 2.19 provides a perfect example of Anna's growing understanding. On the left Anna has drawn the preparation stage of a party, while on the right side (which originally was on the back of the paper) she represents the party itself. It is at this age (7) that the child is desirous to be like (imitate) the parental figure. This taking on of roles is important not only for the child's growing autonomy but for the learning of social roles and codes. Thus, what Piaget terms *imitation* is closely aligned with Freud's defense mechanism of identification.

Classification is what Piaget calls the process of sorting objects into groups. Upon close inspection of Figure 2.19, one can see how Anna at age 7 put this into action. Her drawings of people bustling about show the use of ovals, triangles, circles, and oblong shapes to denote the body, while tables with ready supplies are in abundance even though the space relationship is rather confused. Coupled with classification, Anna also shows

2.19 Anna's Party

Piaget's process of reversibility. "Reversibility constitutes a level of thinking by which the individual is capable of relating any one event or thought to a total system of interrelated parts in order to conceive of the event or thought from beginning to end and vice versa" (Maier, 1978, p. 55). Therefore, drawing the party from conception to actualization represents a major advance in concrete operational thinking.

It is within this stage (by age 8) that children begin to place their objects on a baseline, thus ordering the space relationship considerably. "The base line is universal and can be considered as much a part of the natural development of children as learning to run or skip" (Lowenfeld & Brittain, 1982, p. 240). In Figure 2.20 Anna has not physically drawn a baseline, yet her arrangements have taken on a more orderly approach. This grouping, a process of classification, has now taken us into a comparison of similarities and differences. Her schema of a cat remains basically the same in drawing style, yet each is adorned with its own qualities through the use of color (the cat on the furthest left has been drawn in white and is therefore difficult to see), while the homes are drawn with substantial differences (window shapes, steps, chimney placements).

This ever-growing sophistication is what Piaget likened to equilibration. Equilibration encompasses both assimilation and accommodation, which blends the child's existing ways of thinking with new experiences.

Ultimately, drawings move from a static formation to one of action. This shift in thinking indicates a higher stage of equilibrium than was seen just 6 months prior. In the case of Anna, her ability to reason has moved from

2.20 Anna Begins Classifying

an inductive ability to a deductive one. Thus, by the age of 8, an ability to sequence and comprehend space and time representations will become prominent in her pictorial renderings.

Figure 2.21 provides an example of this growing ability. In storybook fashion Anna relays a tale concerning her cat, Silly. The original drawings were placed one after the other in book form. It must be noted that Piaget stated that until roughly the age of puberty children believe in animism, whereby, for example, the sun is alive and flowers are inhabited by spirits and fairies. Thus, in Figure 2.21 Silly sleeps in a bed (like a child) and begins her morning by getting dressed for the day.

Figure 2.21 begins with a bird singing a melody, while Silly is still in bed. Panel 1 depicts Anna's intellectual advances toward reality (i.e., Silly is

2.21 Anna at Age 8

seen under the covers with his head visible; his feet are also shown, yet they are covered as they would be in reality). In panels 2 and 3, we see Silly leaping out of bed into the air; this concept of spatial distance and perspective is indicated by Anna's clear representation in the drawings. By panel 4, Silly has landed upon the bedsprings; we are therefore given an unimpeded example of sequential actions. After getting dressed (panels 5, 6, and 7), Silly is ready to take on the morning (panel 8).

As time marches forward, a diminished subjectivity that typifies this stage is met with a more realistic appraisal of the environment, and with this growing realism the child moves from his or her egocentric world. It is at age 9 to 10 that the child takes into account color and the object. As rules become ever more important, it is no longer acceptable to paint a blue tree or a purple cat.

In Figure 2.22, drawn by a 9.5-year-old I will call JoAnn, the colors were in direct proportion to the object drawn. The child "has begun to find some logical order in the world and is establishing concrete relationships with things around him" (Lowenfeld & Brittain, 1982, p. 253).

2.22 JoAnn at Age Nine and a Half

2.23 Carpinteria, California

Figure 2.23, drawn by a 10-year-old girl, demonstrates this need for logical order as the child's world branches out beyond the borders of home (see disk to view in color).

Lowenfeld and Brittain (1982) describe the folding over as seen in Figure 2.23 as a mixture of plan and elevation. This type of rendering gives very little consideration to realism and instead focuses on the important points that the child is attempting to convey. However, this stage in the art will soon give way to the child's exploration of whole systems and intellectual experimentation.

In Figure 2.24 JoAnn (age 10) has begun to represent her world in a realistic manner. Therefore, the child's budding interests become topics of the artwork. Her cognitive maturation is exemplified by the increased awareness of the environment and a thrust toward realism.

As children near Piaget's stage of formal operations they continue their immersion with their environment, and it is at this juncture that a greater awareness of and concern for detailing emerge. At this stage their drawings take on a variety of details, from clothing that is decorated to facial features and emphasis on body parts (e.g., breasts, muscles).

In Figure 2.25 JoAnn, nearly one year later, has begun to concentrate on the self. Her figure drawings take on a coquettish air, with great attention to facial features, clothing, and attitude. This emphasis of children

2.24 JoAnn at Age 10

2.25 JoAnn at Age 10 Years 11 Months

on themselves within their surroundings is a precursor to the often-contemptuous stage of endless questions in search of the self.

In the final phase of Piaget's stages (formal operations; ages 11 to 15) youths begin the search for the self. This ushers in a new phase of questioning that encompasses everything: "They think about thinking. They enter into the world of ideas; the road has gone from a world of objects (physical world), through a world of social relations (social world), to a world of many perspectives (ideational world)" (Maier, 1978, p. 64).

In Figure 2.26 a 14-year-old female writes the following questions (obscured within the dark clouds):

> What . . .
> . . . will become of me?
> . . . is life
> . . . will happen to my friends?
> Who . . .
> . . . will I be friends with?
> . . . will I marry?
> Where . . .
> . . . will I die?
> . . . will I live?
> When . . .
> . . . will I die?
> . . . will I leave?

2.26 A 14-Year-Old's Questions

Questions such as these, which revolve around social relationships and the problems that adolescents encounter, weigh heavily on their minds. Hence, their drawings show an increased relationship to feelings, ideas, thoughts, and sophisticated problem solving. It is at this point that they show an increased ability to depict three-dimensional space as the acquisition of complex thinking moves toward equilibrium.

Figure 2.27 shows three very different drawings (using acrylic, watercolor, and pencils respectively) by teenagers (see disk to view in color). These drawings express their individual needs and desires as they continue their march toward intellectual maturity, and the use of varying art media allows this expression to flow unimpeded by outward constraints.

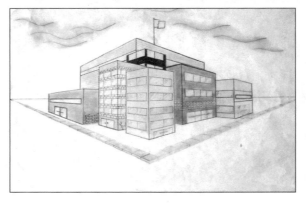

2.27 Equilibrium

As we can see, Piaget believed that learning was tied to maturation; thus, comprehension of the task is infinitely important. In the sensorimotor period children learn to operate physically upon the environment while becoming increasingly goal directed. In the preconceptual phase, children begin to function symbolically, incorporating language with representational communication. By the age of 4, the phase of intuitive thought, there is an increase in social participation and a greater understanding of conceptual thinking. In the concrete operations period, logical thinking begins to emerge along with the ability to order experiences as awareness of the realistic connections inherent in relationships surfaces. It is often at this juncture that children cease drawing in favor of expressing their thoughts through writing. Finally, with the approach of formal operations the growing adolescent grapples with ideas and thinks critically. Piaget likened this stage to the ultimate stage of human development.

These stages of cognitive development are also evident through changes in artwork. Thus, at age 12 months (sensorimotor period) the infant's beginning scribbles become apparent, until the age of 2 years, when increased control allows the developing child to apply a greater variety of pressure, line, and stroke. From ages 2 to 4 (preconceptual phase) the child begins to relate his or her drawings to things known in the environment both physically and kinesthetically. The age of 4 to 7 (intuitive thought) takes us into representational attempts to delineate appendages, clothing, hair, and other detailing. Following this period, ages 7 to 11 (concrete operations) find the growing child utilizing repeated schemas, which soon gives way to less exaggeration and a more logical and realistic relationship in the choice of drawing objects. In the final phase, age 11 and onward (formal operations), the adolescent seeks a controlled and purposeful expression as he or she attains mastery of the art media (Lowenfeld & Brittain, 1982).

Freud

Unlike Piaget with his structured stages, Freud viewed his psychosexual stages as overlapping and therefore deficient in organized configuration. His theory is based upon the belief that deprivation of nurturance (specifically maternal) during infancy results in neurotic difficulties that persist well into adulthood. "In a strict sense Freud was not proposing stages in personality development but tracing the vicissitudes of the sexual energy which he posited and termed *libido* and deemed a motivating force in all human behavior" (Lidz, 1976, p. 85).

Thus, if an individual passes through the five phases (oral, anal, phallic or Oedipal, latency, and genital) without becoming fixated within any specific stage, he or she has achieved sexual maturation through the substitution of new object-cathexes for instinctual object-choices. However, if a fixation occurred, Freud believed the individual would develop a select series of defense mechanisms and behaviors that directly link to specific phases.

Freud's first phase, the oral, is comparable to the age of infancy (birth to 12 months) and represents a stage of dependency. The infant busily places things in the mouth, bites, and sucks, which provides pleasure as well as a sense of protection. However, frustration can develop from the separation of the object (bottle, nipple, food, nurturance) from the infant's mouth, which brings on a reaction to hold on. "The mouth, therefore, has at least five main modes of functioning, (1) taking in, (2) holding on, (3) biting, (4) spitting out, and (5) closing. Each of these modes is a *prototype* or original model for certain personality traits" (Hall, 1954, p. 108). In Piaget's cognitive model the infant has learned to adapt to the environment by the age of 12 months; however, if in Freud's theory, the infant is faced with separation, the manner in which he or she integrates the division will produce a representation that will serve throughout the growing child's adult years.

Therefore, Freud hypothesized that in the early stages of the oral phase incorporation is utilized; either this can be sublimated, as an adult, into a quest to incorporate knowledge, interests, and activities (acquisitiveness), or frustration can develop, and the now adult will incorporate (hold onto) things in order to control their comings and goings (greediness). These symbolic behaviors continue through the phases and can be linked to defense mechanisms that appear and persist in a client's behavior.

As such, projection is often utilized as a defense against dependency in the oral phase of development. If in infancy the child develops a dependent attitude instead of seeking assistance the individual may feel an overpowering need to assist others or purchase lavish gifts. Equally, the desire of dependency may bring on feelings of shame, and a reaction formation may develop that finds the individual resisting dependency on anyone (Hall, 1954).

Oral aggressiveness, the act of biting after teeth have formed, can bring about an adaptation that relies upon sarcasm, verbal retorts, and a dominant attitude. Overall anxiety produced throughout the oral phase of development can cause not only a fixation but also an inability to move into the succeeding phases.

Freud's second stage is known as the anal phase and stretches roughly from the ages of 12 months to 3 years. This phase is identified by the process of withholding and letting go and centers around toilet training and bowel functioning. Freud (1963) describes the process of defecation (expulsion) in the first year of life as a pleasurable activity that reduces tension. However, by the second year of life the child must decide if he or she will let go of feces, at the love object's request, or withhold them for purposes of autoerotic gratification, thus asserting self-will. If toilet training is particularly punitive, the child when grown to adulthood may retaliate against authority figures through irresponsibility and obstinacy. The same punitive toilet training may cause a reaction formation in the adult, and a sense of orderliness may develop in the personality structure that encompasses collecting, possessing, and holding onto objects. This overcontrolled behavior may express itself through compulsive qualities (anal retentiveness) that involve frugality and parsimony. Freud (1963) further states that there are definitive commonalities that exist between an interest in money and defecation.

> Wherever archaic modes of thought predominate or have persisted—in ancient civilizations, in myth, fairy-tale, and superstition, in unconscious thought and dreams, and in the neuroses—money comes into the closest relation with excrement. We know how the money which the devil gives paramours turns to excrement after his departure, and the devil is certainly nothing more than a personification of the unconscious instinctual forces. . . . It is possible that the contrast between the most precious substance known to man and the most worthless, which he rejects as 'something thrown out,' has contributed to the identification of gold with feces. (pp. 31–32)

Freud likens the goose that lays golden eggs in the English fairy tale "Jack and the Beanstalk" to the finding of a treasure in association with defecation. In fact, fairy tales (which is explored later in this chapter) deal with the basic needs of maturation and development. Therefore, the whole of "Jack and the Beanstalk" deals with the growth and regression to earlier stages of a boy as he achieves puberty, while the golden goose can be seen as merely one phase of his development.

In the phallic or Oedipal phase, pleasurable activities shift from the anal erotic zone to the genitalia (phallus). This is also a time when the child begins to exhibit sexual longing for the parent of the opposite sex. Freud termed the boy's shift—from identifying with his father to becoming a rival while sexual wishes emerge toward the mother—the *Oedipus complex.* The equivalent situation for the girl, her desire to possess the father while renouncing the mother, was termed the *Electra complex.* By way of example I am appending a letter (Figure 2.28) that I wrote to my father, which I believe offers an example of Freud's Electra complex. My parents lovingly saved this letter and would retrieve it from its secret hiding place every so

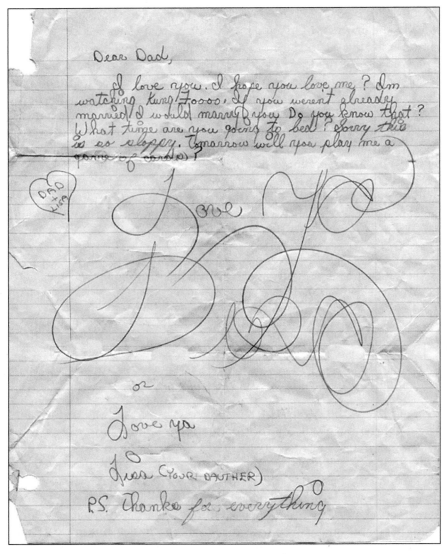

2.28 The Electra Complex

often, usually during family gatherings and such. They had a very caustic sense of humor.

However, the welling up of sexual feelings toward the opposite-sexed parent brings about its own anxiety and fear (the castration complex) and is therefore quickly dispatched to the unconscious, where it is repressed. The child must then identify with the lost love object or with the rival.

In addition, "the super-ego, too, the moral agency which dominates the ego, has its origin in the process of overcoming the Oedipus complex" (Freud, 1959, p. 268).

Lidz (1976) notes that "The 'oedipal transition' is considered a central event in personality development and critical to the patterning of all subsequent interpersonal relationships" (p. 87). Thus, if we compare the prior stages (oral and anal) to the phallic stage we can say that the shift has moved from an egotistical, inward process to one of outward expression, which will culminate in the union of the opposites of sexuality (genital phase).

Freud's latency period, ages 5 to 12, is characterized by sublimatory activities designed to fend off the temptation toward self-gratification. Prepubescent children "tend to become attached to activities (which would later be carried out almost automatically) such as going to sleep, washing, dressing and walking about; and they tend also to repetition and waste of time" (Freud, 1959, p. 116). It is at this point that sexuality lies dormant while feelings arising from the ego, such as shame, disgust, and inhibitions, arise. Beyond repression and sublimation the defense mechanism of reaction formation is employed.

If we refer back to the discussion on conversion (Figure 1.9), this client was molested in the midst of the latency period, yet she had repressed the traumatic experiences until they were not only disguised but also expressed through a reaction formation. The overwhelming shame and belief that she was "damaged" was articulated in its opposite form through the external expression of flawlessness. This continued well into her adolescent years, until the unconscious was made conscious through the artwork.

At puberty, when biochemical and glandular changes take place, the latency period ends and a period of socialization, peer groups, and love interests (which can now be fulfilled physiologically) comes into play. This is a time of adult tasks and responsibility and a phase that lasts until senility. Moreover, as Hall (1954) points out, "the displacements, sublimations, and other transformations of the pregenital cathexes become a part of the permanent character structure" (p. 119).

Thus, Freud and his psychosexual phases traced the origins of adult neurosis and fixations to earlier stages of development, while Piaget outlined adaptive functioning through cognitive development. With these two very different approaches it is important to note that alone they stand for the polarities of human maturity (adaptive and maladaptive), yet together they can yield a wealth of assessment information. And if we apply this knowledge to the art medium, we can achieve a very accurate representation of a client's developmental level.

By way of example, an individual's choice of media and how it is applied will offer a multiplicity of clues. Thus, a client who "regresses" with the use of wet clay (e.g., smearing it or displaying intense dislike at its mention) could be in the anal phase of development. Conversely, the use of pencil and nothing else yields information on a need for safety through a controlled medium (orderly phase of anal development). As children reach latency and are sublimating their sexuality through order (based on collecting), their images often contain a series of objects (e.g., weapons, boats, airplanes, flowers, hearts). However, an adolescent or adult who continues to draw in this manner (a multiplicity of objects on a single page) is expressing a significant deviation from the norm, which suggests a regression to the stage of latency. Figure 2.29, with its violent theme, is an example of such a fixation.

In the end, individuals who compensate for their anxiety through their words and actions become helpless before the art media. The art does not utilize language; it is a nonverbal communication that allows the unconscious mind to speak the truth.

2.29 Belying the Stage of Calm

Erikson

Erik Erikson is noted for his numerous writings on the healthy ego through his theory of psychosocial personality development. In his early adulthood he taught art in an American experimental school in Vienna. The school taught the children whose parents had come to Vienna to join Freud's psychoanalytic trainings. It was through this experience that he met Anna Freud, and soon thereafter he began psychoanalytic training and analysis for himself (Maier, 1978). Ultimately, "he converted the Freudian notion of psychosexual development of libidinal phases to one of psychosocial stages of ego development" (Maier, p. 73). This theory relies upon the premise that within each phase (totaling eight and often referred to as "spanning womb to tomb") emerging conflict must be mastered in order to prepare the individual for future growth and integrity. Each of Erikson's phases identifies a division that incorporates either an encouraging or a detrimental result, and it is society that will help the individual meet his or her needs and surmount his or her struggles by providing the norms of behavior, which ultimately will yield the desired integrated identity.

Erikson attributes five of his phases to childhood (these coincide with Freud's psychosexual stages) and the remaining three to adulthood (thus broadening and extending Freud's theory). Erikson gives much emphasis to the first five stages, as he believed that personality development was based upon the early stages of the life cycle. His first stage, which encompasses birth to the first year, was termed *basic trust versus basic mistrust* and corresponds closely to both Freud's and Piaget's first phases. The child, completely dependent upon the caregiver, incorporates (orally) the objects in the environment through grasping and sucking until adaptive behavior and experimentation develop. The infant experiments with his or her understanding of not only his or her inner world but the external world as well, and it is through this understanding (found through consistency) that trust emerges (both within and from the outside).

In the second year of life, Erikson's stage titled *autonomy versus shame and doubt,* the child's musculature develops and experimentation and exploration become the norm of behavior. Erikson speaks of the same concept as that of Freud's anal phase: holding (on) and letting (go). However, toilet training (self-control) is simply one example of the child's burgeoning autonomy, while shame and doubt are the result of parental overcontrol.

As the child reaches out to his or her environment and symbolization develops, art and play offer a sense not only of self-control but also of lim-

2.30 Release and Adapt

its. Figure 2.30, painted by a 2-year-old (over a 2-week period) with mini-mal intervention from her parents, offers an example of the child's capac-ity to release (top) and to eventually adapt to (bottom) the thick tempera paint; Figure 2.31 shows her ability to retain (see disk to view both figures in color). In Figure 2.30 her paints have combined to form one color, a smeared blue; however, through continued attempts (bottom) yellow and red peek out from beneath the blue brushstrokes.

One month later (Figure 2.31) her colors stand alone; the image is bold, while shapes and boundaries have been established.

2.31 Retain

According to Erikson (1963),

> This stage, therefore, becomes decisive for the ratio of love and hate, coop-eration and willfulness, freedom of self-expression and its suppression. From a sense of self-control without loss of self-esteem comes a lasting sense of good will and pride, from a sense of loss of self-control and of foreign over-control comes a lasting propensity for doubt and shame. (p. 254)

At the end of the 3rd year of life (*initiative versus guilt*) the child's basic family takes on growing importance. It is at this stage that children model themselves after their parents, a process that corresponds loosely to Freud's Oedipal conflict. However, Erikson believed this process to be a power struggle of will against the controlling parent more than a sexual struggle, as Freud postulated. Thus, children's initiative increases as they seek out who they will be and how they will interact within their environment. This shift from egocentricity toward responsibility and increased social partici-pation also sees the emerging superego (conscience) produce guilt and fears whenever conflict surrounding their behavior arises. In contrast, Pi-aget felt that the child exhibited shame and humiliation at this age (3), with guilt predominating from the age of 7 onward. Yet the two theorists agreed that, as the forces of conflict emerge, play becomes an indispen-sable tool with which the child can master and balance the inner and outer worlds. "The child uses play to make up for defeats, sufferings, and frustrations, especially those resulting from a technically and culturally limited use of language" (Erikson, 1940, p. 561).

By the 6th year of life the fourth stage of Erikson's model appears, *industry versus inferiority*. This stage is characterized by the child's radius of relationships branching out into the neighborhood and school. As the prior period was based on a sense of direction and purpose, this phase revolves around a sense of competency. In a stage closely aligned with Freud's latency stage (one of calm), the child now receives approval, regard, and affection based on achievement, which ultimately depends on his or her competence, or conversely, suffers a continuing sense of inferiority (Lidz, 1976). Thus, the ability to complete tasks and be productive is essential for the development of ego mastery. However, if the child feels inadequate, the polarity of this stage becomes a pull toward less production and a satisfaction with slothful behavior. Not unlike Piaget's stage of concrete operations (logical thought about physical objects and their relationship), Erickson's fourth phase sees the child applying his or her thoughts and energy to new skills and tasks. "He can become an eager and absorbed unit of a productive situation. To bring a productive situation to completion is an aim which gradually supersedes the whims and wishes of play" (Erikson, 1963, p. 259).

As adolescence approaches, the child enters the fifth phase, *identity versus role confusion*, which could easily be defined as 'to be or not to be." It is at this point that a search for the self begins just as the adolescent is attempting to consolidate an identity. If we return to Figure 2.26, this 14-year-old is exploring the youthful struggle of "Who am I to be?" through both the artwork and the written word. Erikson believes that phase five (*identity versus role confusion*) is where the prior four phases have coalesced toward an ego identity and mastery of skills. Yet, as with all of his phases, the polarity of opposites exists: If the adolescent has not gained a sense of competence, purpose, and self-control, he or she will be unable to cope with growing frustrations as peer groupings and models of leadership become the norm. It is at this juncture that an individual, feeling a sense of loss and isolation, may turn toward antisocial behaviors, thoughts, and attitudes in order to secure any identity, no matter how dysfunctional. It is this growing identity that often causes parents and clinicians the most problems, for parents often do not know how to deal with the issue, and clinicians often overlook its importance, especially when dealing with an adult population. An individual's sense of identity persists well into adulthood: It knows no barriers but instead is found within. Therefore, if an identity is that of an addict, a criminal, or a dependent mentally ill framework, this will be brought into the therapeutic hour. It will be projected, transferred, and played out in myriad ways. Of the hospitalized patients I have worked with, very few have had a secure job, a driver's license or photo identification, a high school diploma or college education, a viable support system, or even a home to return to: thus, their identities had become linked with institutionalization. As an example, Figure 2.32 shows two samples of work completed in a group with long-term institutionalized adults.

The directive was to draw "Who are you?" and this directive was given seven times over as the patients moved from one self-disclosure statement to another. The drawing on the left (Figure 2.32) was the first drawing completed by one member and expresses quite bluntly his identity in his mind's eye. Another member, in therapy for drug sales and possession, depicted himself with hoards of money in his first drawing (Figure 2.32, right side). Both of these renderings, as the first drawings, are not mistakes but instead unconscious perceptions. It is commonly believed that the first drawing identifies the artist's self-concept and identification (Machover, 1949). The identity diffusion that these gentlemen and this population experience is further complicated by the continuous struggles that were not mastered in adolescence.

Erikson's sixth phase, *intimacy versus isolation*, is directly linked to the previous one, for if the adolescent fails to find a true sense of identity the shift to intimacy with another is difficult at best. One of the major obstacles, therefore, is retaining a sense of one's own identity while becoming involved in a united partnership. Given the same group directive as Figure 2.32, a young adult male answered the question "Who are you?" by drawing four of his seven images with the opposite sex.

The individual who drew Figure 2.33 had been incarcerated after having battered a female stranger he met on the street who rebuffed his advances. These images could be interpreted on numerous levels; however,

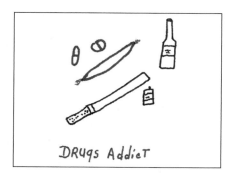 

2.32 Who Are You?

81

2.33 A Young Adult Answers "Who Are You?"

for the purposes of this discussion it revealed that the patient's need to find a partner and a sense of shared identity had become an obsession. Erikson (1963) explains the disadvantages of this phase in the following manner:

> The counterpoint of intimacy is distantiation: the readiness to isolate and, if necessary, to destroy those forces and people whose essence seems dangerous to one's own, and whose "territory" seems to encroach on the extent of one's intimate relations. . . . The danger of this stage is that intimate, competitive, and combative relations are experienced with and against the selfsame people. (p. 264)

As the individual moves into mid-adulthood, production and care become the focus. Erikson referred to his second-to-last phase as *generativity versus self-absorption.* It must be noted that generativity does not merely encompass procreation but also care and concern for society at large manifested through a promotion of values, morals, education, and charity. The difficulty of this phase lies in self-absorption, which can pull the adult away from the community with an all-encompassing focus on self-love.

As with all of Erikson's phases, each depends upon not only the basic virtues (hope, willpower, purpose, competence, fidelity, love, care, and wisdom) but also the inner conflicts that create the paradox. His final phase, *integrity versus despair*, revolves around the ego's integration and the acceptance of the past—a past consisting of all we have been and acknowledging that which we will not be. In this vein, refer to Figure 2.34, completed by an elderly male as part of a group project. The patient was responding to the directive "Separate your paper into threes and draw in the first section where you came from, in the second where you are now, and in the last where you are going."

This patient typically used only a single color (black) and preferred to draw environments rather than people. The patient stated that the first section was a memory of his home as a child. The second section was a rendering of the hospital, with the patient relating numerous experiences in other mental hospitals. Note how the center drawing looks like an oversized home, with the sun shining brightly; this patient had been hospitalized in one manner or another since mid-adulthood, and thus a state of incarceration was truly his home. The final section depicts the board and care home he wished to be discharged to, with the cross denoting "peace" through death. At the end of his description he stated, "Nothing good ever happens to me," which calls to mind Erikson's statement that "De-

2.34 Where I Came From

spair expresses the feeling that the time is now short, too short for the attempt to start another life and to try out alternate roads to integrity" (1963, p. 269).

In the final analysis Erikson—who, one must not forget, was psychoanalytically trained—describes ego development in terms of a supportive social milieu where an individual must ultimately face crisis and conflict. He outlines these crises in terms of polarities that require integration. His basic virtues defined an optimistic outlook that was definitely missing in Freud's psychosexual stages and thus allowed the young adult to continue toward a maturity far beyond adolescence. Yet when one applies information from all three theories (Piaget, Freud, and Erikson), no matter how disparate the theories present themselves, a coherent understanding of personality formation comes to light. For although Erikson in later years discounted the Oedipal conflict and Piaget saw the polarities as a process of temporary equilibrium, while Freud based his theory upon a belief that deprivation of nurturance during infancy results in neurosis, each theorist offered classifications that hold special significance in treatment as they provide a clue to adaptive and maladaptive personality functioning.

To make the comparisons easier to understand, Table 2.3 not only condenses the theories presented but also explores normative behavior in children's art, preferred media, and therapeutic materials as it applies to age and developmental levels.

Therapists must not overlook the information in Table 2.3 when utilizing art with the difficult client. In my work with children, youths, and adults, the majority of my clients were significantly delayed developmentally. However, developmental delay, in this instance, does not refer to the diagnosis of Pervasive Developmental Disorder, nor does it indicate a lack of intelligence. It simply implies what the three theorists postulated: that in every stage of development resolution must occur, for without resolution a fixation may transpire, the individual might not be able to navigate the environment with any level of competence or skill, and thus future growth and integrity could be stunted. Any delay will therefore only gain in intensity as the child ages, making interventions all the more important. Thus, utilizing the proper materials for the stage of development becomes integral to successful treatment. One would not intervene with an alcoholic by suggesting that he or she form new relationships by visiting the local tavern, nor should one utilize the stories of Edgar Allan Poe with a client who is 5 years old or developmentally reacts as a 5-year-old.

By way of further clarification, the next four categories will discuss the use of fairy tale, myth, and literature; collecting; and appropriate media.

Table 2.3 Normative Behavior

Age	Piaget's Stage	Artwork	Media	Freud's Stage	Therapy Materials	Erikson's Stage
Birth to 1 month	Sensorimotor: grasping and sucking; brings objects to mouth; repetition			Oral: oral pleasure; orally aggressive Defense mechanisms (DM): incorporation, projection, introjection		Basic trust versus basic mistrust: social trust, comfort, consistency, coping with urges, hope or despair
1–4 months						
4–8 months						
8–12 months	Adaptive behavior and experimentation	Beginning of scribble; faint lines			Dolls with bottles, toy telephones	
12–18 months	Watching events	Scribble bolder	Crayons	Anal: orderly, parsimonious, obstinate DM: reaction formation	Wet clay, finger paints, toy cars, soldiers, miniature furniture, doll houses, dolls, paper dolls, rhymed stories, puppets, nature tales, animal tales, blocks	Autonomy versus shame and doubt: egocentric behavior, assertion of will, self-control
18–24 months	Forming mental combinations	Increased control	Large crayons			
2–3 years	Preconceptual: hold mental representations; symbolization; language development; play is symbolic or ritualistic	Simple forms, haphazard coloring, tadpole figures	Large crayons/pencils, thick tempera, large brushes, clay	Phallic: Oedipus complex, Electra complex DM: projection, identification, repression		
3 years						
4 years	Intuitive thought: grappling with complex problems; increased social participation; shame and humiliation predominates DM: rationalization	Able to draw a square; generalizing images; images are static	Thick paint, any size crayons, pencils, markers, collage materials, wet and plasticene clay	Latency: sexuality lies dormant DM: repression, sublimation, reaction formation	All of the above and fairy tales, fables, games with definite rules, Legos	Initiative versus guilt: egocentric behavior recedes; emerging conscience (superego); play takes on greater importance, direction, and purpose
5 years		Images are dynamic, logical, integrated; sequencing; drawing diamonds				
6–7 years						

(continued)

Table 2.3 Continued

Age	Piaget's Stage	Artwork	Media	Freud's Stage	Therapy Materials	Erikson's Stage
7–11 years	Concrete operations: logical thought, realism; autonomy is prized; guilt develops; rules become important	Drawings gain consistency; drawing triangles; baseline appears; realistic use of color and space relationships	All of the above and oil pastels, craft projects, watercolor, charcoal, India ink, papier mâché	Latency stage: (see above) DM: undoing, compartmentalization, isolation, identification	All of the above and collectible items, stamps, baseball cards, trading cards, plastic models, dolls, beads, boxes, rocks (early is haphazard, later is organized)	Industry versus inferiority: recognition through production, feelings of ego mastery, acceptance of limitations
11–15 years	Formal operations: search of the self, complex thinking, critical thought	Improved perspective; exploration of past, present and future; three-dimensional space is explored	Any material available	Genital: sexual instinct is coupled with mature sexuality; adult responsibilities DM: displacement, sublimation	All of the above (ages 4 and on) and myth and legends, allegory, historical stories, classic literature, microscopes, telescopes, science activities, hobby crafts	Identity versus role confusion: the promise of finding oneself and the threat of losing oneself
Early adulthood						Intimacy versus isolation: affiliation and love with another; competition and cooperation
Mid-adulthood			Large markers/pencils, thick paint			Generativity versus self-absorption: production and care
Late adulthood						Integrity versus despair: denunciation and wisdom

There Was, There Was, and Yet There Was Not

One must remember that an individual's chronological age can be very different from his or her developmental age. Thus, the use of art therapy and its concentration on symbolization, freedom of expression, and verbal and nonverbal communicative components is perfectly suited to aid in resolution at any stage of development. In addition, the use of fairy tales aids the developing personality to branch out into the world, helping patients to understand others' feelings and thereby removing them from the previous egocentric style of thought that characterized their world. If you recall Erikson's initiative versus guilt stage, the child at age 4 has made a shift from egocentric thinking to one of direction and purpose. However, this growing personality is still incomplete, for the child tends to define good or bad according to the reward or punishment that ensues rather than on a degree of misbehavior. This is due to a lack of critical thinking and super-ego development, faculties that are simply not present in a 4-year-old.

Thus, the use of Edgar Allan Poe, or any other classic literature that deals with true-to-life characters (versus amorphous creatures), will not allow the child (ages 18 months to latency) to move into an imaginative world but will keep him or her tethered to reality and frighten him or her. The characters of fairy tales, though defined as typical people, most certainly are not. They live in castles; they speak to animals, and the animals respond in kind; they are not given usual names but instead are often referred to according to their role in the family or society (e.g., stepmother, youngest child, father, huntsman, etc.). The fairy tale often depicts the youngest and "simplest" child as the hero who ultimately overcomes the odds and succeeds where others have failed. These stories often focus on children's fears in relationship to parents and siblings. These struggles are either familiar to the child or equivalent to familiar ones. Thus fairy tales, fables, and nature stories are customary by the time the child is in the second grade, just as from ages 18 months to 3 years old, when mental combinations are being formed and language develops, rhymed stories (Mother Goose and Dr. Seuss) are the standard books being read and requested.

Unfortunately, many parents believe that the fairy tales of yesterday, particularly the Brothers Grimm, are too aggressive for young children. They look at the fairy tale with the eye of an adult and forget that as children the use of fantasy is a product of the ego structure of latency. Children play. They play with toys, and if these are not available a box becomes a fort while stuffed animals become noble steeds. If these are not available the power of the imagination places tea in empty cups and swords in bare hands. Children at the age of 4 are afraid of the dark, goblins, and ghosts.

By the age of 8, as independence develops, they fear being small, vulnerable, or alone. By age 9 the desire to break free of parental control predominates, and thoughts of being a movie star or an accomplished athlete are prominent. And, alas, by the age of 12 fantasy is forsaken, symbols are lost, reality sets in, and adolescence begins (Sarnoff, 1974). With each of these developmental stages there are nursery rhymes, fairy tales, myth, legend, and literature, all with the power to express in masked forms the affect-laden memories of prelatency.

It is because of this that fairy tales should not be afforded an explanation; the client understands the inner significance without discussion. Just as a child walks into the world without the safety of his family—to school, to sleep-over parties, and the like—fairy tales not only depict that feeling of loneliness but teach autonomy and independence with which to overcome the odds and find a path to riches and love. By the same token, the use of illustration becomes more a hindrance than an aid to the telling of the story. In the telling the imagination has already formed that image, and an artist's depiction will only distract. If the parent, therapist, or counselor has an overwhelming need to discuss the story, then he or she should have the clients draw their own illustration. Therapists can ask what the character looks like and listen to the variations. These nondirected discussions will yield a wealth of information. As anyone who has read these stories will attest, it becomes all too apparent when children have made a connection with the characters in the story, as they will demand to be told the story incessantly. No amount of parental prompting will change their mind. It is at this point that the simplicity, directness, bravery, and value of the fairy tale have broken through. The figures and events have not only illustrated the inner conflicts but offered reassurance and hope for the future.

When one is looking at the developmental needs of a child or developmentally delayed adult it is important to take into account what stage of growth the patient presently possesses. As stated earlier, reading a story beyond or beneath the needs of an individual will fail miserably. Thus, the use of story, fable, and allegory must be tailored to meet changing needs and attitudes. Nursery rhymes such as "Humpty Dumpty," "Hey Diddle, Diddle," or "Hickory, Dickory, Dock" are excellent for the child who is just beginning language development (Piaget's sensorimotor and preconceptual stages) and will learn from and enjoy a symbolic and repetitious cycle. However, for the person who is learning to grapple with complex problems and is focused on the beginning stages of social participation (Piaget's intuitive thought and early phase of concrete operations), nursery rhymes would seem infantile.

Before I illustrate some of the better-known fairy tales it is important to outline the following concerns. The first is that the tales that most touch a child's, and adult's, growing needs are those that have not been watered down. The tale must remain true to its source and related without the benefit of condensing the story. An example would be Carlo Collodi's story "The Adventures of Pinocchio," which was later to be made into the animated film and book by the name of *Pinocchio*. This version, retold by the Walt Disney company, though much beloved, has either deleted or watered down portions of the story. Thus, inner conflicts have lost much of their significance. The differences from the original story are so great that I can only urge the reader to compare the two (especially the beginning and ending) to understand what developmental lessons are gained in the original and subsequently lost through its retelling.

The second issue is in regard to the Brothers Grimm. Their original intention was not to publish stories for children but to record a collection of German tales for science. Yet as time marched on, their original title of *Household Tales* was changed by editors into *Fairy Tales* (Untermeyer & Untermeyer, 1962). These stories have been retold by numerous people, shortened, and altered, yet it is entirely possible to find editors who have kept closely to the originals.

Lastly, there is a significant difference between fairy tales, myths, legends, and fables. In Freudian terms, fairy tales depict ego integration while allowing for id desires that become sublimated. Fables are exceedingly more moralistic than fairy tales and point toward superego development and problem solving. Myths, on the other hand, confront the reader directly with conflicting inner tendencies and are useful in forming the superego. However, their pessimistic quality does not benefit the entire personality. These distinctions are another necessary component when reviewing the use of therapy materials (Table 2.3) for the office.

Before we review select stories it is important that the clinician understand that, when reading a fairy tale to aid in development, the tale should be from the Brothers Grimm, as other versions of these stories have been so condensed that the symbolism and often the struggle or difficulty have been avoided. And it is just this struggle that must be retained, for without multiple unexpected and often cruel obstacles how can one put forth the sustained effort necessary to succeed?

As you refer to the column in Table 2.3 entitled "Therapy Materials," you will note that the stories suggested at 18 months begin with rhymed or nature tales. These are chosen due to the growing child's awareness of his or her environment as well as his or her early struggles to understand language. Thus, the rhymed stories of Dr. Seuss hold a young child's fascination through repetition and humor. The use of nature tales (ages 2 and onward) appeal to the growing child as he or she becomes attentive to their ever-changing world and desires and often demands explanations. These moralistic tales broaden and deepen the child's inner life, appeal to the sense of wonder, and provide a foundation from which to draw moral inferences. One story that is particularly effective is titled "Grandmother Marta" (Souby, 1990) and tells the tale of two girls. The older (and the only natural daughter of a rich woman) is spoiled, while the younger girl is their maid and servant. While the servant is retrieving water from a well she comes upon the twelve months talking among themselves, and since she is pure of heart and loving, Grandmother Marta blesses her. Now each time the young girl speaks, golden coins drop from her mouth. The rich woman, seeing this, sends off her only daughter to achieve the same end; however, because the elder girl has a heart infested with malice and evil, the seasons "bless" her so that from her mouth flow snakes and lizards. Once the rich woman discovers her daughter's plight, she casts out the maidservant, who promptly finds love and marriage with a prince.

The moral of this nature tale points toward love and intimacy: The elder child's (and mother's) insensitivity to the warmth and love of others produces only isolation and bitterness (see Erickson's stage of intimacy versus isolation), while the individual who keeps an open heart finds riches, wealth, and closeness. What child would not enter imaginatively into the characters of this story and grasp the elemental truth of the human experience? In this way all good tales provide that by which we can grow.

If we move on to a story recorded by the Brothers Grimm, "Hansel and Grethel" (Untermeyer & Untermeyer, 1962) revolves around separation anxiety through the children's desperate desire to keep a grasp on their parents. This tale works well for those who require independence and autonomy. As the reader may recall, in the story the two children are led into the woods by their parents (to be abandoned there due to the family's lack of food) but find their way home due to Hansel's quick thinking (he has marked their path with pebbles). In time, food once more becomes scarce and the children are again led into the deepest part of the dark woods (the unknown world); however, this time the children have not planned well, for instead of pebbles, Hansel drops bread crumbs to mark the route home (uses denial and regression). When birds eat the crumbs and the children are unable to return home a second time, they remain in a regressive state and eat of the gingerbread house (primitive orality and greediness). Initially they find the woman who lives in the house to be a gratifying mother figure, but in time she fools and tricks them like their own parents for wicked ends. It becomes obvious that continued regression and denial must be replaced with wit and maturity. Consequently, Grethel tricks the wicked woman, frees Hansel, and gathers the wicked woman's jewels. The children use their newfound intelligence to return home, and having conquered the evil world they are no longer a burden to the family.

Thus, the tale speaks of mastering oral anxieties, sublimating cravings, utilizing intelligence rather than wishful thinking, initiating, and cooperating with others—all in preparation for living happily in their newfound maturity (Bettelheim, 1977).

The last fairy tale that I will relate is "Cinderella." This story affects children between the ages of 6 and 10 and tells of the agonies and hopes that form the content of sibling rivalry. If we analyze this story through Erikson's psychosocial stages, we see that the stage of trust was established with Cinderella's experience with the original, good mother. After her mother's death, being gentle and pious she accepts her new role within the family as a maligned servant (autonomy through self-control and will power). When her father leaves for a fair, she requests that he bring her the first twig that touches his hat on his return home, which turns out to be a hazel branch (symbolically a protection against evil spirits and snakes), and Cinderella plants this twig over her mother's grave and cultivates it with her tears and emotions (initiative, direction, and purpose). The twig becomes a beautiful tree, which Cinderella visits three times a day, and soon becomes home to a white dove (symbol of simplicity and purity), which grants her heartfelt wishes. In time a ball is announced, and the young maiden is determined to attend, but in order to do so she has to complete many hard labors and tasks (industry through method and competence). At the ball (branching out into the larger society) the prince takes notice of her and only her. At the second and third balls the prince awaits her return, and each time Cinderella escapes the ball without his knowing where she lives or who she truly is. It is at the third ball that the prince retrieves her slipper, whereupon he promptly goes in search of its rightful owner. At Cinderella's home her stepsisters attempt to fool the prince by cutting off a toe and a sliver of heel in order that their feet may fit the slipper; however, two pigeons perched in the beautiful tree expose the scheme. On his last try the prince, ignoring the pleas of the stepmother, insists on meeting Cinderella. In this way Cinderella is accepted for herself (identity), as his true bride, regardless of her appearance. They marry (intimacy), while the stepsisters are blinded by the pigeons for their deceit and wickedness (just as symbolically they walked through life blinded by their emotions and hatred).

Each of these tales could be discussed on many levels. From the father in "Hansel and Grethel," who revealed his weak willpower and selfish desires (shame and doubt), to the stepmother's bitterness in "Cinderella," these tales rely on their layers of meaning, so the child can find his or her own answers to budding internal conflicts. However, it must be reiterated that adults and children view these tales of violence in different ways. When the stepsisters' eyes are pecked out by pigeons the adult sees excessive punishment; yet the child, who uses excessive thought, understands that the people reprimanded must have done something very horrid to warrant such a punishment and thus learns unconsciously through the acts of others.

Conversely, myths and fables present problems in the form of superhuman attainments that the young child could never emulate. Instead, the young child requires symbolism that will reward him, provide a sense of optimism, and unite the personality. Therefore, myth becomes important to youths who have passed latency (11 years and onward). As the phase of formal operations approaches, their quests become a search for the self; they branch out into the larger world, looking at their environment with a critical eye. One hopes that they hold within themselves a positive outlook for their future exploits. It is now the time for superego development, and at this stage myth, historical stories, and classic literature come to life. Gone are simplistic first names or general titles (stepmother, father, huntsman); instead, myths tell of specific people, with distinct names and family histories, and in so doing they forsake the generalized formula of fairy tales.

Table 2.4   *Stories That Aid in Development*

Topic	Suggested Stories
Angry emotions	Hans my Hedgehog, The Seven Ravens, Gilgamesh
Giving up dependency attachments	Little Red Riding Hood, Hansel and Grethel
Small achievements made astonishing	Puss in Boots, The Golden Goose
Achieving personality integration	The Queen Bee, The Three Languages, The Three Feathers, The Twin Brothers, The Arabian Nights, Pinocchio, Gilgamesh
Autonomy	The Goose Girl, Jack and the Beanstalk
Degradation	Cinderella, The Ugly Duckling
Problem solving	The Brave Little Tailor, Perseus
Vanity	The Emperor's New Clothes, Echo and Narcissus

Therefore, as part of treatment planning, the clinician should not overlook the use of stories in the therapeutic hour. If you have assessed the stage of development properly, the client will be mesmerized by these timeless stories that speak gently to internal struggles (regardless of age). I prefer to utilize the metaphors within the fairy tale, fable, myth, or legend by choosing the story that meets the client's needs. From time to time as I read the story I stop reading and direct the participant or group members to draw what they see. It is important that the protagonist (main character), family members, helpful or kindly figures, antagonist (evil figure or obstacles), and story ending (the last paragraph of each story) be drawn. In addition, story transformations (repetitious sayings, journeys or quests) and any interaction between the protagonist and antagonist are also good drawing subjects. This technique can be employed with any story that will propel the client forward and can be used with any medium (e.g., clay, watercolor, 3-D boxes, craft supplies).

In short, a story is a work of art. Whether fables, myths, or fairy tales, these stories touch the soul and speak to our unconscious thoughts, needs, and desires. They offer new perceptions and through them a path to growth.

A sampling of stories that aid in development can be found in Table 2.4.

Additionally, Table 2.5 provides a sampling of myths that aid in development through collective knowledge.

Table 2.5   Myths That Aid in Development

Focus	Myth
Unselfishness, honor	Prometheus
Adultery, family dysfunction	Zeus and Hera, Aphrodite and Hephaestus
Grief, suffering, loss	Demeter, Dionysus
Romance and love	Venus and Adonis, Pyramus and Thisbe, Orpheus
Revenge, trickery	Pandora's Box
Ambition brings ruin	Jason, Theseus
Arrogance attracts disaster	Minos
Fight for personal glory and fame	Achilles
Fight within the self	Homeric legend, King Arthur
Hero on quest	Gilgamesh, Siddhartha
Fights monsters, beasts	Beowolf, Bellerophon, Hercules, Perseus

Collecting

As the child moves toward Piaget's stage of concrete operations, collecting objects takes on new significance. If we refer to Table 2.3 we see that the child at the approximate age of 7 not only finds interest in his surroundings but desires to attain them. Thus, he or she will collect all sorts of items in a haphazard array that ends up in a pocket, a drawer, or the floor of a room. Not until the age of 10 does the child's collection take on greater significance. Yet these treasured items are still not classified or ready for display: The 10-year-old simply wants more and more, and therefore selection is not important. However, as the child's interpersonal skills increase (age 11), trading and bartering become central, and with this the need to increase selectivity gains prominence. By age 12 the collection takes on greater meaning, and the child often spends time talking about and looking at the acquisitions. Once the age of 13 arrives, however, collections have all but lost their fascination (Gesell, Ilg, & Ames, 1956).

These developmental phases are important for any clinician to know and understand, as they are a useful intervention tool. The urge to collect is a structure of mid- to late latency (roughly the ages of 8 to 12), and impairments in this structure can show themselves in many guises regardless of age. As an example, the client who is impulsive, destructive, or prone to fights and otherwise exhibits no mechanisms for restraint is acting out not only overstimulation but an impairment in this very necessary developmental phase. It is at this juncture that communicative therapy, which leads the client to talk about the problem at the traumatic root, may be beyond his or her capacity and would indicate a fixation more than therapeutic resistance. A simple method with which to decipher whether a client (of any age) is unable to support latency, through a failure of the symbolizing function, is to ask him or her to relate the plot of a favorite movie, book, or television show. If the client has navigated the age of latency, he or she will discuss the interpersonal details of the chosen medium. However, if the client relates the excitement, noise, or battles for supremacy, then impairments must be addressed (Sarnoff, 1987). This is where collecting becomes important. The act of bringing together not only is good for increasing restraint but becomes a metaphor that promotes sharing (see Erikson's identity versus role confusion stage). Once the clinician has ascertained the developmental level of the difficult client, utilizing the therapy materials listed in Table 2.3 will provide a direction. If the therapist is versed in the types of collecting and their equivalent ages, he or she can stock the office with items to not only pique interest but also move a client forward.

Therefore, it can be beneficial to have at hand a range of comic books, trading cards, dolls, miniatures, stickers, beads, or boxes that the client can organize, handle, and classify. In lieu of collections, plastic models will also serve this purpose. However, it is important to gauge the type of model. It would be inappropriate to allow a client in the early stage of latency to complete a model of a fantasy figure. Instead, offer the client a reality-based model (car, plane, boat, etc.) to move him or her into late latency (early adolescence). If this is not possible due to space considerations, the therapist can assign homework based on the need to classify and organize.

As an example, a severely impaired adult male schizophrenic who had a propensity toward theft, hoarding, and flushing rolls of toilet paper down the commode completed Figure 2.35 in a group session.

When discussing the snake he stated, "I chose a snake because they like to steal and eat. It's my hobby—stealing." This verbal statement, in concert with his propensity toward the toilet, pointed toward the anal stage of development (retention and possessing) when he was psychiatrically unstable.

However, when the patient was stabilized, his art, as well as his delusional system, focused on superheroes and the armed services. Figure 2.36 is a sampling of this patient's drawings taken from an art therapy assessment using the 8CRT.

Beyond this patient's delusional system, these drawings, with their col-

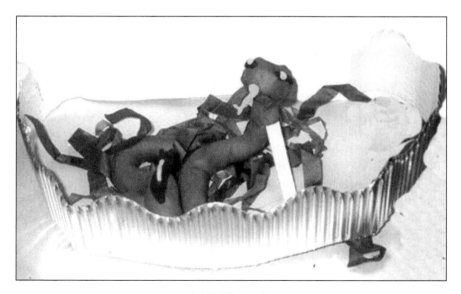

2.35 The Snake

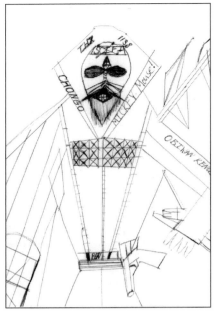

2.36 Superheroes

lection of weapons, minute detailing, and focus on action versus interaction, all point toward a failure in the latency-age adjustment. Since the client was stabilized on his medication it was time to begin a treatment plan that touched upon his delays and promoted autonomy. Thus, the use of plastic models was employed (initially in individual sessions) to provide him with structured play, and then he was incorporated into groups with peers to lessen his dependency on institutional personnel.

The process of collecting, organizing, and classifying is exceedingly important to the growing individual, or delayed client, as it ushers in the ensuing age of adolescence. As a final word on collecting, I am certain that most readers of this book will know an adult in their lives who is an avid collector, thus proving that the art of collecting is not merely a childish activity. Instead it provides a fundamental feeling of power. To own "all" of something and to be able to direct and organize (and in the case of obsessional collecting, to consume) it in whatever fashion one desires offers the individual a special place. As followers of Freud may know, he was an avid collector of antiquities. Freud began his collecting 2 months after his father's death, and it is believed that his collection assuaged the loss and grief that threatened to overwhelm him. At the end of his life these miniature statues lined his desk like an audience (Gamwell & Wells, 1989), offering a much-needed sense of solace and calm, much like what occurs in the stage latency.

Summary

We began the chapter by asking a series of questions: Is the presenting problem a function of the personality? A developmental delay? A failure in the developmental process? A normal repetition of the growth pattern? A product of an evolving identity? A fixation? A dependency reaction? Or regression?

We must end the chapter by stating that the answer most certainly depends upon the client, for the function of personality does not rest on one theory, one belief, or one therapeutic intervention. As humans, we are complex creatures, for we are not the same today as we were 10 years prior, nor will we remain unchanged by life's events 10 years into the future. Thus, a basic understanding of the norms of development can offer the clinician insight into the complexity of issues that may besiege a client at any given point in life. For the purposes of this book only three theorists, out of a host of researchers, are featured, because their models have been useful in assessing the difficult client. In the end, the clinician should seek the repetition of behavior that is calling out for mastery. The recurrence of behavior in clients' life stories; their behavior outside of the therapeutic hour; their self-concept, fears, and defenses; and of course the symbolism inherent in their art is what I refer to as a *symbolic abundance of ideas*.

As an example of how to apply the information, let's return to Figures 2.35 and 2.36. This patient, a regressed schizophrenic, had a propensity toward theft, flushing rolls of toilet paper down commodes, and hoarding found items. All of this information was offered by staff, and these habits were definitely a point of contention in the dorm where the client lived.

Therefore, if we refer to Table 2.3, even before speaking with the client we can hypothesize that he is fixated in the anal stage of development, which corresponds to Piaget's phase of symbolic play and Erikson's autonomy versus shame and doubt. This assertion of will also correlates with Table 2.2, where the anal stage of development (age 2.5) is much like age 11, when behavior worsens as the child grapples with feelings of mastery and his or her limitations. When I met with the client he created a snake (Figure 2.35) and stated, "I chose a snake because they like to steal and eat. It's my hobby—stealing." This verbal statement (even though it had the flavor of some oral incorporation needs) in concert with his propensity toward the toilet led me to believe that beyond his fixation in the anal stage his hoarding was more closely aligned with the need to collect. This assumption also corresponds with the age of 11 (as Table 2.2 pointed out); however, this client's collecting was disorganized, with the main focus on accumulating. Therefore, aligning this client with the age of 11 would gain importance (i.e., increasing his selectivity) when developing a treatment plan.

Arieti (1955) outlined four stages of the progression of the disease of schizophrenia. In the third stage he not only discusses hoarding but also indicates that an absence of symptoms prevails, as the client has learned to conceal his hallucinations and delusions, if only on a surface level. He states:

> The schizophrenic seems to hoard in order to possess; the objects he collects have no intrinsic value; they are valuable only inasmuch as they are possessed by the patient. The patient seems almost to have a desire to incorporate them, to make them a part of his person. . . . The fact remains that this tendency is a non-pathognomonic manifestation of advanced schizophrenic regression. (pp. 356–357)

In Figure 2.36, two of eight drawings were offered to show this patient's continued collecting needs (i.e., as exemplified by the detailing and proliferation of weapons). At this juncture, it was becoming more and more apparent that this patient was "screaming" to collect, to possess. If we refer once again to Table 2.3, at best this regressed client corresponds to Piaget's stage of intuitive thought (age 5 to 7), and it is this age that is incapable of delaying gratification out of a fear that the opportunity will not arise again (hence the theft). When developing a treatment plan, one must meet the client within and slightly above his or her level of development to encourage further developmental growth. Thus, in this case the therapist chose ages 6 to 12: the stage of latency (Freud), concrete operations (Piaget), and industry versus inferiority (Erikson). As Table 2.3 indicates, the most appropriate therapeutic materials all pointed toward collecting and organizing, and the client was offered his choice of materials (he chose plastic models).

It was of the utmost importance for the client to complete this treatment plan with another person (to promote a sense of social participation and action) and for the clinician to follow through on statements in a timely manner (to circumvent the client's feeling that only one chance is available and to promote trust). However, the client was not merely presented with an array of models: He had to earn them through a token economy system and incorporate budgeting into his thinking. Consequently, if he was going to "incorporate" as part of his fixation and collect as part of his need to possess, he should do so in a manner that bespoke of mastery and production.

Ultimately, utilizing the steps outlined in this chapter, therapists can base treatment plans on not only knowledge of the client (their needs, fears, and defenses), but also knowledge of the existing literature by a wide range of researchers, clinicians, and theorists. This process does not merely identify; it also allows for focused interventions.

In the end Piaget believed that the individual must master emerging conflict in order to prepare for future growth and integrity. "Consequently, human development (human learning) is neither purely social nor purely maturational; rather development evolves from individuals' experience of themselves and the patterns of living" (Maier, 1978, p. 21).

It is this pattern of living that provides us with our self-concept, our identity, our abilities, and our worth.

PART II

READING BETWEEN THE LINES

CHAPTER

3

———

Interpreting the Art

I f one believes that experience dictates our self-concept and this self-concept dictates our growth and wholeness, then how does a clinician tap into this sense of self? This ethereal quality that lives nowhere but exists within us all changes for the better or the worse with time and embraces our anxieties, joys, resentments, responsibilities, pleasures, and fears.

How does one break through the well-honed defenses that protect us from psychic pain and emerge with an unvarnished view?

Art.

Art does not censor or distort. Instead it frees. In its use the disguise of language, developed ever so carefully over a lifetime, is dropped, and in its place a psyche is projected onto a blank piece of paper—a reflection of not only an individual's self-concept but his or her concept of others. A projection of ourselves and our environment as we see it, from our own viewpoint, without any influence from external subjective material. This is the power of art.

Projective testing has always had many detractors, and we review this literature later in the chapter; however, it is my belief that although the unconscious nature of art certainly makes its study difficult such study is by no means impossible.

In that vein, this chapter focuses on projective methods of personality analysis and spotlights three techniques: the Draw-A-Person (DAP), the House-Tree-Person (HTP), and the Eight-Card Redrawing Test (8CRT). I have selected the first two procedures because they are the most frequently utilized of the art projective tests. I include the 8CRT because in my own

103

work with the difficult client this assessment tool has proven to be indispensable for evaluating personality decompensation.

The history of art projective testing can be traced to Florence Goodenough's *Measurement of Intelligence by Drawings* (1926). In this seminal work Goodenough focused on the human figure as a measurement of intelligence (IQ). However, as time went by "it was discovered that careful study of the individual drawings often yielded rich clinical material not related to the intellectual level of the subject" (Machover, 1949, p. 20). Since this discovery, the Draw-a-Person (DAP) technique was developed as a basis for using the body as a vehicle for self-expression and thus for personality analysis. Machover has stated, "in a significant proportion of cases, drawings do permit accurate judgments covering the subject's emotional and psychosexual maturity, his anxiety, guilt, aggression, and a host of other traits" (p. 23).

In the mid- to late 1940s John Buck added a house and tree to the existing DAP assessment and called it the House-Tree-Person (HTP). He chose to add these items for three reasons: "(1) They were items familiar even to the comparatively young child; (2) they were found to be more willingly accepted as objects for drawing by subjects of all ages than other items suggested; and (3) they appeared to stimulate more frank and free verbalization than did other items" (Buck, 1948, p. 3).

Buck believed that his approach would yield both a quantitative and a qualitative analysis of an individual's drawing. A few years after the publication of Buck's HTP, Leopold Caligor developed the 8CRT, which he hoped would provide quantification through the use of successive drawings (content) instead of a mere evaluation of detailed signs. Ultimately, the 8CRT was to consist "of eight interrelated drawings, each a development of the immediately preceding one. (Transparent paper is used so that the subject sees the immediately preceding figure as he draws over it.) In this way change can be observed on a continuum" (Caligor, 1953, p. 356). Regrettably, this art assessment never gained popular appeal; instead, it gave way to the other art projective tests that had come before.

Though not reviewed in this book, other art assessments, such as the Kinetic-Family-Drawing (Burns & Kaufman, 1972b), introduced action into family drawings. Subsequently, Burns (1987) expanded the House-Tree-Drawing technique by including a kinetic component that ultimately produced the Kinetic-House-Tree-Person test in the late 1980s.

Although the techniques described make use of differing directives and methods of interpretation, they have one very important component in common: the interpretation of a general system of symbols and metaphor. These images, when interpreted on verbal and nonverbal levels, lead the clinician toward an intuitive realm of functioning.

Yet it is this intuitive functioning that has eluded researchers who have set out to quantify and qualify the methods of art personality analysis through strict adherence to formal scoring systems. Nevertheless, from the late 1950s to the present day, critical reviews have been available that outline a myriad of problems not just with projective drawings but also with the Rorschach test and Thematic Apperception Test (TAT), to name just a few (Seitz, 2002).

In *Handbook of Projective Techniques*, Clifford Swensen (1965) outlined a host of researchers who tested the validity of Machover's DAP technique. From a review of this testing, he found that the DAP lacked sufficient evidence for use in clinical work as a singular test but should instead be used concomitantly as one part of a diagnostic battery. It is not surprising that Swensen's review of the literature found a lack of validity and reliability, as he goes on to state:

> It must have been evident to the reader, in the presentation of the studies reviewed in this paper, that few of the studies reported were designed to test specific hypotheses of Machover's. Studies which attempt to evaluate the significance of patterns of signs on the DAP appear to be more promising than attempts to evaluate the significance of individual DAP signs. (p. 649)

The one test that Swensen finds promising, with regard to research, is the 8CRT. With the test designed to reveal an individual's masked personality layers, Caligor performed three separate studies. The first was in 1951 to determine an individual's unconscious notion of his own masculinity-femininity identification, where results were ultimately compared to the TAT and Minnesota Multiphasic Personality Inventory (MMPI). In 1952 he investigated the use of the 8CRT to detect paranoid trends, and in the following year he created a multi-item checklist in the hopes of developing a more objective and quantitative method for evaluating his 8CRT (Caligor, 1952). However, as noted, Caligor's 8CRT has fallen into obscurity, and the only research completed was by the founder of the technique himself.

Throughout his book *The Clinical Application of Projective Drawings* (1958), Hammer reviews extensive research on various art projective testing, and he sums up problems that face researchers in their attempts to validate the testing as follows:

> Projective data is [*sic*] the product of a multiplicity of variables. In the traditional scientific investigation, one variable is isolated and explored. This is a virtual impossibility in the projective test where a response apparently has many possible origins. Not only is perception involved in the response,

which in itself is a function of many variables, but also the process of re-sponse is involved. (p. 484)

Presently Zoltan Vass (2002) is developing a computer-assisted screen-ing procedure for use with the Kinetic Family Drawing (KFD) projective test. This approach uses computer algorithms that measure both formal and structural graphic characteristics. In this vein Vass stated:

> In a formal-structural point of view, the method described in this study ap-proaches the most demanding methodological requirements (e.g., Swensen, 1957, 1968, 1977; Roback, 1968; Kahill, 1984), which are critical points of the application of projective drawings up to now. As a new and unique ap-proach to the problem, it received positive critiques. (p. 11)

In the end, much of the formal research applied to art projective testing has either relied upon formal scoring techniques, which ignore the sub-ject's own verbal interpretations as well as verbalizations made during the testing process, or centered on testing specific hypotheses as related to per-sonality indicators. In the former case, a strict adherence to scoring tech-niques revealed a lack of reliability or validity to support the data. In the latter, where select issues relating to personality, pathology, and self-image (to name just a few) were explored in a singular fashion, the data were sup-ported (Hammer, 1958).

Consequently, one must utilize an integrated approach to interpretation that includes the following components: the standardization of the sup-plies and directives, coupled with a drawing assessment that takes into ac-count developmental issues; structural and formal aspects; translation of the symbols and symbolic abundance of ideas; the subject's free associa-tions to the art product; and information gathered from the clinical inter-view. As DiLeo (1983) has stated, "the drawing is a personal expression and so is its meaning" (p. 5). As a result, analysis works best when there is a blend of elucidation from the client's own subjective understanding and the use of common interpretive meanings of symbols.

A Picture Is Worth a Thousand Words

As we move into the three projective techniques that will be reviewed in this chapter, it is important to stress that central to the belief of projec-tive testing is the process of projection. Without this core conviction no projective test will satisfy the critic. Laughlin (1970) offers this definition of projection: "Projection is an ego defense or mental mechanism operat-ing outside of and beyond conscious awareness through which consciously disowned aspects of the self are rejected or disowned and thrown outward, to become imputed to others" (p. 221). And it is these inner thoughts, these intolerable wishes and feelings, that are given outward expression. In short, projection provides protection.

Additionally, another concept that I would like to introduce is that of the symbolic abundance of ideas. In *The Psychopathology of Everyday Life*, Freud (1972) discussed the phenomena of remembering and forgetting, giving special emphasis to forgotten material and slips of the tongue. He did not believe that such occurrences were mere chance; instead, he felt that they revealed the inner conflicts of an individual. In much the same manner, a symbolic abundance of ideas, as identified through repeated patterns of specific signs and metaphors within the artwork, overflows with meaning and, when applied holistically, can point the clinician toward the well-concealed feelings of a psyche.

When a clinician employs the concept of a symbolic abundance of ideas in combination with art projective testing, he or she can form a clear picture of the client's feelings, attitudes, and self-concept, a picture that offers light where a shadow once existed. Thus the repressed material, which is destined to repeat in a compulsive manner without the benefit of mastery, is afforded safe and unconscious expression through the projection of art testing. As Whitmont (1969) aptly stated, "In terms of . . . typical human constellations of attributes, anything repressed or lacking in the individual will make itself felt sooner or later in some manner if it is at all vital to his development" (p. 107).

As examples of repressed repetition, refer to any of the figures located in the introduction or Chapter 1. These should offer the reader an opportunity to note how often we repeat that which is important to us. Whether it is verbal—in demands, comments, and queries—or communicated through the use of an expressive therapy, the question is not whether the symbolism exists, but whether we are listening.

As with any expressive therapy, applied familiarity cannot simply be replaced with pure theory. It was for this reason that I asked the reader in the introduction to complete two drawings and answer a series of questions in written form. If you have completed this directive, please retrieve your renderings. If you have not, either do so now or utilize the figure I provide later as a guide.

The assignment that I gave in the preface was a loose variation of the DAP projective test. In its purest form the test, as Goodenough (1926) originally designed it, related to intelligence, with each addition and omission relating to "points." The interpreter counted these points to arrive at an estimate of intelligence. As Machover (1949) broadened this test, she sought out personality analysis. Consequently, after requesting that the client draw a person for the first rendering and a person of the opposite gender for the second, she asked a series of 48 questions. These questions were "designed to elicit the subject's attitude toward himself and toward others" (Machover, p. 30). They ranged from the benign ("What are they doing?" "What is their age?") to the personal ("How often do they masturbate?" "When was their first sexual experience?").

In the procedure that I utilize, I generally replace the 48 questions with the directive "Tell me about these people" and the query "What did you think while you were drawing?" Although my process is much abbreviated, I have found a level of consistency with regard to the formal and structural aspects when interpreting, as Machover and others established.

For ease of interpretation, I have broken down the drawing assessment into three aspects: (1) the structural or quantitative, which implies the design of the rendering (i.e., size, placement, line quality, shading, color, and overall impression); (2) the formal or qualitative, which relates to the recognized symbols and metaphors from the literature and research; and (3) the client's or subject's free associations and verbal statements in the post-drawing inquiry.

From a structural standpoint you will need to record the following information (refer to Appendix A for detailed interpretations):

1. Size of the drawing
2. Placement
3. Detailing or reinforcement
4. Line quality
5. Shading
6. Use of color (if client is not offered only one color)
7. Overall impression (from the viewer's standpoint)

Figure 3.1 is provided to offer a quick visual reference to significant quantitative details. As you will note, it is broken down into three distinctive parts: size, placement, and shading. When assessing the drawing, one should first employ a structural perspective. This will benefit the clinician by affording him or her a general idea of the client's relation to his or her environment. In addition, the structural aspects and the manner of interpretation do not change regardless of the projective test utilized.

In Figure 3.1 the upper drawing (two DAP assessments by one individual) expresses the use not only of size but of paper chopping (where a portion of the drawing item is "chopped" off, or goes beyond the edges of the paper). Hammer (1958) has stated that the average full-figure drawing is

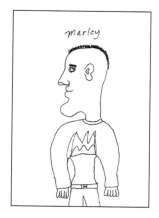

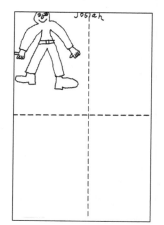

3.1 *Structural Analysis*

"approximately seven inches long, or two-thirds of the available space" (p. 101). In this example the male (Marley) is paper chopped, and if he was to remain in proportion the remainder of his body would stand roughly 12 inches, while the female (Sharna) is 7 inches high. If we, like Hammer, look at the size of a drawing as relating to the client and the environment, then the obvious discrepancy in size is suggestive of feelings of aggression and expansion in the environment (male) coupled with feelings of subservience or denouncement toward the female. However, this drawing also combines paper chopping of the male's legs and feet, which conveys "feelings of helpless immobility within the environment" (Buck, 1948, p. 57). Thus, from a purely structural standpoint, at this juncture the aggression suggests impotency with regard to masculine concerns.

In the center example, this client combined a regressive use of color with an unhealthy and patterned use of shading. He applied this stylized treatment to very distinct aspects of his HTP (tree bark, crown, and body of person), and therefore we can interpret it as invading every aspect of the client himself. Machover (1949) has stated that the use of a patterned or stylized shading "serves to rationalize and so reduce shock with regard to the particular area of conflict" (p. 99). As a result, a combination of structural analysis and a formal review of the signs will offer the clinician further elucidation into this client's relation to the environment and personality formation/integration.

Two separate individuals completed the bottom drawings of Figure 3.1. The assessment on the left is one half of a DAP, while the drawing on the right is a completed HTP. The broken line separating the vertical and horizontal planes (in the DAP) and separating the HTP horizontally were added to aid in the discussion of placement. If we review the bottom left figure first, the person is located in the upper left-hand corner of the paper (as was the client's female drawing, which is not shown). This placement is often found in the work of elementary school children and tends to move toward the center of the page by the eighth grade (Hammer, 1958). Buck (1966) has called this area the "quadrant of regression" or "never was" due to his finding that it is often used by deteriorated psychotics or individuals who have not attained a high level of conceptual maturity. In addition, he emphasizes the importance of horizontal placement of the figure, having found that the further the rendering is placed to the viewer's left, the more concerned the client is with the past and the self, while placement to the viewer's right signifies controlled overconcern with the future.

As we move to the bottom right of Figure 3.1, we see a completed HTP assessment. Although this application of the HTP differs from Buck's original design (my use of one page for all the items versus his use of one page per form item), the placement interpretations remain relevant. In this rendering the items are located, not uncommonly, on one plane, yet they are placed relatively high on the page from the midpoint.

> The farther above the average midpoint of the drawing form page that the midpoint of the whole is located, the greater is the likelihood (1) that the S[ubject] feels that he is over-striving toward relatively unattainable goals; (2) that the S tends to seek satisfaction in intellectualization or phantasy rather than in reality. (Buck, 1966, p. 104)

It is also important to note that this client's house is positioned in the "quadrant of regression." Therefore, the therapist must make interpretation from a vertical as well as a horizontal placement perspective.

Finally, the structural analysis of line quality must be mentioned. Generally speaking, most people draw with a free-flowing, controlled stroke whose average length is one-quarter to three-quarters inches long (Caligor, 1957). Any variation from this type of line could "suggest a functional personality maladjustment or a central nervous system disorder" (Buck, 1966, p. 122).

Appendix A will serve as a guide; it was compiled from multiple sources (Buck, 1948, 1966; Caligor, 1957; DiLeo, 1983; Gilbert, 1980; Hammer, 1958; Knoff & Prout, 1985; Machover, 1949; Matthews, 1986; Payne, 1948) among art therapy literature, research studies, and available manuals associated with select projective testing. I provide this information in this much abbreviated and condensed form to offer the clinician a quantitative analysis with regard to personality differentiation and to aid in the interpretation of the three art projective tests we review in this chapter.

Draw-a-Person (DAP) Examples

Those of you who completed the DAP (from the introduction) will refer to those renderings. Everyone else should use Figure 3.2 which was completed by a "healthy" female who works in the mental health field (see disk to view these figures in color). If you completed your drawings when first reading this book, you may not have any free associations at hand, but with a client these are of the utmost importance. How we approach a new, requested task is central to how we approach anything original and unknown in the environment, and it is the clients' spontaneous statements that offer us a glimpse into their ego strength.

In addition, you will notice in the sample write-up that there are responses behind select structural and formal aspects. You will find these

3.2 Draw-a-Person Sample #1

responses in Appendix A (for the structural components) and Appendix B (for the formal aspects of the human figure). Once all three areas (structural, formal, and verbal) have been completed, a clear picture will emerge.

If you are assessing your drawings before reviewing the sample cases, please retrieve them now. At this juncture write down what you see as you look at the completed renderings. What do you like? What stands out? What immediate visceral response do you have to the drawings?

Now refer to Appendix A and assess the drawing from a structural perspective for both the male and female separately.

Before returning to Figure 3.2, I would like to take a few moments to introduce the formal aspects of the human figure drawing. When you are assessing a projective test, these signs or details take on great significance, for "details are believed to represent the subject's awareness of an interest in the elemental aspects of everyday life" (Buck, 1948, p. 49). In view of that, when you draw information regarding a client's personality and his or her reaction and behavior in the environment, you must combine any structural assessment with a qualitative interpretation of the signs. A study by Goldstein and Rawn (1957) focused on seven symbolic details and two structural aspects to assess whether aggression could be deduced from drawing style using the DAP. The seven signs comprised the following: slash-lined mouth, detailed teeth, spiked fingers, clenched fists, nostril emphasis, squared shoulders, and toes on a nonnude figure. The two structural aspects were heavy line pressure and large figure size. In the end the structural aspects did not yield significant results, yet "the seven specific drawing details, as a group, did in fact relate to aggression" (p. 171).

Through studies and observations completed by various clinicians, a body of interpretive details has become available. Appendix B is offered as a guide when assessing the human figure in any projective test. These interpretations, as with Appendix A have been compiled from numerous sources (Buck, 1948, 1966; Burns & Kaufman, 1972a; Caligor, 1957; Cirlot, 1971; DiLeo, 1973, 1983; Freud, 1950; Hammer, 1958; Jung, 1964; Klepsch & Logie, 1982; Machover, 1949; Matthews, 1986; Ogden, 1977; Oster & Gould, 1987; Reynolds, 1977). However, I caution the reader to not take these signs individually, but as an inter-related abundance of ideas. It is only in this manner that a complete and accurate picture of the underlying personality dynamics can be appraised.

When assessing the formal aspects found in Appendix B it is best to begin at the top of the drawing (head) and work your way toward the bottom (feet) for each rendering. In so doing you will be describing each detail and adding the interpretive data (from the appropriate appendices). When you have illustrated each rendering in this way you should find that certain themes will not only emerge but repeat. These notes make up the symbolic abundance of ideas that will be the foundation for your assessment.

After you have completed this step, read the written responses to the questions that were posed in the introduction and take notice of any verbal statements that tend to recur. Finally, compare these responses to the structural and formal aspects of each drawing to arrive at an overall symbolic abundance of ideas.

The sample case given in Figure 3.2 will serve as a guide toward formulating all the disparate aspects (structural, formal, and verbal) into one cohesive whole.

In Figure 3.2, drawn by a "healthy" female, the artist undertook the directive with multiple self-deprecating statements. She emphasized that she was not a good artist, that she could not draw, and that she was doing a terrible job. She drew the female, her first drawing, two times before this, her third attempt (threatened by the content and needing to draw a safer image). Her first drawing was named Jen (the name was changed for confidentiality). The person fills the entire page, is centered (self-directed) and is outlined in orange. The artist used long strokes (apprehensive, requires support and reassurance) to draw the outline and short bursts of tensional intensity shading (anxiety) to fill in the figure detailing. The total number of colors used was seven (excessive use of color-emotional responses). For the male, named Mat, she did not start over (not threatened by the content of the projection). He too is in the center of the page and is the same size as Jen, yet he does not appear as large (less intimidating). His body is drawn with short, sketchy strokes, especially in the arm region. She spontaneously commented, "I'm doing much better with my male. He's much more proportionate." The total number of colors used was three (well within average use). As the drawing progressed, she had far fewer verbal complaints about her ability.

Thus, from a structural point of view we see increased apprehension with the female rendering. She has used excessive color and shading, which has made the figure larger and more imposing. Drawn with long strokes, the projection conveys apprehension, while the male figure is the same size yet appears less intense and intimidating. In fact, all interpretation of the male figure points toward a less intimidating viewpoint. She did not begin the drawing over (as she did on the first drawing), and the number of colors is within normal range. The shading appears anxious, as does the use of short strokes, yet this figure's expression in contrast with that of the female is confident. At this juncture interpretive focus is placed on the imposing female figure.

Now we will assess the image from a formal point of view. In this portion we will be looking at how the image is drawn, from head to toe. This part of the assessment will provide us with information on conscious feelings regarding body image and self-concept.

From a purely formal viewpoint, Jen's hair is multicolored and flows down the front of her body (anxiety, overthinking). Her face is round, with a quizzical look to the mouth. The mouth is reinforced (conflict relative to that part) on the upper lip and has a dimple mark on the left side. Due to the flowing hair, her neck is almost nonexistent and gives the overall impression of a head floating above the trunk of her body (organ that joins control area with that of impulses). Her arms are thick, dangling at her sides (views self as dependent and helpless) and overly long (overambitious striving, desirous of isolation and withdrawal, rejection of others). They extend toward her feet, have four fingers (helplessness), and are bulbous and ineffectual in shape. Her shirt is well decorated and billowy, and you can see trunk lines through the shirt (thought pattern disturbances). Her pants and shirt are colored in anxious strokes, with her legs being significantly out of proportion to the rest of her body (emotional immobility). Her shoes are resting on the bottom of the page and colored in with black.

In contrast, the male's head is rounded, with no pupils in his eyes (immaturity, egocentrism). The schema is the same for the mouth in both drawings, but there is no reinforcement on Mat. He exudes a confident look toward the viewer. His neck is proportionate to the rest of his body. He wears a tight-fitting T-shirt and stands with his hands behind his back (interpersonal reluctance, evasive). The transparency we see in the trunk lines visible through the shirt on the female is not present in this drawing. His legs are colored in with brown pants, and his feet appear clubbed.

From a formal aspect the symbolic abundance of ideas points toward feelings of helplessness and emotional immobility. Interestingly, the reinforced area, or conflict, surrounds the mouth. In contrast, however, the male figure shows little to no conflict, with the only details of concern being the lack of pupils and placement of the hands behind his back. Once again, interpretive focus is placed upon the female.

At this point we will review the artist's verbalizations about the two drawings. The questions should always remain the same, but prompting or elaboration is fine once the initial questions have been asked. It is exceedingly important that the interviewer does not impose interpretations or projections onto the drawing. Any inquiry should be based on what one has noted in the formal and structural aspects of the test. It is important to form questions from your instincts, and once you have interpreted a fair amount of artwork, with the aid of the appendices provided, you will begin to notice more aspects of each drawing and your questions will then be tailored more specifically.

When I asked her to tell me something about the two figures, the artist started with Jen. "I patterned her after me. She's smiling and has curly hair; she doesn't dress like me, though. . . . She has funky arms. What does that say about me?" In response to my silence she stated, "I feel big and gangly and wear loose clothes." When asked about Mat she said, "He's athletic, built, good upper body. He's the outdoorsy type. He's wearing a muscle shirt." When I asked her to elaborate she stated, "I can't tell you about them because they're not real. I'm so concrete" (laughter). When I asked her to try to say more about Jen, she said, "She's a nice person, I should have drawn her embarrassed because I get embarrassed easy. I would have added red cheeks" (nervous laughter). When I asked her why Mat's arms are behind his body, she stated, "I learned from Jen and put the arms behind. I can't draw arms."

As we interpret the drawing from a verbal level, it is apparent that the female subject feels highly threatened by her feelings of inadequacy and embarrassment at feeling "big and gangly." In fact, while drawing she commented on how "proportionate the male was over the female." However, it must be stated that in real life she is in no way "big and gangly." Her weight is appropriate and balanced. This exaggeration of physical features was a clear projection of internal issues. Thus, if we return to the structural aspects, her apprehension at drawing the female becomes all too clear. Her preoccupation with her imagined defects in appearance and her subsequent embarrassment were symbolized by the inability to begin and her need to start twice (only for the female). Her use of excessive color, as compared to an average use in Mat, is also a symbolic repetition of her need to hide behind an expansive camouflage. However, this camouflage, instead of helping (in the drawing), has made her appear imposing and large.

From the formal aspect, the symbolic abundance of ideas that was noted with regard to feelings of hopelessness, isolation, and immobility is apparent in her body image feelings. It also becomes clearer why the mouth was emphasized on the female and not on the male figure, as the mouth is the means by which food is brought in. In addition, the transparency that was noted in the female's trunk is not a thought disorder as in schizophrenia but certainly a thought disorder in her own body image and dysmorphic thinking. Finally, the apparent lack of neck (due to the way the drawing was colored) symbolizes her issues with control (wanting to be thinner) over the inner desires (wanting to consume food/nurturance).

On the whole, the interpretation from a purely structural and formal standpoint directed us toward an emphasis on the female figure and a de-emphasis on the male figure. However, it was the verbal comments after the drawing that allowed the full understanding of the projection to fall into place by giving us a picture of the individual, her fears, and her anxieties. In the end, this information can be of assistance to the therapist in the formulation of treatment planning goals and objectives.

This single example has been replicated time and again. Whether with a difficult client or a volunteer, the blank page is a safe and nonthreatening forum to project the worries and anxieties, real or imagined, that a client hides from view.

At this time I would like to present a selection of art projective tests that have been used for assessment purposes in a variety of settings and have proven effective with a wide range of clients.

Draw-a-Person (DAP) Art Assessments

The DAP technique, as devised by Karen Machover, operates by reflecting a person's self-concept. This self-concept is not only projected onto the blank paper but also expressed through the client's verbalizations. As I have noted, Machover designed her technique to be utilized in conjunction with a series of carefully designed questions (which can be found in her book *Personality Projections in the Drawing of the Human Figure*). However, for the purposes of this book I have replaced these questions with a request for the client to invent a story about the completed figures.

For ease of administration I will outline the components necessary for introduction of the technique. First I must state that prior to any art assessment I perform a verbal interview (which includes a mental status exam). This procedure affords an opportunity to bond and often offers information that will later clarify issues that arise during the art production. Some clinicians prefer to offer the client a single pencil with eraser; I, on the other hand, prefer to offer a pack of fine-line markers or colored pencils. I have found that giving the client a range of colors with which to work yields another layer of personality dynamics, diagnostic indicators, and information that is missing from an achromatic drawing. In addition, the client is unable to erase with a fine-line marker, and the client's reaction to this limitation offers information on frustration tolerance and problem solving. Secondary to the markers, I offer each client the same type of 9" × 12" drawing paper (80-pound weight). This paper allows the client to work with a large drawing surface and is a weight that works well with markers, pen, pencil, and watercolors. The room should have ample space for the examinee to rest comfortably while drawing. A sturdy table where the examinee and examiner can sit is preferable. With these considerations in place we are ready to introduce the projective test to the client.

Give the client this directive: "Using as many or as few colors as you like, draw the best person you can. The person should be a whole figure, not just a floating head." Often the client will ask a series of questions or make statements about his or her inability to draw. It is best to counter these statements with gentle prompting, such as "this is not a test of your artistic talent. This is simply a nonverbal means of communication." However, if the client asks specific questions about what gender to draw or how to draw the figure, a general statement without further elaboration is best (e.g., "Any way you want will be fine. Just do the best you can and make certain it's a whole figure").

Once the figure is complete, have the client give it a name and write it on the paper. This helps to identify the sex, as sometimes clients will draw a figure in a manner that is at best asexual. Once you have deciphered the gender, provide the client with another sheet of paper and ask the examinee to "draw a male/female/boy/girl," whichever represents the opposite sex to the first figure. After the client has completed this drawing, ask him or her to give this drawing a name and write it on the paper. I then place both drawings side by side and request that the client "tell me something about these two." I do not prompt any further but instead allow the client to grapple with the projection. If he or she is having a difficult time, I ask the client to "choose one that you want to talk about first." This is normally enough to get the examinee started talking, at which time I will ask clarifying questions based on the invented stories.

Before we review sample cases, it is important to illuminate two issues. The first is the examiner's anxiety at having a client draw (e.g., "Will they really do it?" "What do I do if they don't?"), and the second is an examiner's preference regarding whether to take notes during an interview. As for the first concern, the client will draw as you request, sometimes only with the aid of positive reinforcement, but they will draw regardless of age or gender. Most clients' objections arise from the thought of having to draw and their lack of ability rather than an outright rejection of the task. If you are comfortable with the request and sensitive yet firm in response to your client's protestations, you will end up with an art production.

With regard to note taking, this is a matter of comfort and personal preference. Depending upon your training, you may have been instructed to take copious notes, use recall after the session, or use some combination of notes and recall. Throughout the years I have developed an ability to write in a shorthand that allows me to combine the two. However, when the client is relating the story of the figures I prefer to take notes verbatim. It is important not only to have this as a record for later use but also to use the statements, as noted earlier, when seeking a symbolic abundance of ideas. Often the words of an examinee can convey a metaphor that becomes important when looking at the assessment as a whole.

Before we review case illustrations, the directives for the DAP art assessment are as follows:

- Direct the client: "Using as many or as few colors as you like, draw the best person you can. The person should be a whole figure, not just a floating head."
- Once the figure is complete, have the client (1) give it a name and (2) write it on the paper.
- Once you have deciphered the gender, give the client a second piece of paper and ask him or her to "draw the best male/female [as the case may be] and include the entire body."
- After this is complete, ask the client to give this drawing a name and write it on the paper.
- Place both drawings side by side and begin the postdrawing inquiry by requesting, "tell me something about these two."

Case Illustrations

As with all case illustrations within this book, the information concerning clinical matters is factual. However, the client's personal information has been replaced to retain confidentality.

Personal Profile 3.1

This case involves a male in midadulthood. When he was a preteen his father died from cancer. He lived with his mother until the age of majority, when he married. Within a few years he divorced and was diagnosed with Bipolar disorder. From this period forward he began to experience hallucinations and paranoia. He stated that he had heard demeaning voices inside his head but that since starting antipsychotic medication he had not reexperienced the auditory hallucinations. However, during this time of stability he assaulted his girlfriend by kicking and punching her and slamming her head against the ground. Additionally, he threatened (with a knife) a stranger in the community who was walking past his house with her children.

Throughout the interview the patient's thought content was grandiose, and he tended to be abrasive in his responses. His attitude was guarded, his appearance neat and clean, his eye contact good, his motor activity normal, his speech at times rapid (he responded in flowery verbiage to both impress and intimidate), his affect congruent, and his mood euphoric. His insight was poor, and he employed intellectualization and minimization. The sensorium mental grasp showed good attention and concentration, an excellent fund of knowledge, and poor judgment and insight. He responded to questions about similarities well if not interestingly. To the question "How are an apple and orange alike?" he replied "fruit." To the question "How are an elephant and a tree alike?" he replied, after a long thought, "organisms." His responses to proverb interpretation ranged from grandiose to mildly paranoid and bizarre. To the prompt "A rolling stone gathers no moss," he stated, "Keep a direction that's healthy; then you won't have to be concerned about things that come from an illness." To the proverb "People who live in glass houses shouldn't throw stones," he replied, "You could be doing something to someone else, but you stand back and make a comment and you may have the same imposition."

Figure 3.3 is his completed assessment.

Prior to the art assessment the patient had emphatically stated that he enjoyed drawing; however, once given the directive he became oppositional. He asked curtly, "a male or female?" When told either would be fine he hur-

3.3 Bipolar Disorder with Psychotic Features

riedly drew a stick figure (evasion) in the upper left-hand corner. Instructed to draw an entire figure, he drew a female head and called it "Jane." I then gave him the choice of either drawing an entire body or leaving the head suspended in space. He then worked diligently on the drawings.

He drew the female first (possible difficulty in establishing a masculine identity). Both figures are excessively large in size, with the female measuring 10.25 inches in height and the male 11 inches (impulsive, grandiose, possibly aggressive), and the male floats higher on the page than the female (keeps self aloof and relatively inaccessible). Both are drawn with long strokes (requires support and reassurance). The shading is patterned (rationalizes) and geometric. The female was drawn in nine colors and the male in six colors (inability to exercise self-control and restraint over emotional impulses).

Although both heads have overemphasized hair (overthinking, anxiety, fantasy), the female drawing has multiple reinforcements with regard to color and aggressive line quality. The female has tiny half-moon eyes, a squiggly mouth, and bushy eyebrows (uninhibited), with no neck (body drives threaten to overwhelm, regressive). Her face is heavily shaded with yellow (seriously disturbed, poor self-concept). The body is multicolored with an exceptionally heavy trunk (confusion of physical power, maternal symbol), a small waistline, long arms, oversized hands (hostility), tiny sticklike legs with knobby knees or joints (faulty and uncertain sense of body integrity), feet drawn like hands, and a transparency in the feet (pathological aggressiveness) with large clunky shoes that feature aggressive detailing. The client drew squiggles that look like knife slashes on the forearms, thighs, and chest area, as well as the bottom of the dress leading toward the genitalia. Overall the image is menacing, hostile, regressive, and manic in appearance.

I then instructed him to draw a male. He worked quickly on this image and drew the head and face last (disturbance in interpersonal relationships). The image is drawn with angular strokes (masculine), as compared to the first image, which is rounded. The hair is again prolific (virility strivings), the eyes are closed (not wanting to see), the mouth is drawn in a heavy slash like a "V" (verbally aggressive, sadistic personality), and the nose is drawn in the same manner. There is no neck; the trunk is large (unsatisfied drives) and the hands are in proportion, but the left has pointy fingers (aggressive) and the arms are excessively long and thin (weakness and futility). He has drawn pockets on the pants and shirt front (dependency issues, infantile, maternal deprivation). The legs are exceedingly thin, with long feet (striving for virility) and no transparency; the shoes are decorated high-tops (impotence). The "knife slash" squiggles appear on the male also, but not in such proliferation.

He titled this drawing "Bob" and declined to talk about either of the images. The lack of postdrawing inquiry, though unfortunate, does not hinder the interpretation: The clinical interview that preceded the art projective will serve as a guide.

From a structural perspective this patient exhibits not only a sense of grandiosity and egocentricity but poor inner controls and restraint over his impulses. His initial reluctance to complete the task (evident in the stick figure) with concomitant redirecting yielded a hostile response in the drawing of his initial figure (female) with a much less regressive rendering for his male figure. He is overly focused on the past and his own needs for support and reassurance. In addition, the drawings show excessive difficulty in coping with environmental stressors.

From a formal perspective this patient both denigrates women and yearns for a maternal figure that will meet his needs. This infantile dependency takes the form of hostile reactions when he feels deprived or dismissed. His multiple assaults revolve around not only these dependency issues but also his confused sense of manhood, his virility strivings, and power, which is tied into maternal symbols. He feels futile and weak when compared to females and attempts to stave this off through verbal aggression and intellectual defenses. However, when these methods fail, he resorts to physical aggression and sadism.

His history shows that he became excessively hostile after the birth of his first child and was verbally threatening toward a mother and her children. These issues, coupled with his emotional dependence on women and his mental illness, make him pathologically aggressive toward others (especially women) whom he views as thwarting his needs. In addition, significant signs of psychotic decompensation appear in the regressive features, joint emphasis, transparency, unusual coloring, and distorted body parts.

In the final analysis, due to this patient's propensity toward coping with environmental stress with either ambivalence or violence together with psychotic decompensation, the prognosis for this patient is poor.

Personal Profile 3.2

The patient is a single adult male whose father died many years prior to the assessment. When discussing his family, he spoke briefly of the loss of his father and mentioned a younger sister. Of his mother he stated, "She's a basket case like me. She's authoritative . . . but she's also my best friend, but is she ever controlling. I love her, don't get me wrong; she's just a high-strung person." In fact, with each question, regardless of the topic, the patient interspersed every answer with a discussion that revolved around his mother.

The patient was charged with making terrorist threats after having made multiple phone calls to his girlfriend. He has no arrests as a juvenile but many as an adult. Since early adulthood he has been treated for Bipolar disorder, and he describes his illness as follows: "I believe I have a partial mental illness. I do things without thinking, I make bad decisions: . . . I have a Bipolar disorder." As the interview progressed, his mood became increasingly grandiose, and his speech was pressured. He spoke in a rambling manner about his extensive substance use and his prison terms and verified that his relationship with his mother was symbiotic in nature.

His appearance was neat, his attitude was friendly and cooperative, his motor activity was restless, and his affect was mood congruent. The mental status exam showed concrete thinking in response to similarities, with a fair fund of knowledge. His proverb interpretation was expansive and bordered on the bizarre. To the proverb "Even a dragon that walks along the river has small fish biting its tail" he replied, "Even the poor little folks are trying to keep up with the big folks . . . (undecipherable sentence) or vice versa." He denied any suicidal ideation, gestures, or plans, although he did state that he was depressed because of his present circumstances.

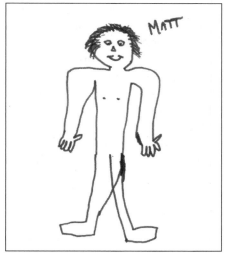 

3.4 Bipolar Disorder without Psychotic Features

Figure 3.4 is the completed art assessment.

When administered the DAP assessment, he began immediately and without complaint. He drew both figures on the lower left side of the page (seeks immediate and emotional satisfaction, over-concern with self and past). The male stands five and one-quarter inches high (normal height) while the female stands four and three-quarters inches high (environment experienced as overwhelming). The line type is a long stroke (apprehensive, requiring support and reassurance) with below-average graphic control. Both drawings face forward, with each figure rendered naked but with only the nipples (no genitalia) visible. There is a significant blackening on the male's left hip (anxiety from the waist down) as well as on the male's left hand (preoccupation with that part). In addition, the groin area is crossed over with a double line (conflict relative to that part). On both figures only two colors are used—blue and pink (constricted, emotionally shy).

The patient began by drawing the male figure, which he named Matt. Matt was initially drawn in all blue, and the patient spontaneously stated, "He's a big blue, for boy." The face is round with a triangle nose, simplistic smile, and rounded eyes with pupils. The patient added the features of the head last (disturbance in interpersonal relationships). Once the examinee had added pink, he gave the figure an abundance of hair (anxiety, virility strivings). His shoulders are squared (preoccupied with the perceived need for strength) and misshapen with a shortened neck (uninhibited impulse expression). The long arms are muscular (frequent with adolescents, concerns of masculinity) and end in looped hands with prominent thumbs that point in the wrong direction and toward the reinforced and darkened areas. The trunk is exceptionally thin (frailty, weakness) and has no enclosure (immaturity; regressed, disorganized) with pinpoints for nipples. The trunk extends toward the legs into a block foot (immobility).

The female figure (Jeana) was drawn with the head first (in contrast to the male), an elongated neck (problem with anger management or primitive drives), broad shoulders (confusion of physical power and maternal symbol), and hair excitement or chaos (infantile sexual drives). The trunk has a hint of enclosure (hip line) but again is drawn long and thin. The legs have thin, functional feet. The nipples (infantile nurturance needs) are more pronounced than on the former drawing.

In the patient's story he described Matt as a hardware store manager who fishes with his friends for leisure, whereas Jeana is a cocktail waitress and very social at work. However, at home she reads books and is not social, having few close friends. She gets angry when she has to rush around. Matt becomes angry when he is not being listened to, and he wants to be a productive member of society. The patient finished the story by saying that Matt and Jeana have not yet met but that when they do they may get married.

From a structural perspective the patient, while reserved, exhibits a narcissistic quality, with anxiety and concern focused on the opposite sex and sexual satisfaction. It is difficult to ascertain whether the female is a projection of his mother or his girlfriend, or an amalgamation of the two. However, it seems likely that the female represents the patient's symbiotic relationship with his mother, as this relationship has impinged upon any intimate adultlike instincts. The crossed-out groin also points toward a symbolic feeling of castration.

From a formal aspect the male has an abundance of ideas that point toward frustrated virility strivings and significant conflicts in his personal relationships. In contrast, the female stands on firm footing, yet problems with anger management emerge. In addition, the drawing's representation of reinforced nipples expresses infantile nurturance needs. Once again, whether this is a sign of the patient's needs, the mother's, or a combination of the two is not evident.

In the postdrawing inquiry, the patient verbalized a combination of the structural and formal aspects. Jeana, though displaying appropriate social skills in public, prefers to have only a few close friends and becomes "angry when she has to rush around" (problem with anger management). Matt feels neglected and ignored and desires "to be a productive member of society" (immobility). To complete the story the patient has Jeana and Matt not merely meeting but possibly marrying.

Ultimately, what emerges is the patient's unresolved Oedipal issues and confusion not simply over frustrated sexual desires but also with his anxiety and the attendant fear of castration. Therefore, requiring punishment for his guilty thoughts, he has been symbolically castrated (concerns of masculinity), which is evidenced in his reinforcement and shading on the male figure from the palm of the hand to the crossed-out genitalia. In addition, this narcissism has not found outward expression, and he has found himself overwhelmingly frustrated when seeking mature sexual relationships and adult responsibilities. Overall, psychotic processing difficulties were not evident; instead, infantile nurturance needs emerged.

The prognosis for this patient at the present time is good if he can receive individual counseling, group therapy, independent living skills training, and anger management or stress management classes. However, a return to his maternal home, instead of placement in the community at an adult group home, is not recommended—for obvious reasons.

House-Tree-Person (HTP)

The HTP art assessment was introduced by John Buck in the late 1940s and was "designed to aid the clinician in obtaining information concerning an individual's sensitivity, maturity, efficiency, degree of personality integration, and interaction with the environment, specifically and generally" (Buck, 1966, p. 1).

The structural elements of DAP interpretation explained in the DAP section and Appendix A remain the same in the HTP. However, this is where the similarity ends. The HTP's formal details offer a degree of breadth to the art projective test that also encompasses the individual's relation to the environment. The elements that Buck has added (house and tree) "are believed to represent the subject's awareness of and interest in the elemental aspects of everyday life" (Buck, 1948, p. 49). If we hearken back to the cognitive theory of Piaget, the child gains an increased interest in his environment with each passing day until, in the 9th year (concrete operations), he or she looks within a larger system—the system of deductive thought. It is this deductive thought that allows the child to examine rules for all their details—the rules of space, time, proportion, and size. Consequently, in the interpretation of the HTP the therapist must assess all of the drawing's interrelated parts for their relationship to one another as well as the degree of essential detailing. By applying developmental theory to the assessment process a clinician therefore gains a glimpse into the intelligence of any given client. With time and practice it is pos-

Table 3.1 Normative Stages in Children's Art

Age	Characteristic
3	Able to draw a circle; head and limbs; little or no trunk
4	Able to draw a square; head and limbs; little or no trunk; navel makes an appearance; objects seem to float on the page; no understanding of proportion, placement, or size relationships; one-dimensional arms and legs
5	Able to draw a triangle; beginning of sexual differentiation of figures; recognizable figure representation; draws hands with fingers; navel is generally not drawn any longer; no understanding of proportion, placement, or size relationships; one-dimensional arms and legs
6	Able to draw a diamond; trunk is expected; hands and fingers; arms are connected to the trunk (not the head); no understanding of proportion, placement, or size relationships; one-dimensional arms and legs
7	Able to draw a diamond; rows of buttons make an appearance (more than seven may denote too much dependence on others); mixed profile is common; clothes, hair, and other detailing expected; figures show no interaction; baseline appears; space representation is confused; folding over is common; human body tends to be geometric shapes; size and proportions dependent upon emotional value
8	Begins to draw a whole body rather than segmenting; draws shoulders; two-dimensional arms and legs; figures show little to no interaction; size and proportions dependent upon emotional value
9–12	Detailing increases; size of objects indicates depth, interrelationships between objects and people begin; baseline disappears and plane and elevation begin; drawings appear stiff
12–14	Drawings show depth, proportion, shade, and shadow; perspective makes an appearance
14–17	Perspective improves in accuracy; exaggeration of detailing

sible, just by looking at a client's drawing productions, to deduce the cognitive level of the artist by applying the principles of normative art expectations.

To that end, I have provided Table 3.1 (compiled from DiLeo, 1973, 1983; Gardner, 1980; Levick, 1983; Lowenfeld & Brittain, 1982) as a basic guide to the normative stages of children's art. However, this table is not all inclusive, and I direct the reader to Lowenfeld and Brittain's book *Creative and Mental Growth* (1982) for further information.

Table 3.1 Continued

Characteristic	Emergence
Perspective/proportion	Perspective begins at age twelve, with accuracy by age fourteen. Proportion equals emotional value placed on object/person by child at age seven; by age nine proportion increases in accuracy as depth, plane, and elevation appear
Omission of arms	Normal until ages 4 or 5; expect arms and hands after age 6
Transparency/X-ray drawings	Normal under the age of 8.5–9
Human figure is definitely recognizable	By age 7
Baseline appears consistently	Age 8
Mixed profiles (two eyes and one nose)	Should not be seen after age 9
Figures show no interaction (looking forward rather than at one another)	Seen between ages 7 and 9

As you review Table 3.1, you will notice the gradual progression of detailing, perspective, and proportion, which parallels select developmental milestones. Buck scores these details on a quantitative level and integrates them into his qualitative (formal) interpretation. The use of symbols is therefore woven into the analysis through metaphor and reliance on empirical studies and observation.

Additionally, through his standardization studies, Buck found that formal detailing that is omitted is just as significant as items that are included. One example is chimney smoke. Buck (1966) found "that chimney smoke was drawn by 40% of the standardization Ss of the moron group, and by 35% of the Ss [subjects] of the above average group, but by varying lesser percentages of the Ss of the other groups" (p. 36). The differential values that make up Buck's scoring system were obtained through standardization studies of varying levels of adult intelligence (ages 15 years and above) that ranged from imbecile to superior. Thus, the HTP assessment, when applied to Buck's quantitatively scaled point system, yields information relating to the client's intellect. The therapist gleans this information by scoring each item drawn (the house, tree, and person) on an elaborate objective system that can be found in Buck's *House-Tree-Person Technique* (revised 1966).

In short, this scoring system appraises the drawn item's descriptive matter, classifies the information based on factor levels coupled with adult norms, and compares the good and flaw scores to arrive at a rough intelligence quotient. This system, however, differs greatly from the present-day administration of the HTP. In Buck's original design the client was given a pencil and three separate sheets of paper (7" × 8.5" in size) and was instructed to "draw the best picture of a house that you can." The client was then instructed to draw a tree and person, respectively, on the remaining pieces of paper. As the client drew these images, the examiner recorded a meticulous account of the elapsed time, spontaneous verbal comments, and sequential details in each rendering. When the nonverbal phase of the test was completed, the examiner then asked the client a series of questions (19 total for the house, 25 total for the tree, and 20 total for the person) that were grouped and staggered to provide gaps between each question item. At this point the patient was then offered eight crayons and was given the same instructions as have been outlined, with a postdrawing inquiry that included five questions for the house, eight for the tree, and nine for the person. The examiner then scored both tests (achromatic and chromatic) on a qualitative and quantitative scale using scoring folders. Buck (1948) states:

> Once the examiner has completed his scoring, he is in position to compare the subject's HTP per cent of raw G IQ with his IQ on other and more structured tests which have been designed specifically as a measure of general intelligence. One of the greatest values in estimating an IQ on the HTP seems to lie in the information derivable from its comparison with the IQ's attained by the subject on other tests. (p. 46)

In many cases the HTP IQ is as much as 10 points higher for individuals who find verbalization difficult, whereas the HTP IQ scores for those who are depressed or anxious tend to be significantly lowered. Nevertheless, I must stress that the HTP was intended to be used not as an intelligence test but as a signpost for aptitude. It assesses a client's intellectual level as one aspect of the personality, and Buck has stated that this assessment may more accurately be described as an efficiency quotient instead of an intelligence quotient.

Before we review some HTP evaluations it is important to add the formal aspects that make up the house and tree respectively. These drawn items, and the ensuing content, are as important to a qualitative interpretation of the HTP as the formal aspects of the completed person were for the DAP. For this reason, I provide Appendixes C and D, which have been adapted from multiple sources (Buck, 1966; DiLeo, 1983; Hammer, 1958); when combined with Appendix B, these appendices will present the clinician with a complete appraisal of a client's personality and functioning within the environment.

In order to illustrate a comparison of Buck's initial design with the method in current use, I have completed two HTP assessments on one adult male. The first set of drawings (panel A of Figure 3.5) is based strictly on Buck's initial design, without the chromatic assessment, while the second (panel B of Figure 3.5) is the presently utilized shortened version of the

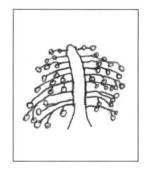

3.5A Schizoaffective Disorder, Depressed Type

3.5B Schizoaffective Disorder, Depressed Type

HTP art projective test. Both tests were completed within one month, and the Wechsler Intelligence Scale for children (WISC-III) score was collected one week after the final projective test was completed.

House-Tree-Person (HTP) Examples

The client is a single young adult male. Records indicate that his parents were divorced when he was a toddler, and he has focused his anger on his mother. She states that while in preschool he threw a burning stick at her and was later found standing over her with a pair of scissors. These episodes never resulted in any physical injuries but would end in screaming matches. From this time forward he lived with his father, who physically abused him on numerous occasions. He has been incarcerated since late adolescence, and he attempted suicide while in prison. The patient has also spoken of sexual incidents that occurred during his incarceration, many of which were consensual in nature. He reports a history of visual and auditory hallucinations that have convinced him that demons are after him. He states that in the past he saw demons, a bright light came through his bedroom door, and two shadows of demons paralyzed and levitated him. He further reports that he has felt an "evil wind blowing through my soul." Presently, he believes he has a mental illness, but he is hard pressed to describe or identify the illness. Instead he states, "I worry, I'm confused. . . . It's a lack of faith." He states that he has not had any delusional thoughts for some time, but he doesn't believe that his medication is the cause; instead he believes it is because he "reads the Bible, has faith, and prays."

Throughout the interview he was cooperative, with normal motor activity. His speech was soft but coherent, his appearance neat. His mood was depressed; he made self-deprecating remarks, and his thoughts were preoccupied with religion. His insight was fair to poor. He was able to answer similarities without problem, and his fund of knowledge was excellent. His response to proverb interpretation was appropriately abstract. To "even a dragon that walks along the river has little fish biting its tail" he replied that the proverb said "that we're all made alike." The patient has an extensive substance abuse history. In his early adulthood a screening measure used to identify persons fabricating psychological and physical symptoms found that he had a tendency to exaggerate symptoms, and the patient gets secondary gains from his delusions. He has often stated, "I know I'm the Antichrist."

In early adulthood the Culture Fair Intelligence Test measured his full-scale IQ at 77; however, by late adulthood he was retested using the WISC-III and garnered a full-scale IQ of 85.

I gave the client the HTP art projective test based on John Buck's original design. Panel A of Figure 3.5 shows his three drawing items. Following the analysis (as recommended by Buck), panel B of Figure 3.5 will illustrate the second and most frequently employed method of HTP assessment to compare and contrast the two techniques.

Qualitative Analysis: Details (Figure 3.5A)

House: (1) There is no chimney (lack of warmth in the home situation, lack of psychological warmth, or difficulty dealing with a masculine sex symbol); (2) the house lacks a bottom wall baseline (poor reality contact); (3) the door floats above the implied wall baseline (interpersonal inaccessibility).

Tree: (1) The trunk of the tree was completed first in a clearly phallic shape (feeling of basic power and ego strength); (2) the client placed special emphasis on the apples and branches through erasures (anxiety, dependency, and oral needs); (3) the branches are one-dimensional (pathoformic) and drop toward the bottom of the picture (trauma with regard to contact in the environment); (4) the amount of detailing for the tree is in direct contrast to the detailing for the house and person.

Person: (1) The hair was drawn first, erased, and then emphasized (virility striving, freedom); (2) the shoulders are large and excessively squared (defended, preoccupied with need for strength); (3) the neck is nonexistent (body drives threaten to overwhelm); (4) the person is clothed in a trench coat (security and protection, defensiveness).

Qualitative Analysis: Proportion

House: The door is drawn excessively large (dependent).

Tree: (1) The tree is small compared to the form page (feelings of inferiority, insignificance); (2) the branches of the tree dwarf the size of the trunk (inadequacy coupled with striving for security and satisfaction within the environment).

Person: The person is small compared to the form page (feelings of inferiority, insignificance).

Qualitative Analysis: Perspective

Tree: (1) The tree is placed high on the page and toward the left corner (seeks satisfaction in fantasy, aloof, insecurity with environmental factors); (2) it leans definitely toward the left (seeks immediate and emotional satisfaction, overconcern with self and past).

Person: (1) The person is placed in the exact position of the tree (seeks satisfaction in fantasy, aloof; insecurity with environmental factors); (2) the person has a slight lean toward the left (attempts to suppress the future with preference to the past).

Qualitative Analysis: Time

House: (1) After completing the garage door and prior to beginning the upper story windows, the patient ceased drawing for many moments and spontaneously stated, "It's hard to tell people about what bothers me. . . . I have to look at people and then I forget it's hard to get across. I worry about things . . . all this little paranoia" (feelings of alienation regarding home and family); (2) after completing the upstairs window (which he identified in the postdrawing inquiry as his room) he spontaneously asked, "Do you think there's anything wrong in being religious? I don't think there is. I think there's a time and destiny for everyone" (found solace and acceptance in religion through the escape/withdrawal of his bedroom).

Qualitative Analysis: Comments, Drawing Phase

Tree: (1) After erasing and adding a second berry to the bottom right row of branches, he made a superfluous comment: "It's a little bit detailed" (insecurity); (2) he then immediately made a series of unrelated comments ("I stay up late at night chewing tobacco or reading a book"), and at this point his speech became so rapid that I could ascertain only his general topics. These comments focused on his medication, his drug use (present and past), and confrontations by peers in his dorm. After this comment, he then added the rounded top to the trunk of the tree (regression as the tree took on a more phallic form).

Person: (1) After completing the person's hair he stated, "This was old-style long hair. I never grew my hair long" (virility strivings); (2) after completing the trench coat he stated, "I was thinking, I know it looks like a warlock or something" (constant struggle between good and evil, God and devil, superego and id).

Qualitative Analysis: Comments, Postdrawing Inquiry

House: (1) The house is above the client, and while he was drawing it it reminded him of his mother's house (personal relationships regarding home and family; feels insecure, insignificant); (2) he stated that it was a friendly house but then added, "I wish I had better memories of being there, but when I was there, I was mentally ill" (contradicts statement of happy memories with unpleasant experiences); (3) he added that what the house needed most was "to be taken care of. . . . You have to fix it" (patient needs to be taken care of, fixed).

Tree: (1) The patient stated that the tree was feminine because "with her caring heart she shows her fruit," which was determined by "lots of nice apples" (sexual and maternal symbols combined); (2) the tree reminded him of "how a person should grow up and produce good fruit" (concern and obsession with his mental illness as a "defect," with resulting religious metaphor relating to fruit of her womb; sexual, maternal, and religious symbols combined).

Person: (1) The male's name is "Werewolf," and the patient is attempting to convert him to Christianity by "talking about the Lord," but Werewolf is thinking about "how good a feeling hard rock music gives him" (religious delusional thoughts surrounding struggle to remain pious; good and evil thoughts comingling); (2) the person is "sick in the mind" because "he won't stop using drugs and he's into witchcraft" (projection of patient's internal struggle); (3) unlike in the drawings of the house and tree, the weather in this rendering is "cold and rainy. A light drizzle" (depression, external pressures); (4) in response to the question "what does this person need the most?" he said, "support and love from a higher power" (retreat into delusional or religious belief system for dynamic needs).

Qualitative Analysis: Concepts

House: His house should be built on a ranch, which is a frequent topic of this patient (i.e., living on a ranch, being a "cowboy"; desire to retreat to open spaces, anonymity through a masculine and "tough" symbol).

Tree: The tree is a healthy apple tree because "you don't see hardly any dead spots" (infantile dependency and oral needs ill disguised).

Person: The person is a werewolf (sexually predatory symbol) who prefers drugs and witchcraft to religion and conventionality (powers that threaten to emerge from within the patient).

Quantitative Analysis: Summary

According to Buck's scoring system the patient's raw G IQ is 73 and his net weighted score IQ is 77, which places the patient in the Borderline Intellectual Functioning range. His good IQ score correlates to an IQ of 83 and represents his ability to interact in his environment. However, his interests are relatively simple and material in nature. An overview of his detail, proportion, and perspective scores basically yields difficulty surrounding critical and analytical judgment regarding the more basic problems that are presented by the environment. The patient's lowest overall scores appear in the drawing of the tree, where individuals generally attain their highest score. This expresses significant conflict in the patient's basic feeling of ego strength.

Evaluation of his HTP reveals the presence of the following characteristics: (1) feelings of insecurity and inferiority regarding masculinity, resulting in an attendant withdrawal into masculine symbols of power; (2) infantile and orally dependent traits that cause sexual symbols and maternal symbols to be united, creating possible Oedipal conflicts; (3) a tendency to retreat into a delusional or religious belief system to meet his dynamic needs when body drives threaten to overwhelm.

In the end, this patient is essentially immature, with infantile dependency needs and predominant feelings of shame and humiliation that impede his general functioning within the environment. He therefore seeks a sense of superego through religious preoccupation. Yet, in the fantasy of finding himself through his delusional belief system, he instead loses himself.

The same patient also took a shortened version of the HTP art projective test (panel B of Figure 3.5). He began this drawing with meticulous lines that are minimally wavy in appearance but otherwise well drawn. The house is completed in one color (constricted use), the tree in two (brown and green), and the person is outlined in a pale yellow with brown belt, hair, and feet (constricted use). All items are placed one third of the way up the page, with the person to the furthest left (seeks immediate emotional satisfaction; concern with self and past), then the tree, and then the house. There is no ground line under any of the renderings.

The house has three outlined roofs, which makes it look like a Tudor style. It has a large, rounded doorway (overly dependent) with a multiplicity of windows. Each window has a centerline designating the pane of glass. The house, though drawn well, appears impersonal and daunting.

The tree is to the left of the house and has a long trunk (feels constricted by and in the environment) with three branches on either side and one on top. It is very symmetrical in appearance (ambivalence regarding course of action). The leaves are carefully drawn as circles emanating from the branches (clinging to nurturance, dependency issues), again very symmetrical. There is no ground line delineating the base of the trunk (vulnerable to stress).

The person was drawn last and is outlined in yellow so that the body is almost invisible. The client began by drawing the feet first and ended with the head (disturbance in interpersonal relationships, possible thought disorder). The arms are raised in a gesture of hopelessness or a bodybuilding pose. While drawing the arms the client stated, "I didn't draw the arms very big" (critical comment regarding power and strength). There is no face indicated (poor interpersonal skills, withdrawal), only hair (expression of virility striving; masculinity and strength), which is drawn with quick bursts (infantile sexual drives), a midline belt on an otherwise naked figure (emotional immaturity, mother dependency, feelings of inadequacy, sexual issues), and frantically drawn large balled feet (striving for security and virility). The figure has one hand (the right) with fingers indicated, while the left hand is merely a pointed line (guilt, insecurity, difficulty dealing with the environment). The figure's legs are long in comparison with his torso (striving for autonomy). When I asked him if he wanted to add anything, the client added windows to the bottom story of the home, including two beside the arched door. He titled the drawing "Eastern U.S. Home."

He told the following story: "He's happy. This room [pointing to window beside the door on right] is the kitchen [oral needs, need for affection]. This room [pointing to window beside door on left] is a bathroom [elimination]. Behind this is a living room and family room [social intercourse]. This room [pointing to upper story, center windows] is one large room. His room is that room. He lives in the house alone. . . . He built it with the hopes of finding a wife and having two kids (a son and daughter). . . . He's 34 years old and the house is on ten acres."

Summary

Overall, the patient's completed drawing indicates feelings of constriction within the environment, a concern with the past, and marked disturbances in interpersonal relationships (dependency, helplessness) coupled with a desire for intimacy. His spontaneous comment regarding the drawn figure's lack of strength and power is in proportion to the symbolic abundance of ideas that focus on emotional immaturity, dependency issues, insecurity, and infantile sexual needs. The patient generally feels insignificant and inadequate. Even though the tree is drawn well, the figure shows that in the environment the client desires virility and security, yet the figure's yellowed outline bespeaks of emotional and physical withdrawal. The absolute symmetry that he applied to the tree (and home) also points in the direction of the patient's ambivalence toward intellectual or emotional satisfaction. Therefore, unable to decide, he withdraws into the comfort of an oversized and impersonal world (institutions, religion, fantasy) where his basic living and dependency needs are provided. The drawing does not indicate overt psychotic thought processing, and it would appear that the patient's medication regime has circumscribed his delusional subsystem. He does, however, exhibit a high degree of depressive features in concert with dependency issues.

When we compare the two panels of Figure 3.5 from a qualitative perspective, the information we glean about the two HTP assessments is remarkably similar. In both instances we see feelings of insecurity and infantile sexual needs. However, Buck's original design produced a richer picture of this client's internal struggles. Although his delusional retreat was evident in the adapted HTP, it was in no way as detailed with regard to internal processing difficulties, especially those related to his mother in concert with his body drives. The postdrawing inquiry consequently allowed a closer scrutiny, which permits the clinician to apply a wide range of theoretical constructs to the therapeutic hour.

Thus, if we were to provide treatment for this institutionalized client, Table 2.3 offers three distinct stage theories of development, and one can see how the client is fixated within the Piagetian stage of formal operation, the Freudian genital stage, and the Eriksonian phase of identity versus role confusion, and any of these theories offers an appropriate starting point for the treatment plan.

As we move into a comparison of the two HTPs from a quantitative examination, the raw G IQ score and the good IQ score remained relatively the same (73/83 on the original and 74/80 on the adapted test). The tests differ in the net weighted score IQ (points toward the client's potential level of functioning), with 10 less IQ points measured on the adapted projective test. Taken as a whole, both tests pointed toward Borderline Intellectual Functioning, while the WISC-III score of 85 placed this patient in the low average range.

Yet the testing that was administered when the patient was in early adulthood should not be overlooked. The Culture Fair Intelligence Test, an instrument that measures intelligence that is not influenced by cultural background or scholastic training, produced an IQ of 77. In comparison, the IQs from both HTPs are within mere points of each other, which may be due to the fact that both the HTP and the Culture Fair Intelligence test rely little on verbal training; as Craddick (1980) has stated, "Projective tests (such as the Rorschach) are by their very structure more likely to elicit pathological responses than will the WAIS [Wechsler Adult Intelligence Scale], for example" (p. 914).

Although this client was able to fully participate in a battery of verbal testing treatment, a clinician's work with the difficult client often requires a broad knowledge of diverse cultures. These diversities are not relegated only to cultural traditions, religion, and generational differences, but also encompass clothing and food preferences, communication styles, morality, control of aggressiveness, and socioeconomic differences. Consequently, cultural variations affect patterns of communicating, behaving, understanding, and problem solving. However, as related to art therapy, research has indicated that "children up to age five, regardless of cultural or ethnic origins, follow a specific pattern. . . . These [patterns] in turn become the basis for recognizable images . . ." (Levick, 1983, p. 45). If you review Table 3.1 you will notice a guide to normative stages in children's art. This guide was taken in part from Lowenfeld and Brittain's (1982) research on childhood developmental stages, yet a quick search of their index for cultural issues finds them linked only with aesthetics. There is no mention of how culture affects art development and no discussion of any cross-cultural commonalities that may exist within childhood renderings.

To address this deficiency in the research Alter-Muri (2002) began "an informal inquiry into how Lowenfeld's theories might function today" in which "one hundred and fifty-six drawings by children ages 3 to 11 from schools in Switzerland, Denmark, Germany, France, and Hungary were collected" (p. 178). Just as childhood developmental stages (art) paralleled Piaget's cognitive theories (see Chapter 2), the results of Alter-Muri's study found that Lowenfeld's methods were applicable across cultures in Europe. Unfortunately, the research inherent in a qualitative breakdown of a projective test is often based upon Western criteria. For that reason, when taking cultural variations into account "projective techniques are found useful when the researcher is investigating a specific hypothesis, using an objective system of scoring" (Al-Issa, 1970, p. 495).

Figure 3.6 provides an example of the use of HTP with a patient from a different culture: in this case, a male from India who spoke rudimentary

3.6 Major Depressive Disorder with Psychotic Features

English and required specialized interpreters, as his village dialect was obscure. I chose the HTP projective test for its previously noted ability to measure independently quantitative details and for its objective scoring system. However, I must state that Buck's study (not unlike Lowenfeld's) focuses on research developed by Western participants and standards. As Machover (1949) has observed, however, common social meanings are inherent in artwork, especially in human figure drawing, and facial characteristics transcend variations in culture or in drawing skill. Thus, the human figure should contain (with exception made only for consequences of figure positioning or an absence accounted for verbally) a head; a trunk; two legs, arms, and eyes; a nose; a mouth; and two ears (Buck, 1966). Additionally, Figure 3.6 contains two drawings completed within two months of one another. The HTP on the left was completed without an interpreter present and therefore was not accompanied by a postdrawing inquiry, while the session that produced the drawing on the right utilized an interpreter. I performed the projective test twice to see if the client's drawings would differ after the client had settled into the milieu of institutionalized living. As you will note, they differ very little, with the exception of the form page's having been turned vertically for the initial drawing. However, the second rendering shows two significant differences: the omission of the mouth and the presence of a seemingly barred door. These differences could be attributed to the patient's inability to communicate in his natural language (the absence of the mouth) and his separation from his family and culture (the barred door, which may also imitate the locked and impersonal institution in which he now resided). For purposes of this discussion I will be interpreting the second rendering (as this was accompanied by a brief postdrawing inquiry), and I have administered the test based on the shortened version of Buck's design.

The client is a married adult male. He immigrated to the United States with his wife when he was in his late 20s. He is the oldest child in a middle-class family. He stated that he prefers living in the United States, "because of the opportunities here." The client was being interviewed due to his unprovoked assault on a coworker. Apparently, family difficulties had created a situation in which he was sleeping poorly and had stopped taking his prescription medication. On the day of the assault others had noticed he was acting bizarrely, and his supervisor had offered to send him home. However, he declined the offer, as his family needed the income from his job. When questioned about his mental illness he stated, "I have a weight on my brain. My doctor [in India] said I imagine things in my brain." Although he denied hallucinations or delusions, he did admit that historically he had heard voices. Throughout the interview the patient's attitude was pleasant and cooperative, his motor activity slow, his speech soft, and his appearance disheveled. His responses to similarities (a measure of general intelligence) were appropriately abstract. His affect and mood were depressed. He showed no signs of thought disorder or delusional content. He denied a substance abuse history and admitted to depressive tendencies when he heard voices. He stated that he had completed the 10th grade in India, a level of education that the interpreter characterized as being equivalent to a high school education in this country with some college. The diagnostic impression was Major Depressive Disorder with Psychotic Features.

Prior to reviewing the art therapy assessment, it is important for us to discuss some issues related to cultural considerations. The first revolves around the dedication to family and community inherent in the region from which this patient came. Morris Opler (1959) explored a village in India and found that the beliefs and customs of the villagers were characteristic of the region. Although Western influences have penetrated the area, many traditions and festivals continue to be observed. In fact, these villagewide rites are integral not only to culture but to the family as well; 25 of 40 rites "revolve around family needs and purposes" (p. 288). One such traditional celebration is called Divali (festival of lights): As recently as 1959, this ritual found a villager entering homes where the owner had gone to sleep and "calling loudly for the Goddess of poverty to leave the home and for a God or Goddess of wealth to enter" (p. 281).

Furthermore, the caste system, while no longer sanctioned, is a long-established classification in India. This system organizes the social classes in the following order: (1) Brahmins—priests; (2) Kshatriyas—royals, rulers, or warriors; (3) Vaisyas—merchants, farmers, or professionals; (4) Sudras—workers; and (5) Pariahs or Harijans—beggars or the diseased (Kipfer, 1997). Under this system the client's family and personal doctor would fall within the Vaisyas. With regard to cultural influences on depressive symptomatology, Wittkower and Rin (1965) tested Cohen's (1961) hypothesis that "psychotic-depression [sic] is generally more frequent among those persons who are more cohesively identified with their families, kin groups, communities, and other significant groupings" (p. 392) and found it to be valid. Thus, the protective agent of these close familial bonds provides for safety and protection within the community. However, "a Hindu family leaving India . . . will experience the forces of transition from the security of a close traditional extended family to the isolation of a nuclear family" (Landau, 1982, p. 555). If this isolation is coupled with stressors and further decompensation of family bonds, then one can assume that the depressive features could reach dizzying heights.

Finally, Alter-Muri (2002) refers to research conducted on art symbolism in other countries and states, "Wilson (1985) noted that human figures drawn by 9–12 year olds in Islamic countries had rectangular-shaped torsos and fused necks" (p. 176). Wilson (1985) states:

I have observed this feature in the drawings of children from other countries with Islamic populations—Saudi Arabia, Qatar, Turkey, Iran, India, and Kenya (although I have not determined the percentages). The feature occurs with such regularity that I have called it the *Islamic torso*. (p. 92)

Although the patient stated that he was exposed to Western culture prior to his immigration, his drawing ability is in keeping with Table 3.1's description of a 9- to 12-year-old. Thus, I took this into account when scoring and interpreting the final art product (Figure 3.6).

Qualitative Analysis: Details

House: (1) There is no chimney on either drawing, and this is in keeping with the patient's culture, as homes in India do not possess chimneys; (2) the patient places a barlike emphasis on the door of the home in the second figure only (feelings of entrapment, inability to escape present living situation).

Tree: A ground line exists under both trees, with the first being longer and bolder (insecurity in the environment).

Person: (1) The first rendering contains a mouth, which is omitted in the second drawing. The omission could suggest the patient's ongoing difficulty in relating to others due to the language barrier rather than intellectual deterioration. (2) Neither figure's eyes contain pupils (visual processing or learning problems associated with language barrier and/or reluctance to accept stimuli); (3) the fingers are drawn one-dimensionally and without hands (infantile aggression) on the second drawing, while the first drawing's hands are enclosed by a loop (wish to suppress aggressive impulse, repressed aggression).

Qualitative Analysis: Proportion

House: The home is the smallest item in the first drawing and is even smaller in the second (sees, feels, views his family connections as far away in relation to his present environment).

Tree: The tree is very large in comparison to the page in the second drawing (feels constricted by and in the environment).

Person: The person is drawn large in both drawings but is further away (spatial distance) from the home in the second rendering and devoid of a mouth (feelings of helplessness and frustration produced by a restricting environment and physical distance from his home and family).

Qualitative Analysis: Perspective

House: The house in the second drawing is shown from a bird's-eye view and appears far away (rejection of the home situation; however, due to bars on door, may instead indicate a rejection of his present circumstances).

Qualitative Analysis: Comments, Postdrawing Inquiry

Rather than asking the formal questions designed by Buck, I administered the shortened version (for the second drawing only) and requested that the client tell me "what's going on in this picture?" He stated (through an interpreter) that the man has a job and is coming back home. When questioned about the man's age, he said he is 43 years old and that his family lives in the house. He further added that the man is a doctor who is very busy and a nice person. When asked to give the drawing a title or name, he decided to title it "Village Town," which I wrote out (on the left) and which he copied in his own hand.

Qualitative Analysis: Concepts

House: The perspective and spatial distance of the house from the person indicates that in the first rendering the patient may have had more hope for a return to his community and family, while in the second drawing the home is obviously dwarfed by the present circumstances and literal distances.

Tree: In the second drawing the tree is extremely large as well as separating home and person.

Person: Assigning the role of doctor to the person in the second drawing is an interesting mixture of hope for renewal (the doctor has always provided well for the client in the past) and trepidation as the client's present circumstances place him in the position of having to trust unknown professionals. The lack of mouth may symbolize not only the client's growing frustration due to the language barrier but also the family doctor's lack of input into the patient's treatment. In addition, a row of buttons is normal in drawings by Western children until the age of 7 or 8 but afterwards comes to symbolize feelings of inadequacy or dependency. Additionally, the midline that separates the trunk vertically "is frequently seen in schizoid or schizophrenic individuals whose physical inferiority and mother dependence are in the forefront" (Machover, 1949, p. 89). Although the meaning of this may differ in other cultures, it is interesting to note that it is the second drawing that contains references to dependency and not the first.

Story: The title of the drawing, "Village Town," may represent a combination of two cultures, with the village suggesting India and the town indicating America. It is apparent from this titling that the traditional bonds of family and community remain strong.

Qualitative Analysis: Summary

As noted under cultural considerations, the art of select Islamic countries is typically different from its Western counterpart. Therefore, the score of this projective test takes that into account. In addition, due to the patient's initial drawing of the mouth, I gave him credit despite its subsequent omission, as I consider the exclusion to be due to his increased frustration with his inability to communicate and therefore not an indication of pathology.

Consequently, the HTP raw score is 86 and the net weighted score IQ is 85. This would place him in the low average range of intellectual functioning. His good IQ score correlates to an IQ of 85 and represents his ability to interact in his environment, with a flaw IQ score of 85. Analysis yields that his interests are relatively simple and material in nature. An overview of his detail, proportion, and perspective scores represents an overall stability of functioning with the exception of his perspective good score, which is a measure of insight. This low score coupled with the low score in the proportion flaw indicates difficulty surrounding critical judgment in the more basic problems presented within the environment. The patient's lowest overall scores appear in the drawing of the person, which expresses a significantly low degree of functioning with regard to interpersonal relationships.

Evaluation of his HTP reveals the presence of the following characteristics: (1) feelings of entrapment, helplessness, frustration, and insecurity produced by a restricting environment; (2) a conviction that his family connections are far away and possibly unattainable in relation to his present environment; (3) a growing despondency and dependency.

In conclusion, the patient, estranged from the traditional systems of security previously rooted in his family system, is experiencing increased feelings of inadequacy, despondency, and helplessness.

House-Tree-Person (HTP) Art Assessments

Not unlike Karen Machover's DAP assessment, the HTP has been modified from its original design and now tends to be shortened both in degree and application. However, as outlined earlier, this modified version can still yield accurate data when combined with Buck's scoring system for aptitude and intelligence.

In the end the HTP yields both conscious and unconscious information concerning the client's personality, interpersonal relationships, and interactions with the environment. As a result, it offers a broad spectrum in which to appraise all clientele, especially children who are beginning to branch out into their growing world. For this reason, in an initial evaluation, I prefer to administer the HTP to children and the DAP to adults.

Before we review case illustrations, the directives for the modified HTP assessment are as follows:

- Offer the client one sheet of 9" × 12" paper.
- Give this directive: "Using as many or as few colors as you like, draw the best house you can."
- Once the house is complete, ask the client "draw the best tree that you can" on the same piece of paper.
- Once the tree is complete, ask the client to draw "the best person" he or she can on the same piece of paper, adding, "The person should be a whole figure, not just a floating head or stick figure."
- After this is complete, have the client give the picture a title and write it on the paper.
- Begin the postdrawing inquiry by requesting, "tell me what's going on in this picture."

Case Illustrations

Our illustrations include a pair of sisters, and an elderly male.

Personal Profile 3.3

This case involves two sisters who are resistant to visiting their biological mother. The psychosocial history reveals that the biological parents divorced when the children were toddlers. The mother quickly remarried, and the children's stepfather was physically abusive to the children as well

3.7 Dysthymia

as toward the mother (which they witnessed). At this point they were re-moved from their mother's care and placed with the biological father.

The 10-year-old (Figure 3.7) is currently experiencing difficulty con-centrating, is hostile and resistant, and is overly dependent upon her fa-ther. The 8-year-old (Figure 3.8) is expressing numerous somatic com-plaints in the form of stomach aches and headaches as well as experiencing nightmares. A medical exam found no medical etiology to cause the so-matic complaints. The assessments were conducted on the same day and separately for each child.

From a quantitative perspective the height of Figure 3.7 is exceedingly small (environment experienced as overwhelming and self as inadequate; infantile tendencies), and all the form items are drawn utilizing the bottom edge of the page as a ground line (insecurity, feelings of inadequacy). The house and tree are drawn in long strokes (apprehensive; requires support and reassurance), while the entire person (without face) is shaded and col-ored orange in an aggressive manner (concealment). Color usage is appro-priate; however, the roof of the home (orange) matches the color utilized for the person and points toward tensional intensity (anxiety). The use of distant detailing that dwarfs the person (i.e., sun) indicates anxiety re-garding environmental intrusions, with poor intellectual defenses.

Heather's creation!

3.8 Adjustment Disorder with Mixed Anxiety and Depressed Mood

A qualitative analysis notes that the house uses the paper's edge as a ground line (basic home insecurities). It has an inverted V roof, windows that are attached to the wall edge (need for support, fear of autonomy and independent action), and a door that floats above the baseline (interpersonal inaccessibility). The chimney is detailed with cross-hatched brick (enriching detail devoid in other items) and a line of thick smoke emanates from it (inner tension). The tree is to the viewer's right and has two lines for the trunk and a looped crown (oppositional tendencies) in both brown and green. A person stands to the left of the home with outstretched arms (desire for affection), a circular face, dots for eyes, a nose, and a single line for the mouth. Overall, the lack of facial detailing gives the impression of concealment. The head is connected directly to the squared trunk (body drives threaten to overwhelm). The hair is profuse (striving) and yellow. The figure has a rectangular body with reinforced shading of the body walls (need to contain and delineate ego boundaries); however, the figure has no hands or feet (inadequacy, helplessness, withdrawal). In addition to the HTP items, distant detailing appears in the upper left-hand corner in the form of an oversized sun with large rays (need for love and support; representative of parental love), and two blue clouds float over the home (generalized anxiety).

When asked to tell something about the drawing, the patient stated that the person was her and that the house was her home where she and her sister live. Clarifying questions did not yield any further information. She titled her drawing "Me and my Home."

The symbolic abundance of ideas found within this assessment points toward significant feelings of inadequacy, insecurity, and fear in conjunction with anxiety. Her dependent reactions are in direct conflict with her need for industry and accomplishments. Moreover, the reinforcement found in the rendering of her person illustrates the struggles surrounding her sense of self. Another area of concern is the lone detailing found in the chimney. This, coupled with the thick smoke, exemplifies her overconcern with the emotional turbulence that is occurring within the home as well as the client's own inner tension.

In comparison, in the 8-year-old's-drawing (Figure 3.8) the person is within normal height, while the home is drawn tall and thin with a tiny doorway (reluctant to permit access). This, however, is normal for this client's age, when size and proportion are dependent upon emotional values rather than reality. The remainder of the drawing shows adequate line quality, strokes, shading, detailing, and use of color. There are ground lines added under both the tree and the house (provides stability and structure within the environment to reduce the stress when drawn by young children). The manner of scribbling or shading for the ground under the tree, however, bodes poorly for her ability to cope.

The house is placed to the viewer's left and is drawn tall and thin. The roof is patterned (normal use of detailing) as is the overly large chimney (exhibitionistic tendencies). A circular plume of smoke is seen escaping the home (emotional turbulence within the home). All windows are drawn high on the front of the house, and there is a tiny door (reluctant to permit access) that does not connect to the baseline (interpersonal inaccessibility). Outside the home a purple-spiked ground line is drawn (provides measure of security but also appears foreboding). An extremely tall tree (aggressive tendencies, need for dominance; feels constricted by and in the environment) is found just right of center and has a colored trunk with branches and foliage located on each branch. Under the tree is a highly shaded ground line. The person is placed on the right side with a circular smiley face (typical for age group), thin neck, and long flowing red hair, wearing a brightly colored blue dress. She has well-detailed hands, considering the use of markers and difficulty associated with drawing fingers. Her one-dimensional legs appear slightly regressed (indicative of 6-year-old); however, the addition of high-heeled shoes shows her attention to detail and focus on shoes versus the legs. Just above the home is found a sun (representative of parental love and support) wearing sunglasses with a "Charlie Brown" smile (normal for age group).

When asked to tell what was going on in this picture she said the girl was her and that she lived in the house with her sister, Dad, and her Dad's girlfriend. She titled the drawing using her own name (which has been changed): "Heather's Creation."

Not unlike her older sibling, this client is apprehensive due to the turmoil found within the home and the prospect of reestablishing visits with her biological mother. Since a medical etiology was ruled out for the somatic complaints, it would appear that she is experiencing a kinesthetic sensory system (Mills & Crowley, 1986) whereby anxiety is revealed through physical symptoms. In spite of this, the overall drawing shows good adjustment. The difference between her and her older sibling is that this child finds stability and structure within the environment, allowing her to move through the necessary stages of development. It will be important to ascertain the level of abuse that occurred, and it is possible that the younger sibling was not the primary victim of the attacks but was protected by her older sister.

In evaluating the two renderings, the 10-year-old's drawing (Figure 3.7) should show variances with regard to increased accuracy in depth, plane, detailing, and elevation (see Table 3.1). However, her drawing items appear more in keeping with a 7-year-old's with attendant expression of moodiness and anxiety. This inward thrust (see Table 2.1) keeps her tethered to feelings of shame and humiliation, and it also correlates to the age when the abuse first began. In contrast, the younger sibling shows adequate development within her artwork and an increased attention to the environment. Therefore, her adjustment parallels the use of age-appropriate intellectual defenses together with age-appropriate expansive symbolism (note size of person).

At this juncture the older sibling appears to be having a much more difficult time adjusting even though the younger sibling is experiencing a wealth of somatic issues. However, her symptoms are not merely focused on physical complaints, and this signifies an etiology focused on worry and anxiety that should resolve itself with individual and family therapy as well as ongoing structure and safety. Overall, the older child appears to be withdrawing from contact with the outside world and clinging to infantile qualities within her relationships. This indicates a lower level of functioning, increased depressive features, and the possible utilization of the defense mechanism of regression.

If we review the postdrawing inquiry, although both girls showed a paucity of response, the younger sibling placed the entire "protective" family within the home (the tiny door perhaps not allowing others within this protective circle), while the older child added only herself and her sister. This is a curious situation and makes one wonder whether the older child views herself in the role of protector yet is emotionally and physically unable to perform this role and is consequently struggling with feelings of inadequacy, guilt, and shame at her perceived failure. Additionally, this child may be harboring resentments that the father did not rescue his children and may therefore be undergoing a sense of distress that anyone can provide protection.

Overall, there are many unanswered questions that will require further exploration. However, the older child may benefit from involvement in individual, family, and group therapy to increase her contact within the environment and focus on her own feelings and issues without the younger child being the topic of discussion or concern. Due to the level of resistance, an expressive therapy approach (in individual and family therapy) may prove beneficial until she can build sufficient trust and rapport to communicate her feelings rather than repressing or regressing.

Personal Profile 3.4

The client is an elderly male who has been divorced multiple times. He presently has no contact with any of his ex-wives or family members. He states that he left home as a preteen and has lived on the streets the majority of his life. He is being evaluated because of concerns that he suffers from dementia and is presently unable to attend to his basic, daily living needs. The patient denies the presence of mental illness and states, "I don't have an education, no job, no place of my own. I don't have a mental illness." When questioned about a possible head injury he replied that at the age of 7 he was in a car accident and hit his head on the windshield, which according to him has caused him problems with memory.

Throughout the interview his speech was so soft that I had to lean in and request him to repeat his answers. His appearance was appropriate, his attitude casual, his motor activity normal, his mood depressed. His thought content appeared unrelated to delusions or paranoia, and he was not responding to internal stimuli. The sensorium mental grasp showed significantly concrete answers to all questions: To the question "How are a tree and elephant alike?" he replied, "both give you shade"; to the question "How are an apple and orange alike?" he replied, "they have seeds and you peel them." His immediate and recent memory was fair. However, when answering questions regarding remote memory, he would fill in the blanks with tangential rambling or mumble incoherently. When asked to touch his right arm's index finger to his left ear, the patient touched his right ear with his right index finger. To the proverb "A bird in the hand is worth two in the bush" he at first refused to answer and then answered rapidly, "he wouldn't be welcome in my hand all the time, or under the bush all the time . . . ," and at this point he spoke so tangentially and softly that I could not understand the remainder of his answer. His tendency toward tangential speaking appeared to be related to dementia and not psychotic thought processing. He reports that he began drinking alcohol before he was in the sixth grade and continues to drink excessively to this day. However, he does not feel that he has an alcohol abuse problem. The patient states that 10 years prior he attempted to hang himself and admits that he was drinking and very depressed at the time.

Figure 3.9 is his completed assessment. Prior to starting the drawing, the patient stated that he used to be a good artist but now can only draw boxes. Consequently, his house is a three-dimensional drawing of a box. On the bottom he added two windows and the semblance of a door. On the side was an attachment that looks like another window. The house is drawn from a bird's-eye perspective (rejection of the home situation). Its lines are wobbly (organicity, motor control issues) and connect poorly. He next rendered the tree by drawing three lines upward that fall back toward the ground line. He then placed cloudlike outlines on the ends of the tree branches and added a squiggly line for the base with grass growing on either side of the tree. All branches are one-dimensional and connect segmentally (organic style of branch development). Writing the name "boy" and then taking the letters and making them into eyes, ear, and head (the

3.9 *Organic Brain Syndrome Secondary to Substance Abuse*

"b" is the left eye, the "o" is the right eye, and the "y" is the ear, with a quick loop to make the head), he drew his person. He then added the mouth, nose, and a thick neck while reinforcing the eyes. I instructed him to complete the body, and with one line (apprehensive, requiring support and reassurance) he outlined the arms and legs like a gingerbread man. The body leans toward the right of the drawing and is clearly off balance. I asked the patient how he learned to draw a person like that and he proceeded to draw another, this time with a female head, and told me that he had made up the procedure one day and that you can make the girl by writing out "Boy" or "Loyd."

He titled the image "Village" after much contemplation. In addition, he spoke spontaneously about the two people, "The two need to build the house, live in it, and clean it; if they build it, they're a couple living there, keeping it clean. . . ." He then started to talk about the box home and said, "They weren't happy with things I did, they never were satisfied, they couldn't be happy." When questioned on who "they" were he stated, "the children at school."

A structural analysis shows that each item is placed high on the page (anxiety and insecurity in coping with environmental factors) with the home drawn in the uppermost left-hand corner (normal in young children; in adults organic, poor concept maturation). The line quality is heavy throughout the entire drawing (organic quality) with obvious impairment in motor control. The patient's insistence on writing out the word *boy* in the drawing of a person indicates his reliance on structured patterns to complete tasks.

Overall, the entire rendering takes on the qualities of neurological impairment. According to Buck's scoring system, the patient's IQ fell in the range of 49 with a high of 51. This would place the patient in the mild range of mental retardation, yet, having no premorbid testing available, I was unable to compare his level of functioning. However, the characteristics of his drawing are highly suggestive of organic mental deterioration. If one looks at all three form items, each lacks appropriate motor control, detailing, proportion, and perspective. This organizational difficulty indicates a major organic collapse and perhaps emotional disturbance. Machover (1949) has found that with chronic alcoholics or in conditions of senility "the placement of the figure is relatively high on the page, and often gives the impression that the figure is adrift in space" (p. 90).

Assessing the image from a formal point of reference shows a rejection of the home life, feelings of insignificance, a need for protection, trauma (tree size and branches dropping to bottom of image), and an inability to navigate in his external world.

Eight-Card Redrawing Test (8CRT)

The last projective test that we will review is the 8CRT, developed by Caligor. Unlike the HTP or the DAP, this assessment procedure never gained favor among working professionals. In fact, in my schooling experience I never even heard of the 8CRT; it was only through a fluke that I stumbled upon a review of the process in a journal article. However, once I began incorporating this test into my routine, I found it to be an indispensable tool.

In 1957 Caligor lamented the restriction posed by the single-drawing projective tests and developed the 8CRT, which utilizes a series of eight interrelated drawings. He defines his test in this manner:

> In the progression from drawing one through eight scores may tend toward the more pathological, remain essentially the same, or tend more to the statistical norm. This *pathological weighting* is an index of the individual's ability to maintain his functioning level under stress, and whether he is able to show recoverability after responding to stress. (p. 66)

Furthermore, this ever-increasing and interconnected use of the client's drawings allows for an interpretation that explores the varied layers of an individual's personality structure. And it is these layered concepts of interpretation that make use of the structural analysis and formal or symbolic analysis found in Appendixes A, B, C, and D.

Additionally, Caligor created a scoring system to impartially measure the structural elements based on deviations from statistical norms. If we return to Buck's scoring system for his HTP assessment, many of the same elements are also stressed in Caligor's study. These surround the ratio of heights, amount of detailing, proportion, and paper chopping. Yet this is where the similarity ends. Caligor's method is not intended to measure intelligence; instead it "should be seen as a reflection of the individual's approach to life situations" (Caligor, 1957, p. 65).

Caligor has provided examples and an outline of his system for scoring the 8CRT in his book *A New Approach to Figure Drawing* (1957). For the purposes of this discussion, I prefer to utilize an adapted version. Therefore, rather than assessing the client's completed test based on Caligor's 36 structural dimensions, I have adapted his table to offer a quick overview of the eight drawing pages. This approach (Appendix E) allows me to observe and note simultaneously any deviations, repetitions, or patterns throughout all eight drawings while completing my assessment on quantitative and qualitative levels.

Eight-Card Redrawing Test (8CRT) Art Assessments

In contrast to the HTP or DAP, the 8CRT requires that an examination booklet be prepared prior to administration of the test to the client. This is completed by taking eight sheets of 9" × 12" tissue paper (Caligor recommends 8.5" × 11"; however, this is not a standard size of precut tissue paper) and stapling the sheets to a piece of same-sized white drawing paper. This provides a background for the first drawing (page 1). In addition, during the test, another sheet of drawing paper is required to place between the drawings so that only two are showing at a time (i.e., previous drawing and fresh sheet on top). I prefer to use a firm clipboard and place the completed booklet in place under the clasp. The interviewer then takes seven of the eight sheets of tissue paper and rolls them over the top of the clipboard (not under the clasp). This leaves the eighth sheet of paper exposed to be used for the client's first drawing.

After this is accomplished, the directives for the administration of the 8CRT are as follows:

- Offer the client the premade booklet and one pen or a pencil with an eraser.
- Ask him or her to "draw a picture of a whole person."
- Once this is completed, roll the seventh sheet of tissue paper out from behind the clipboard and lay it on top of the finished picture. You can now see the prior drawing (page 1) underneath the fresh sheet of tissue paper (which will be page 2).
- Instruct the client, "Do anything you like to this picture. You can add to it, take away from it, change it, or leave it alone. Only make certain you have a picture of a whole person."
- Once this is done, roll the next sheet of tissue paper out from behind the clipboard and lay it on top of the second drawing (page 2). Taking the second sheet of white drawing paper, slide it in between pages 1 and 2. You should see one fresh piece of tissue paper overlying page 2. Page 1 should no longer be visible.
- Tell the client, "Do anything you like to this picture. You can add to it, take away from it, change it, or leave it alone. Only make certain you have a picture of a whole person."
- Once he or she completes this drawing (page 3), repeat the process until no tissue paper remains behind the clipboard (page 8).
- It is imperative that you slide the second sheet of white drawing paper in between every completed drawing. The client should only see the latest drawing through a fresh piece of tissue.

Case Illustrations

The following profiles illustrate the use of the 8CRT in specific situations.

Personal Profile 3.5

The client is a teenaged male in therapy due to extensive drug use with a series of juvenile arrests and probation violations. His parents are presently separated, but both are appropriately involved in his treatment. Throughout the initial interview, the client presented with an elevated and grandiose mood, an animated affect—especially when recalling his probation violations—glorification of past substance abuse, and frequent testing of limits with a mixture of flippant and apathetic responses. His single goal is to improve his communication with his mother.

The client showed appropriate attention and concentration, with a good fund of knowledge. His responses to similarities were concrete and showed a lack of abstract ability. To the similarity "How are an apple and orange alike?" he replied, "because they're big." To "How are a chair and table alike?" he stated, "because they're made of wood . . . no, wait, because they fit together." To the proverb "A rolling stone gathers no moss" he replied, "rolling stone going through grass or something." It should be noted that these vague responses may be a function of his lack of effort toward the task rather than one of inability.

Figure 3.10 is his completed art assessment.

Page 1 of Figure 3.10 is drawn over eight inches high (self overemphasis and environment underemphasis; impulsive, possibly aggressive) with an abundance of hair (virility, masculine symbols) and a prominent mullet. He is wearing sunglasses (guarded) and has a detailed ear, heavy beard growth, large jagged teeth (aggressiveness), muscular bicep, and tiny forearm. His fingers are pointed (aggressive). His jeans are detailed with two pockets (maternal issues), and his shoes are also detailed with laces, while his left foot rests on a box of sorts. He is drawn in profile view (avoidance of the environment).

Page 2 is superimposed over page 1, but the right foot is missing and the jeans are drawn with a heavier line. The figure has a stump for an arm (helplessness), a prominent eye (hypervigilant), and heavily shaded hair (anxiety, overthinking), and instead of a nose he now has a bird beak (phallic drives). The drawing remains large (grandiosity, poorly developed inner controls).

Prior to drawing page 3, the client was redirected to draw a person, not a hybrid. This figure has the same body superimposed, with the right foot

Page 1

Page 2

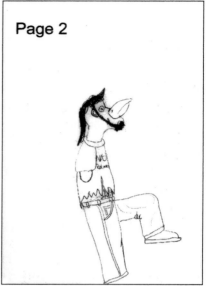

Page 3

Page 4

3.10 Conduct Disorder, Adolescent Onset, Severe

154

Page 5

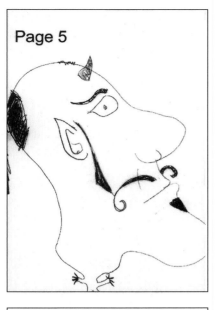

Page 6

Page 7

Page 8

3.10 (continued)

155

now added. The stump of the arm remains, and a belt is now present. This figure has a prominent chin (need for social dominance), with a small beard on the chin edge, and a bulbous nose with nostrils (aggression) replaces the beak.

By page 4 the same instructions were given, but without the tonal emphasis on "person." This image is now an amorphous ghost overlapping page 3 (interaction is detached, denial). The snakelike ghost has a skull for a face, one nostril (aggression), aggressive teeth, large ear (sensitive to criticism), clawlike hands, and a large knife extending from the index finger on the figure's left hand.

Page 5 is yet another overlap (avoidance and running away from problems/interpersonal relationships). The Dali-esque figure has an extremely large, profiled head (focus on self, preoccupation with fantasy, grandiosity), decorated like a warrior with a topknot for hair, goatee and mustache, long sideburn, quizzical eyebrow (masculine symbols, virility strivings), and a single horn on the forehead. The body is tiny with sticklike fingers (aggression).

Page 6 ignores the directive almost entirely and is yet a third in the series of overlaps (extreme denial). The drawing has a naked human body with the head of a cat (detachment, self-centeredness, feminine symbol). The figure takes up three quarters of the page, and it is squatting, with a singular belly button (maternal dependence, infantile needs) as the only body detail.

Page 7's overlap shows a significant size decrease with the body of a teddy bear (infantile needs) and a skull head or human face, which appears berating. Again aggressive teeth are prominent; one eye is significantly larger than the other, a nostril is drawn in heavily, and there is anxious shading under each of the eyes.

In page 8 the figure is seated (dependency, inhibited energy, lack of drive) in profile and is similar to page 1. The person has a prominent head of hair (virility) and a goatee; the eye is looking at the viewer, and the right arm has an extremely large index finger (pointing toward the ground), which is reminiscent of an oversized middle finger (oppositional; hostility). The figure has a huge belly that extends beyond the shirt with a prominent belly button (nurturance, dependency needs). The midline is stressed (emotional immaturity, mother dependency) and the legs are long and thin.

In the final analysis this client is initially highly defended and tends to approach life situations in this manner. Yet, left unchecked, he will quickly return to dependency and nurturance needs (pages 6, 7, and 8). However, it is important to note how he attains control. By page 2 the client began to show his oppositional traits in order to engage the therapist in a manner that required redirection. When this was provided (external control), his image returned to human form (page 3). However, by page 4 only the directive was offered, and the client continued to draw nonhuman figures until the final one at page 8.

This indicated that he does have internal control but relies heavily upon authority figures to guide and caretake. In addition, this client is sensitive to criticism, yet he seeks out verbal reprimands, which causes me to wonder if that is his only mode of interaction with his family and subsequently the environment. Furthermore, his projected aggressiveness, coupled with his dependency needs, appears to be focused on the parental dyad and related to his conflictual feelings of infantile dependency and his need to exhibit virility with a frustrated adolescent's mind-set (i.e., grandiosity, poorly developed inner controls, recognition through antisocial activities).

That his drawing went from a cloaked (sunglasses) and belligerent person to a seated and defeated male shows the patient's grandiosity toward masculinity, yet feelings of inferiority cannot be held at bay and therefore become prominent in his drawings as the layers of personality are stripped away. Unfortunately, his hostile pride does not allow the affect, and he therefore denies these desires by avoiding emotional attachments and shuts out the overwhelming feelings through antagonism, substance abuse, antisocial relationships, and ultimately the defense of reaction formation.

It will be imperative that future sessions concentrate on increasing decision-making ability and autonomy. Helping professionals and family members will have to make a conscious effort not to enter into a codependent relationship and must therefore provide consistent structure and consequences for choices of behavior, setting realistic goals for his future, becoming involved in peer interventions and group therapy, and in due course exploring his grandiosity as overcompensation for feelings of dependency.

Personal Profile 3.6

The final 8CRT assessment we will review is based on two projective tests given to the same client. The first examination is called "Draw-a-Person in the Rain" (Figure 3.11), which is loosely based on the DAP projective test and measures an individual's ability to deal with stress from the environment. The second test (Figure 3.12) was the 8CRT and was administered over 1 year later. This test was utilized to assess the patient's functioning with regard to stabilization as the treatment team looked toward community placement.

3.11 Draw-a-Person in the Rain

The patient is a middle-aged male, who had molested his latency-aged daughter. When questioned as to why he did so the patient replied, "she never called me Daddy, and I wanted her to know she came from my bloodline. . . . I was drinking. . . . I feel sorry I did it." He has a long history of hallucinations and delusions and has stated, "I thought I was Jesus; my mother called the paramedics." Throughout the interview, the patient's speech was coherent but at times disorganized, with mild thought blocking evident. His motor activity was normal, his attitude cooperative, his appearance appropriate, his eye contact good, and his affect congruent to the topics discussed. He showed no overt signs of hallucinations or delusions but did have mild disorganized and tangential speech. His insight was fair. His proverb interpretations ranged from bizarre to concrete. To the proverb "A bird in the hand is worth two in the bush" he replied, "gonna make an egg"; to "People who live in glass houses shouldn't throw stones" he replied, "because it will shatter."

3.12 Schizophrenia, Paranoid Type

Page 5

Page 6

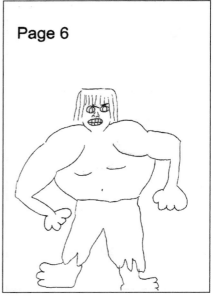

Page 7

Page 8

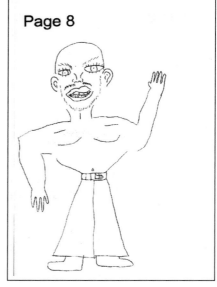

3.12 (continued)

A review of the client's body of work from art therapy groups together with his verbal statements and delusional subsystem showed a symbolic abundance of ideas focused on his father, on his being recognized as a father, and on God (the "universal" father) and the Bible. Looking at this client's abundance of ideas from a psychoanalytical point of view Gay citing Freud (1989) states, "that his personal relation to God depends on his relation to his father in the flesh . . . and that at bottom God is nothing other than an exalted father" (p. 504). And it is this parental engulfment that had become incorporated into the client's psychotic processing, resulting in a regressive fixation that was both delusional and incestuously pedophilic.

In Figure 3.11 the patient drew the reinforced clouds and long rain splatters first. It is important to note that the rain is not merely falling but also splashing upwards once it hits the ground. The oversized head shows a preoccupation with fantasy life (focus on mental life), the tightened legs indicate sexual maladjustment, and the overemphasized nose suggests phallic preoccupation. His closed eyes indicate his self-absorption, while his outstretched arms provide a feeling of strength and power. Yet it is only the lower half of the body that is reinforced and detailed. The patient stated, "the man was standing in the rain with his shirt off; he's happy because it hasn't rained for 40 days and 40 nights."

In short, the image suggests sexual difficulties, fantasy preoccupation, hostility hidden behind a powerful persona (possibly a reaction formation), and a storm that not only falls from above but also surrounds the person with external pressures. The patient's verbal statements indicate his religious preoccupation.

One year later the client was administered the 8CRT (Figure 3.12) as a continuing assessment of his functioning. He entered the testing session apprehensive and mildly paranoid about how the results of this test would be utilized, so I informed him that this was a follow-up to earlier testing (Figure 3.11) and would be used to determine the degree of his stabilization.

Page 1 shows an extreme presence of "Spiderman" squatting. The figure has hollow eyes, emphasis on the chest area (muscles), small rounded fingers, and no feet. In addition, in the genital area of the figure are two heavily shaded testicle-appearing shapes with a straight line that runs from the midsection to the base of the "testicles" and gives the impression of being a vagina.

Page 2 also shows extreme presence. It depicts a woman with a rounded head and a bobbed haircut that does not touch the head, appearing to hover. The nose is prominent, and the mouth has large cupid's-bow lips. A tiny neck connects to broad shoulders. The biceps are muscular; the forearms are tiny, and the hands have splayed fingers. The waist is cinched with a belt; there are no hips. The figure wears a long skirt, boots, and a pearl necklace. There is emphasis on the chest area that does not look like breasts but like male pectorals. The overall figure is drawn in the same schema as the patient's male figures but with female endowments (skirt, necklace, and bobbed hair).

The child figure on page 3, the first regression, is placed at the bottom center of the page and leans precariously toward the right side. The drawing is below average in presence and tiny in comparison to the first two. It is drawn in profile, and the patient stated, "I used to draw this when I was seven." The male figure has an Afro, an emphasized ear (sensitive to criticism; hallucinations), and a line slash for a mouth (tension, shutting the mouth against something). His chest is overly large (virility strivings), and there is a hump on the back of the figure. A pocket (dependency issues) adorns the shirt, and his right arm extends into the pant pocket (evasiveness), with a belt at midline (dependency issues). His leg is short (immobility), and the drawing only indicates one leg (unbalanced).

Page 4 depicts a female child who is placed in the center of the paper and has wiggly lines for hair, empty eyes (hallucinations, desire to see as little as possible), an emphasized nose, and cupid's-bow lips (sexualized). Her hands are on her hips; her trunk is short with a cinched waist. She is wearing a skirt and has two sticklike legs with rounded balls for feet. Due to the hair excitement (infantile sexual drives) and hollowed eyes, she appears to be scowling.

Page 5 is yet another child, but at this juncture the client has reverted to drawing cartoon characters. This is a drawing of Charlie Brown on his pitcher's mound. He is drawn in profile with a large chest and squared trunk that give him the appearance of having a hump on his back. His hat is worn backwards, and he has an ear, an empty eye, and a line slash for a mouth. His arms extend out from either side of the trunk, and one hand has a mitt, while the other is holding a baseball. He has a belt, and again the drawing indicates only one leg. This figure resembles page 3 in many ways (the drawing style, appearance, and symbolism) and is interpreted in that manner.

Page 6 continues with the cartoon character theme with a drawing of the Incredible Hulk. This figure has an extreme presence and takes on an aggressive tone of uncontrolled rage or lust. He has an aggressive face with squared head, large staring eyes, circular mouth, and teeth (aggressiveness). He is overly muscular, with pectorals, and has a belly button (maternal dependency issues). His feet are oversized, as are his hands, which are large closed loops (desire to suppress aggressive impulses).

The client identified page 7 as Supergirl. She has outlined hair, empty eyes, and a cupid's-bow mouth. Her arms are indistinct, and she has no hands. Her legs are thin, and she is wearing boots. A cape with a large "S" logo flies out from her left-hand side. At her midsection is a shape that looks like pantaloons or a diaper. The patient commented, "I like superheroes."

At this point the patient had drawn many superheroes, and I requested that he draw a real person, rather than a cartoon figure, for page 8. The large head (delusional; fantasy life) is rounded, with no hair (lack of virility) and an oversized forehead. The patient drew a moustache and beard (phallic substitutes) and stated, "I wish I could grow a better beard." The figure has large, prominent eyes (paranoia, watching all the comings and goings), nose, and cupid's-bow lips with a profusion of teeth visible (aggressiveness). His ears are emphasized (sensitive to criticism; auditory hallucinations). His neck is short and thick, and he has broad shoulders, a muscular chest, a belly button (dependency), strong forearms, a cinched-in waist, and a detailed belt (maternal dependency). His legs are drawn together (sexual maladjustment) with toes pointing in the opposite direction (ambivalence). His left arm is waving in the air, while his right is squared and toward his side.

From a quantitative standpoint, the figures present with two polarities: adult figures with extreme presence (pages 1, 2, 6, and 8), and figures of average height that are regressions to childhood (pages 3, 4, 5, and 7). This polarity presents us with an adult who exhibits an immature self-concept while reflecting discomfort with his adult role. He experiences the environment as demanding and reacts with impulsivity and excessive fantasy. Additionally, each figure shows a continuity that is overlapped.

From a quantitative analysis, this level of detachment is unusual, as most subjects are unable to sustain the emotional distancing and tension that overlapping requires (Caligor, 1957). Due to this detachment, if we were to look at each rendering placed one atop the other, they appear a haphazard lot. However, if qualitatively we look at the renderings and take them into account as one would a story or book, the patient appears to be communicating his sexual confusion, dependency issues, fantasy preoccupation, regressive tendencies, and fears that his anger and passion will engulf his identity.

Thus, page 1 is the superhero Spiderman, who is virile, capable, honest, and dependable. In addition, this figure is endowed with testicles but also confused sexually as he has a line representative of female genitalia. This confusion from the patient is symbolic of his own internal uncertainty surrounding virility/manliness and shame, which point us toward Oedipal issues in page 2. The only adultlike female figure is overlapped and found standing on the genitalia of page 1, while page 3 is an unbalanced drawing that the patient stated he used to draw as a young child (the same age as his victim), and this image culminates in page 4, where the female child appears scolding. Page 5 is a facsimile of Charlie Brown, a symbol of all that is inadequate, insecure, and fearful within the child. As we move into page 6, the preceding drawings are now overcome by the uncontrolled rage (lust) of the Incredible Hulk.

One may recall that the Hulk story is based upon the premise of a mentally ill (multiple personality disordered) male who turns into a "monster" when angered. The desire to repress and deny the hostile impulses is unfortunately overrun by anger and inner desires. We can view this symbolism as a projection of the patient's own feelings of lust and uncontrolled passion. Page 7 continues the theme of superheroes and shows Supergirl. A companion to Superman, she possesses the same powers, yet the patient has infantilized her in diaperlike pantaloons without hands with which she could repel or maneuver. In addition, the patient returns to fantasy preoccupation and comments on this by stating, "I like superheroes." By page 8 I had prompted the client to draw a person rather than a superhero (compare the similarities in Page 6, Incredible Hulk, and this figure). This drawing again indicates the struggle for opposites within the patient, with an overwhelming sense of dependency and neediness offset by a vision of sexuality and virility (the patient stated that he wishes he could grow a better beard).

Overall, it appears this patient's psychosis is mainly stabilized through his medication regime; however, it remains an activating force. The drawings when taken as a whole symbolize the forbidden sexual desire (mother figure) that leads this patient to renounce adult females, focusing instead on an immature sexual fixation and delusional material that when circumscribed produces humiliation and guilt. These feelings lead him to self-reproach, which heightens his feelings of guilt and shame and thus brings on stress that could result in a psychotic decompensation, especially if his defense mechanism of incorporation remains strong. This patient is infantile in his thinking, and the combination of his extreme dependency issues and his need for virility and regard from without is a lethal combination. This patient's struggle with opposites has left him in a precarious position that threatens to overwhelm his weak sense of self.

On the whole the client does well with the structure and safety of institutionalized living, where schedules are set and orderly. It is the community issues that he must tackle with their myriad difficulties, frustrations, and disappointments. Therefore, this patient needs to increase his independent living and real life skills by learning to cope with situations that will in some form replicate life traumas while he remains in a safe environment. It is also imperative that he receive one-to-one individual therapy that explores his struggles (e.g., Eriksonian work with personality and psychosocial development) to help the patient progress from an infantile manner of relating to one that is autonomous and healthy. However, this patient has a delusional makeup that may preclude any further work, because his fixation in infancy/dependency, coupled with the defense mechanism of incorporation, fuels his delusional thought processing. Yet, in the words of Erikson (1963),

> In psychopathology the absence of basic trust can best be studied in infantile schizophrenia, while lifelong underlying weakness of such trust is apparent in adult personalities in whom withdrawal into schizoid and depressive states is habitual. The re-establishment of a state of trust has been found to be the basic requirement for therapy in these cases. For no matter what conditions may have caused a psychotic break, the bizarreness and withdrawal in the behavior of many very sick individuals hides an attempt to recover social mutuality by a testing of the borderlines between senses and physical reality, between words and social meanings. (p. 248)

Summary

In this chapter I have outlined three distinct assessment tools to illustrate the power of art and symbolism. In my work with the difficult client I have not found any singular projective test, therapeutic intervention, or isolated process that applies to the whole population. Instead, it is often the use of varied methodology that offers a path for the clinician to begin the process of personality integration.

Although the debate on projective testing rages on, I hope that I have shown that a multileveled interpretative stance can prove fruitful. Whether you are using the HTP, DAP, 8CRT, or any derivative of these tests, combining symbolism with the client's verbal statements or fantasy productions can open a door to hidden defenses, metaphor, and meaning. It is the quest of the client to find personal significance, tradition, and hope. Just as the Babylonian myth of Gilgamesh began with a self-centered tyrant (toddler) who was transformed through contact with the community and friends (childhood) into a selfless adult possessed of wisdom and generosity, we all have a myth by which we operate. It is myth that gives meaning to human life and metaphor that implies comparison, an "as if" quality that is experienced by all of humankind. As children we physically played games "as if" the blocks of wood were a large fortress or "as if" we were the mommy or daddy. As adolescents we imagined ourselves in famous roles of industry and influence. Ultimately the physicality of childhood was replaced by the physical reality of our environment and regaled to an unconscious level of hopes, dreams, and wishes. From the artwork we choose to display on our walls to the collectibles in our professional and private corners, we communicate indirect messages about our personal myth.

If we return to Figure 3.12, this client's first drawing of the 8CRT was of Spiderman; however, this was not the first time he had spontaneously rendered Spiderman. In the Spiderman comic book series, Peter Parker, an orphaned, nondescript Charlie Brown type of character, is transformed into a hero after an unusual spider bite. In a youthful act of defiance he allows a burglar to escape, but the same criminal eventually robs his own home and ultimately kills his uncle (Peter's father figure). From this point forward he focuses his powers on the betterment of the community. However, his arch-enemy The Green Goblin is his best friend's father, who, after being transformed through a premature scientific experiment, is now psychotic. Thus, the repetitious father theme coupled with the battling of a psychotic nemesis becomes a metaphor for our client's internal struggles.

By the sixth drawing of the 8CRT, another comic book figure, the Incredible Hulk, makes an appearance—a significant departure from the prior theme, and one that calls for discussion. The back story for Bruce Banner (the Hulk) begins with his grandfather, who meted out severe psychological abuse toward Bruce's father, Brian Banner. Consequently, Brian looked upon his father as a monster. Fearing that he had inherited a "monster" gene, Brian was determined to have no children. After an evening of excessive drinking, he returned to his laboratory and accidentally released an overload of gamma radiation, which in time brought to the forefront his repressed feelings of rage and anger (recall the client's excessive drinking and subsequent molestation of his daughter). Meanwhile, he fell in love, married, and had a son, Bruce. As time moved on, his repressed feelings turned him into that which he despised, an abusive husband and father. He was sent to a mental institution while his only son withdrew into his own world. At this juncture, Bruce Banner began to exhibit symptoms of Multiple Personality Disorder (MPD) with a myriad of personas ranging from the Incredible Hulk to Guilt Hulk (brought out only after a doctor attempted to cure Bruce of his MPD diagnosis). In time the father was discharged from the hospital, and ultimately Bruce kills him in a fit of anger (Yarish, 2002).

In both comic books, significant issues arise from the protagonists' relationships with their fathers or father figures and guilt reactions. If we recall not only this client's symbolic abundance of ideas, but also his delusional material, his focus remains the father. One wonders if these "mythologems" are powerful symbols for the ultimate of Oedipal concerns and bespeak of hostility toward the father coupled with forbidden sexual desires for the mother figure—an identity centered on an infantile incorporation of aggression, power, dependency, pleasure, and guilt (Jung & Kerenyi, 1963).

A pattern of personal myth and life metaphors is not merely observable through art projective testing but is also found within the imagination of artists. One example is the artwork of Frida Kahlo, who "suffered illness and isolation as a small child and overwhelming physical trauma as a young woman. Examples of her art are used to support the hypothesis that her traumatic experiences are reflected in her artistic self-expression" (Feldman, 1999, p. 388). At the age of 6 she was quarantined for 9 months due to polio. Twelve years later she was involved in a horrible bus crash that broke her spinal column, collarbone, ribs, leg, pelvis, and foot. Ultimately, her right leg was amputated. After a series of 30 operations, the confinement necessary for recovery left her unable to pursue her dream of attending medical school, and instead she began painting self-portraits. "Following each surgery, during long periods of confinement, she sought ways to paint, even lying flat in bed using mirrors, in order to absorb her attention on documenting her survival" (Feldman, p. 390). The repetition of the self-portraits was not merely serving to transform the fearful drives and trauma but also serving as an "as if" within the monotony to say, "See me. Look at me. Listen to me. I exist." Kahlo's awareness of each moment within her existence calls to mind the myth of Sisyphus, with its loneliness, cunning, and tedium. Kahlo's pleasure arose not only from cheating death (as did Sisyphus) but through the process of painting herself boldly, not as a pale reflection.

Conversely, Vincent Van Gogh is one in a long list of artists who suffered from mental illness. The majority (including his close friend Paul Gaugin) exhibited depressive symptomology or the hypomania so common within the Bipolar Disorders (Jamison, 1996). The elevated, expansive, and irritable moods that produce a flight of ideas coupled with extreme goal-directed activities have been meticulously recorded by Van Gogh through his extensive letters, now archived. An excerpt from one such letter, written roughly 1 year prior to his suicide, states:

> My dear brother, it is always in between my work that I write; I am working like one actually possessed. I think this will help to cure me. And perhaps something will happen to me like what Eugene Delacroix spoke of: 'I dis-

covered painting when I had no more teeth or breath,' in the sense that my unhappy illness makes me work with a dumb fury—very slowly—but from morning till night, without slackening. (Stone, 1937, p. 443)

Van Gogh's struggle with love and death, two warring factions of our higher and lower natures, calls to mind Goethe's story of Faust. The myth not only asks what life is and what the purpose of humanity is (in Van Gogh's last letter before his suicide, he states, "you can still choose your side, acting with humanity, but what's the use?" [Stone, 1937, p. 480]) but also argues that creativity thrives on madness. In the end, much like Frida Kahlo, Van Gogh became obsessed with self-portraits, a symbol of agony— see me, I exist.

A symbol, especially in the case of literature or art, evokes an emotional response. If you have ever looked into the eyes of pain represented in Frida Kahlo's portraits or the sweeping movement of Van Gogh's brush strokes, both stirring and tragic, you have felt the rejection of realism and the power of symbolism. The feverish vitality of Van Gogh's painting and the duality of Kahlo's portraits transmute their mental states from inhibiting factors into hopeful solutions.

As an example, let's consider the symbolism behind fire. In my discussion of Figures I.5 and I.6, I spoke of this adolescent patient's unconscious memories of sexual abuse, indicated by his spontaneous drawing of flames after a family visit. Early in my therapeutic career, I was informed that clients who present with arson histories also have a tendency toward molestation histories. When I inquired how these two issues connected, the response was unremarkable. However, as time passed, I not only found the hypothesis to be accurate but found much of the answer within the symbolic metaphor. Fire, a precious resource, was revered as a god by primitive cultures (Tresidder, 2000). It was not until our early ancestors learned to control its power and created techniques to call it forth at will that it took on the symbolism of power, love, and sexuality. This new perception is found within "the ancient Hindu Vedas," for whom "creating fire by rubbing two pieces of wood together represented copulation" (Gutheil, 1951, pp. 212–213), and later in the writings of the Marquis de Sade, which feature frequent and not so subtle references to fire's sexual characteristics. One of the best observations on fire as sexual symbolism comes from Shattuck (1996): "Fire speaks a single message: My lust will destroy all" (p. 278). Presently, fire is often represented in the popular media as a manner in which to pay homage: the candlelight vigil, sacred in its use of undying flame, epitomizes our spirit of togetherness and community. Yet fire continues to stand as a duality of destruction and protection, a symbol that can both inhibit and offer hope.

Ultimately, art projective assessments should not rely simply upon formal scoring systems that quantify and qualify results. This manner of study removes all expression and perception from a very personal and intimate production, one created from a simple directive that begins and ends with the client's unconscious selection and one that contains interrelated patterns found within the symbolic abundance of ideas, the client's personal history, his or her verbal statements, his or her choice of defense mechanisms, and in due course a personal myth that provides meaning.

It is my belief that this multifaceted approach yields a plethora of clinical information that will help to define treatment success with a client who historically has been labeled as resistant. As an adjunct to psychotherapy, art projective testing can see beyond the conflict and delve within the extreme anxiety and pain that conceals the self.

In the words of Anderson (1951), "projective tests, as such, test not only projection but practically all conceivable mental mechanisms, both expressive and defensive" (p. 23).

CHAPTER

4

Directives

J ust as art projective assessments offer the clinician guidance for treatment planning, directives provide a framework for the therapeutic hour.
Throughout the first part of this book the great majority of drawings resulted from directives. These directives were not offered haphazardly but
were designed around the client's maturation process. Based upon Erikson's
premise that emerging conflict must be mastered in order to prepare the individual for future growth and integrity, the use of directives allows the client to reveal unconscious material in a safe forum. Consequently, I cannot
overemphasize the importance of directives in a process-oriented framework.

It is the therapist's responsibility not only to evaluate where the client
is developmentally but to take into account the defense mechanisms that
protect the individual and block communication. To this end, art therapy
directives allow a freedom that purely verbal therapy deters. Directives can
be designed to meet the client's changing needs and thus allow each individual to produce, share, and express on a multiplicity of levels.

As a result, if we return to Erikson's (1963) theory on psychosocial development and distinguish each period by the client's inner conflicts, we
see that directives can be developed to enhance ego functioning, confront
maladaptive patterns, identify similarities, and clarify life transitions.

Table 4.1 provides an example of how inner challenges to the basis of
an identity can be delineated through directives. However, it is imperative
that the clinician arrive at the client's developmental stage, regardless of
chronological age, to assess the most effective directive in any category.
Additionally, note that this list of directives is not intended to be all

Table 4.1 Directives and Psychosocial Crisis

Psychosocial Crisis	Sample Directives
Basic trust vs. mistrust: Constant testing of relationship due to need to define inside drives and outside experiences; literal and figurative biting (i.e., sarcasm), intense need to consume	*Provision of soothing comfort and focused attention* • "Draw a picture showing what you want from _____." • "Select pictures of people and write down what they are thinking and then what they are saying."
Autonomy vs. shame and doubt: Gains power through stubborn control; destructive holding (control) or letting loose; obsessed by own repetition; feelings of being exposed	*Firmness, outer control required* • "Select a picture that shows how you see yourself." • "Make an animal. Discuss its characteristics." • "Make the scariest animal you can." • "Draw a person in the rain."
Initiative vs. guilt: Jealous rage; desirous of favored positions; aggressive manipulation and intimidation	*The need to learn and plan with others* • "Draw a dream." • "Draw a wish." • "Draw pictures of animals to symbolize each member of your family."
Industry vs. inferiority: Thoughts of inferior abilities produce withdrawal, isolation, or feelings of inadequacy; refuses to attempt new tasks	*Recognition through task completion, skills* • "Choose 4–5 pictures that appeal to you and write why underneath." • "Choose one color of clay and create a group sculpture."
Identity vs. role confusion: Tests of trustworthiness, insistence on uniqueness, a search for belonging	*Concern lies with how you are perceived* • "How do others perceive you? How do you perceive yourself?" • "Draw your problem and solution."
Intimacy vs. isolation: Avoidance of relationships produces self-absorption and/or isolation	*Empathy and mutuality toward others* • "Draw a gift you would like to give to someone. Draw a gift you would like to receive."
Generativity vs. stagnation: Feelings of personal misery or impoverishment	*Encouragement and direction required* • "Draw a picture of the past, present, future." • "Draw something you would like to change."
Ego integrity vs. despair: Outward disgust hides internal hopelessness, fear of death	*A return to the need for trust and reliability* • "How do you feel when your needs are met? Unmet?"

inclusive; instead it is merely a sampling of how directives can be relevant when applied to developmental stage theory.

You will note in Table 4.1 that Erikson's psychosocial stages accentuate the polarity of conflict and integration. Therefore, many of the directives are offered as "polarities" (e.g., "Draw your problem and solution"). This type of directive translates well when looking toward personality formation that favors a hopeful outlook.

However, it is imperative that the clinician, when evaluating the developmental progression of a client, take into account a complete assessment of the individual and the artwork, lest an inaccurate picture of maturity emerge. As an example, see Figure 4.1.

Both drawings were completed by teenage females in separate group therapy sessions in response to the directive "Draw anything you wish." In each rendering, issues related to defecation figure prominently (this was a frequent drawing subject for both clients). For that reason, one may assume that both of these adolescents are fixated in Freud's anal stage of psycho-

4.1 Letting Loose

173

sexual development or Erikson's autonomy versus shame and doubt (to let go, to hold on). However, a review of the drawing style (see Table 3.1) imparts further information relating to developmental progression.

The upper drawing shows a cat endowed with human facial features and a stick figure with balloon hands (5-year-old style), while the lower image shows an attempt at perspective with a female's back turned from the viewer (teenaged style). It is evident that the upper drawing appears regressive (lack of proportion and detailing, repetitive schema for facial features) when compared with the bottom rendering's obvious statement of disdain (back to viewer while defecating).

If we now add the client's history to the evaluation, we learn that the upper drawing was done by a chronic schizophrenic who when decompensating tends to add fecal matter to her images just prior to destroying property or assaulting others. Thus, the upper rendering bespeaks of the anal stage of development or Erikson's shame and doubt with its concomitant destructive forces and residual rage, confusion, and mistrust of the environment. The bottom image was completed by a female who challenges the environment with her "uniqueness" of being; the intensity of her persona influences all of her interpersonal relationships, and she is cruel toward peers who are perceived as different from her. This drawing signifies the quest for identity— so important to an adolescent who is fearful of her own sense of self.

In the end, an assessment of these two females that incorporates the completed drawing, normative stages of art (Table 3.1), client history, and developmental stage theory (Tables 2.3 and 4.1) offers a progressively thorough appraisal of maturation. Although both of these clients were chronologically 16 years of age, only one was operating within the adolescent years of developmental stage theory. The other client, delayed by numerous years, would not benefit from a treatment plan that only took into account chronological age.

In this vein, if a directive (or intervention) is too advanced for the individual's developmental capabilities, then an already frustrating environment will further come to seem unsafe, confusing, and chaotic. Conversely, directives that are below the developmental age for any given client will seem infantile, and the client is likely to either manipulate or reject such directives out of hand.

The same consequences apply to the clinician's choice of media. As such, the use of pens or pencils with a child in the scribbling stage would be too advanced, while an offer of crayons for an adolescent is infantalizing. Table 2.3 discussed select varieties of media as they applied to developmental stages and abilities. However, this list was not all-inclusive, and at this point I would like to introduce other materials into consideration.

The use of scrap materials and found objects is particularly helpful for clients who are navigating the stage of latency. It is within this phase of the developmental process that individuals move from parallel play to joint interactions. They can now understand another's point of view and are actively seeking competency through the completion of skills and tasks.

For this reason, not only is the tactile quality of cardboard, tissue paper, fabric, felt, and scrap paper appealing, but the act of creation from raw materials provides a feeling of accomplishment.

Figure 4.2 offers an example of a three-dimensional task created by a group of adolescent males (see disk to view in color). The project began as individualized designs (cardboard bases and toilet paper rolls) to which they added odds and ends until they were satisfied with the results. At this point they were instructed to combine the individual projects to form a single foundation. The final phase revolved around relating a story, and the group ultimately arrived at one that focused on power and the reward of female companionship.

Figure 4.3 (a detail of the finished directive) followed similar steps, yet this project was completed by a group of institutionalized adult males. The final theme paralleled their daily experience, with rivalries and scapegoating taking precedence.

4.2 Power and Control: Adolescents

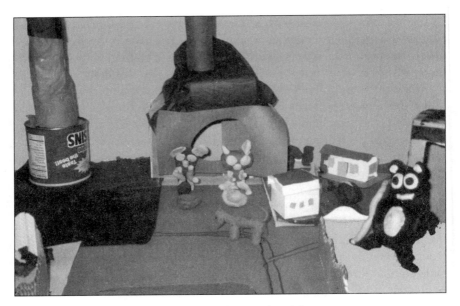

4.3 Power and Control: Adults

In both instances, although the chronological ages of the patients were separated by numerous years, their developmental skills were evenly balanced, and thus the use of mixed media provided an opportunity for recognition of individual skills through the completion of a hands-on group task.

The left side of Figure 4.4 was created by an adolescent male whose maternal grandmother had recently died and whose father was terminally ill (see disk to view in color). The family, as a whole, had never dealt with the feelings of loneliness or the associated anger and resentment of loss. Due to this situation, grief work based on a family systems approach was instituted. Utilizing a technique outlined in Maxine Junge's (1985) article "The Book About Daddy Dying," the client began to construct his own book based on events and recollections to aid in the mourning process.

This image illustrates a single page insert created out of fabric, tissue paper, and string (all media chosen by the client) that recalled comforting memories of his grandmother's favorite quilt. It is important to note that this was the only page of the completed project for which the client required mixed media. All other pages were drawn or utilized collage imaging.

Similarly, the right side of Figure 4.4 is an example of a memory box. This project, completed in stages, placed a variety of materials at the cli-

176

4.4 Grief Work

ent's disposal and ultimately provided a safe environment to communicate and explore issues related to self and others. In this session the client was instructed to incorporate the theme of family while "decorating the outside of the box." When this was completed, he was asked to "decorate the inside" and finally to create items for inclusion. The final objects (incorporating mixed media) represent his feelings of isolation surrounding missed holidays, birthdays, and events and his enduring need for a familial connection.

In each example (Figures 4.2, 4.3, and 4.4) these clients were served by the palpable quality of their mixed-media creations. With this in mind, the therapist should choose art materials carefully in order to take individual needs into account. These needs encompass everything from physical ability to environmental concerns to developmental requirements, as well as attendant emotional complications.

Directives as Interventions

Ultimately, the value of using directives lies in the flexibility it offers the clinician in individualized treatment planning. Their application in the therapeutic hour not only permits continued growth but can also provide a resolution of conflicts at any developmental stage.

As interventions, directives are as far-reaching as your imagination will allow. Whether in a group, family, or individual setting, they provide an integration of thought and feeling that in due course will heighten the interaction between the individual and his or her environment.

For the purposes of this section, directives are organized into five separate categories; however, I must state that this categorization is only for the purposes of illustration. Generally it is not possible to decide prior to a session whether to use specific directives during the therapeutic hour; instead, directives develop out of the unique requirements of the individual and his or her interaction in the here-and-now. For this reason, these categories should be utilized as a starting point for intervention rather than as a comprehensive guide.

The Introduction

Not unlike the stage theory of development, the phases of therapy can be distinguished by the progression of growth toward a mature identity. In this fashion, the initial encounter, with its need to join and build trust where mistrust often resides, is as important to the relationship as the stage of closure. For it is the introduction, the initial meetings that impart the tone for the relationship. In this stage, as Erikson (1963) noted in a discussion of the infant's social achievement goals, "the constant tasting and testing of the relationship between inside and outside meets its crucial test" (p. 248). Although Erikson's focus is infants, this statement easily applies to the client's first steps toward social relatedness regardless of age. Characterized by a struggle surrounding dependency (reliance upon another) and power (testing the environment), the initial stages of therapy seek an integration of inside and outside.

4.5 Hands of Love

For that reason, the individual requires a combination of comfort, control, and focused attention—the focused attention that directives and art tasks can provide.

The following illustrations typify directives that are useful in the early stages of therapy.

Figure 4.5 was completed by a group of adult males and entitled "Hands of Love." These gentlemen were instructed: "Trace your hand on your paper and draw a symbol inside the hand that represents something friendly about you. Once this is done, cut out the hand and glue it to the mural paper" (which was taped to the wall).

In this first meeting the task of forming connections was completed through not only the drawing phase but also the discussion that followed. Each group member explained the symbols that he had produced and how it related to the self. From verbal descriptions of faith (second from the left) and sobriety (fourth from the left) to the unconscious rendering of jagged lines framing the fingers of a male who the evening before had put his hand through a window (first on the left), these institutionalized men focused on the basics of their personality as they interacted beyond material needs.

In Figure 4.6 the same directive was given to a group of preadolescent females, yet the differences are profound. In this figure hands in one group

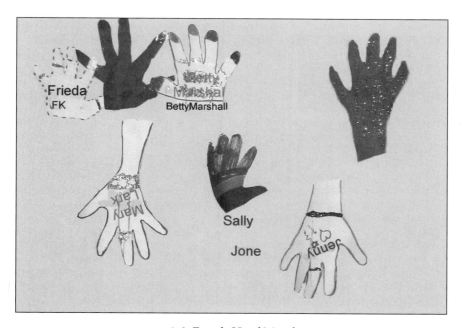

4.6 Female Hand Mural

overlap and intrude upon their neighbors, while others languish on the outskirts or are placed upside down (the same individual created two hands—one for herself and another for her friend). Additionally, the group prominently labeled their hands with their names (digitally changed); rather than using their hands to symbolize the self, they preferred to affirm the connection physically with a name.

This example of closeness and distance contrasts with Figure 4.5's arrangements, which are evenly spaced and divided. There is neither closeness nor distance, only an equal sharing of space. This may be due in large part to the unspoken credo of the institutionalized that physical contact is always to be avoided, since in an institution even an innocent bump can create a dangerous situation.

Consequently, while the adolescent females seek a connection, often intrusively, the institutionalized male distances himself for protection and safety. Yet the objective of both groups remains the same: the provision of a safe haven where individuals can share, express, and build a foundation for improved trust that breaks down the division of internal wants and external needs.

In much the same way, a collage directive, with its prefabricated imagery, offers the individual a nonthreatening medium with which he or she can clarify interests and provide information in an atmosphere of support

4.7 Collage of Me

and acceptance. The directive for Figure 4.7 was "Choose four to five collage images that tell me something about you, and write down why underneath." This completed collage not only presented interests related to the procurement of basic needs (the nurturance of food and joy of leisure) but also provided insight into this adolescent's relationship with the environment (a desire for knowledge and a generalized love).

In the early stages of therapy, the clinician is responsible for providing an environment of supportive safety as well as outer control. These conditions are necessary if the new client is to learn productive methods of communication within the environment. Yet for some clients the intensity of such a personal interaction creates a sense of fear and vulnerability, which is often juxtaposed with the use of defense mechanisms to protect from ensuing anxiety.

The client who completed Figure 4.8 relied upon the defense of undoing to resolve conflict and assuage the feelings of shame and guilt that threatened to overwhelm her fragile sense of self. For this reason I employed a dual scribble drawing. Not unlike collage work, this technique

4.8 Help

offers a measure of safety as well as a manner of connecting. The process for this directive (although many adaptations can be utilized) was that I quickly scribbled random lines and asked the client to help me find a "picture" within the scribbles. She identified the bunny, and I colored in the disparate areas to flesh out the image. Understanding her issue with control and her frequent forays into destructiveness, I commented aloud, "he looks out of control," to which she responded, "turn it away, don't look at it." This metaphorical interaction continued with the client adding a "hammer" and bumps on the head as a means of discipline, while I commented that I didn't find the rabbit offensive, although others might, and symbolically toned it down with the use of color (rather than aggressive shaming techniques).

In Figure 4.8 the discomfort created by the client's conscious and unconscious guilt feelings drove her interactions within the environment. Along these lines, a directive that I make use of not only to facilitate trust but also to assess the level of identity formation is one I call the initial game. The procedure for this directive is to instruct the client to "draw your initials as large as you want on the drawing paper. Using the initials and the design they make, find ideas for pictures. Once you see a picture, color it in. Feel free to remain within or outside the lines, and use as much color as you desire."

4.9 The Flames of Anger

Figure 4.9 is an example of a completed initial directive (Landgarten, 1981, p. 25) drawn by an adolescent male. Instead of using his initials he used a combination of his first and last names (digitally changed). From an interpretive standpoint, the client's verbal explanation is as important as the visceral response of the viewer examining the drawn-form items. In the discussion phase he excitedly named his drawings as (from left to right) a video character, a fire pit, a flame, a man's face, a profile view of a woman, a woodpecker, and a polka-dot moon—fairly benign symbols as named verbally.

However, if we view our initials as emblematic representations of the self, then these details take on an increased significance. As reviewed in the last chapter, fire continues to stand for a duality of destruction and protection, a symbol that can both inhibit and shower hope. Unfortunately, the excessive use of fire and fire symbols in Figure 4.9, together with the renderings of male and female figures (accompanied with prominent genitalia on the woodpecker and female), appeared more destructive than encouraging. In this case the use of an expressive medium coupled with this client's past familial trauma (fire had destroyed his home) offered a process that was far too exciting.

Thus, not every introductory directive will create a safe and serene haven for feelings, thoughts, and emotions. An individual's past experiences will often find voice in unconscious expression, allowing the personal meaning to be brought forward—a personal meaning that has been formed from the cumulative experiences of his or her life.

Ultimately, the therapist must never forget that art has the power not only to bind but to intensify both existing and unconscious thoughts and memories.

Feelings Expression

If introductory directives can correspond to the first and second stages of developmental theory (*basic trust versus mistrust* and *autonomy versus shame and doubt*), then feelings expression can be said to correlate to the third stage of development (*initiative versus guilt*). It is imperative as clients leave infantile dependency needs behind that their emerging identity and ensuing efforts toward integration be tempered with acceptance and validation as they move in the direction of cooperation, increased self-sufficiency, and collaboration with others in the environment.

Because of this stage's thrust toward direction and purpose, the clinician needs to offer an atmosphere that allows for exploration of the emerging self as well as an opportunity to give vent to any associated negative expressions as the evolving individual seeks his or her course in an expanding world.

One way to provide for feelings expression in the use of directives is to allow the client to simply create, to experience the art materials without any instruction other than "Draw or create anything you wish."

The adult male who created Figure 4.10 recalled fond memories of feeding birds and the serenity of open space. Over the more than 20 years that he had been institutionalized, his hopes for release had turned to a fantasy that alternately produced depression and rage. His lack of freedom did not encompass the entire reason for his despair, however; much more important than his verbal protestations were the internal feelings of worthlessness and a lack of accomplishment. With little purpose other than to sit and wait, his sense of isolation grew while initiative waned. Throughout numerous groups, this gentleman's art took on a similar appearance: With open expanses, rocky crags, and secluded surroundings, his images spoke of his failures to attain. However, each week he voluntarily returned to express his feelings and communicate the meanings of his experiences in a forum that offered recognition and validation.

In much the same way, a preteen explores her feelings of depression and loneliness as she both resists and reconciles herself to the dawning insight that family reunification will not occur (discussed in post-drawing inquiry).

4.10 Rocky Mountain

4.11 Clouds of Loneliness

In Figure 4.11 she has spontaneously drawn an image that expresses the anxiety of outer forces (rain, storm clouds) but also offers partial protection (umbrella) from these external pressures. Interestingly, this client has symbolically presented the problem (lack of parental support) and the solution (mastering the challenge by providing protection for the self), neither of which, at this point, requires conscious discussion. What she requires at this juncture is her own initiative to explore, absorb, and accept.

Along with an exploration of the self, the importance of negative expression cannot be underestimated. Whether it is in a group setting or individual session, this stage of the life cycle draws a parallel to the emerging personality as the individual tests not only his or her own limits but also the limits within the environment.

For this reason, in group therapy a client in this stage of development will often undertake challenges directed toward the group leader. Often a test of what will be acceptable and how the individual will be tolerated, these challenges are a necessary part of the developmental cycle as the client moves from an individual identity into a group identity.

In Figure 4.12 an adolescent completes a pass-around directive (Wadeson, 1980, p. 336) with a group of peers. In this directive the group was instructed to "draw anything you like on the front of your paper. When done, on the back list three things you want the group to complete. As we pass

4.12 Evil Child and Happiness

the drawings [to the right], each of you will draw one item in order. Once you have your original drawing, give it a title." This female wanted her peers to draw (1) an evil thing, (2) a happy thing, and (3) all evil and happy things.

In another pass-around directive, a group of adult males was instructed to "choose a collage image and draw one thing on your paper. After passing it to the right, add a second collage image; with each subsequent pass you will be told to add one thing. Once you have your original drawing, add anything you wish and give it a title."

This completed task (Figure 4.13) met with vocalized disdain from the original artist. During the discussion phase, he criticized nearly every aspect of what his peers had added while belittling the directive that I had chosen. In so doing, he, not unlike the female artist of Figure 4.12, was testing the environment's ability to withstand condemnation while employing early stages of learning in which working cooperatively with others aids the individual as he or she moves from "playful" expression to one focused on industry and competence.

Problem Solving

As the relationship matures and challenges related to power and control diminish, the client can benefit from directives that focus on problem solv-

4.13 It's G.O.D.

ing and the attainment of frustration tolerance. The sense of industry that
develops during this stage is often coupled with skills acquisition arising
from an increasing desire to expand the knowledge base through learning
and responsibility.

Accordingly, directives that encourage a collaborative effort, centered
on resolution and completion, provide an experience that counters feelings of inferiority with teamwork.

Regardless of the individual's cognitive ability or diagnosis, problem-
solving directives shape the growing child's personality to prepare him or
her for the increased intimacy involved in the sharing of him- or herself.
Figures 4.14 and 4.15 provide an example of the use of a problem-solving
directive with clients diagnosed within the pervasive developmental disorder spectrum. The project resulting from this directive (Figures 4.14 and
4.15) stretched over a period of 5 weeks and involved a group of boys with
varying ability levels and communication skills.

4.14 Beethoven and His Home

When you are working within this diagnostic category, teaching team-work skills becomes exceedingly important in order to improve issues related to reciprocity, conflict resolution, and empathy. However, it is also important to recognize the high levels of anxiety that these clients experience when tasks outside of their normal routine are introduced. Therefore, it is beneficial to ease into the assignment by first creating individual projects and then combining these to form a larger whole.

The project began with the directive to each group member to "make an animal out of clay" (Figure 4.14 on left), and over the following 2 weeks group members were instructed to "choose a home for your animal and decorate it using any of the materials provided" (Figure 4.14 on right).

Once this was completed, the group was presented with a butcher paper–covered board, and a discussion followed that focused the group on pretend play. Each group member decided where their clay animal would

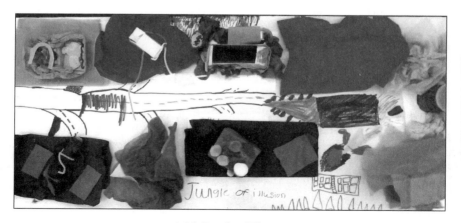

4.15 Jungle of Illusion

live by placing their home and animal on the board; then they negotiated with one another when instructed: "As a group, title the project." The final step encompassed further negotiation and problem solving as group members worked as a team to complete the task by adding reality-based objects to the living environment. Figure 4.15 presents the assignment in its entirety (see disk to view in color). In keeping with the developmentally delayed child's symptomology, tissue paper not only predominates the project (fascination with tactile media), but six of the eight clay animals are hidden and in some cases sealed within the home, which symbolically points toward their preference for isolation over socialization.

In another directive, the same group of children used collage to explore facial expression as it pertains to the communication of feelings and emotions. The directive began with each group member choosing a series of collage images (two each, facial expressions only). I then introduced the group to the emotion pie on the wall which had four wedges. The wedges were labeled Serious, Hurt, Worried, and Happy. They were then instructed to "One at a time, glue your collage face where you think it belongs on the emotion pie." We then explored as a group the feelings as they applied to the task. In some instances the group did not agree with a particular placement. A situation such as this produced a spirited discussion about how feelings can confuse in their duality.

In the end, when you are working with a developmentally disabled population, "an essential component of these programmes [sic] is to describe and explore the event and comments that produce a particular feeling, both within the child and other people. . . . This is the start of acquiring empathy" (Attwood, 1998, p. 60).

Insight and Self-Disclosure

In keeping with developmental stage theory, the ability to understand and abide by rules is as critical to social competency as the attainment of a sense of self, empathy, and intimacy. The emerging personality possesses a rising motivation toward mutuality as well as self-exploration. However, in working with difficult clients I find that they have found much of their affirmation from self-absorption. In the avoidance of intimacy the individual has failed to master the ability to share his or her thoughts and feelings. Thus, the polarity exists whereby the client shows an intense need for social support at the same time that he or she prefers isolation, an isolation that is often motivated by the fear of a shared and intimate encounter.

Therefore, in this stage of therapy it is important that the clinician encourage a sense of responsibility and reciprocity, for the ability to compromise, share, respect dissenting opinions, and discuss frustrations is the foundation upon which genuine interpersonal relationships are built.

Figure 4.16 provides an example of a polarity directive that was given to a group of recovering substance abusers. These adolescent males were instructed to "draw what drugs or alcohol have done *for* you on one side of the page, and on the other side draw what drugs or alcohol have done *to* you."

Through the process of member-to-member interaction, the group initially chose to focus on their glorification and idealization of the past. Thus, at first their discussion focused on the right side of Figure 4.16 with its abundance of buxom girls, expensive cars, copious cash, and other accoutrements that defined their sense of self. However, as the dialogue turned to the left side of Figure 4.16, a more sobering discussion ensued. It was through this side of the polarity that the group stepped away from their fantastical recollections and processed the subsequent consequences. As a result, a range of emotions emerged that focused on the false sense of courage that substance abuse afforded, the physical ramifications (jaundice, weight loss, etc.), the legal implications, and the severed relationships with family and friends.

Although not every member of the group agreed with the feedback, the act of sharing, listening, exploring, and debating set in motion an intimate exchange.

4.16 *2 Me, 4 Me*

In much the same way, a group of adult males redefines anger as not a driving emotion but one that is often driven. In Figure 4.17 the group was asked to "draw the feeling behind your anger and label each emotion that applies." This male, though initially focused on the theme of the stalled car, was ultimately able to process his feelings of sadness, betrayal, and isolation, which related less to automobile difficulties and more to familial problems. The helplessness and misery that this image illustrates is not only experienced viscerally by the viewer but was intuitively experienced by the creator as his discussion progressed.

When exploring feelings and emotional expression, the therapeutic hour, coupled with the therapeutic relationship, is often the first arena where the client not only practices the skills but feels safe enough to communicate and share them with others. Thus, this safe haven, whether it be in an individual or group setting, allows the growing individual to work at a pace that is comfortable while learning something about him- or herself.

4.17 The Feeling behind My Anger

Yet this situation can become dangerous if the skills learned remain only within the relationship and are not generalized. This type of dependency does not promote the continued growth that is necessary for future productivity in the larger world.

Therefore, it is imperative that any insights acquired are generalized outside of the protection of the treatment setting. One way to do this is to link directives so that they apply to both internal and external states. In Figure 4.18 an adult was instructed to "decorate the outside of the bag to represent how others see you. On the index cards provided, write down what you do not show the world and place them inside the bag."

When discussing Figure 4.18, the client stated that the stripes on the left denoted brightness while the inner circles symbolized calm. However, what he verbally focused on was the dark shading that surrounded the bag. This represented his darkness, which always encircled anything calm or

4.18 I Don't Let People See

bright and was how he believed others viewed him—sinister and threatening. Looking inside, he completed two index cards; the first said, "I don't let people's [sic] see how I fill [sic] about my life," while the second stated, "I don't let people's [sic] see the hurt I have in my heart." If we compare his drawing (how others viewed him as sinister and threatening) with his written word (how he doesn't show the world his hurt), these two states are polar opposites. Externally, he believes himself to be a representation of all that is ostracized, while internally he experiences the distress associated with isolation, apprehension, and secrecy.

This directive allowed him to explore his identity through symbolic expression while giving voice to internal fears and solitude. Once expressed, the secrets of his internal concerns were now available for discussion and offered the opportunity for change when treatment looked toward a future-oriented framework.

The same holds true when working with clients who not only are cut off from family relations but fail to acknowledge the role that family dynamics have played in fostering present-day issues. In the case of one male, his sense of isolation was profound, and he often voiced his feelings of loss through stoic verbal comments coupled with intellectualization as it applied to his and his family's propensity to substance abuse. Considering that secrecy and denial were this individual's personal tenets, I introduced a pictorial family genogram directive. As Holman (1983) defines it, a "genogram is a valuable assessment tool for learning about a family's history over a period of time" and "usually includes data about three or more generations of the family, which provides a longitudinal perspective" (p. 68).

Figure 4.19 not only offered more visual impact for the client than the traditional genogram circles and squares but also provided a factual response to a pervasive situation. Based upon the client's previous drawings, it combined his verbal statements to embellish his family history and consequently guided a discussion on multigenerational substance abuse through an empathic and respectful exchange of ideas.

Alone, the pictorial family genogram did not provide the change needed, but it offered the client a safe forum in which to discuss and explore the family system and their interactions, communication patterns, and structure.

Closure

As the therapeutic relationship comes to an end, the expression and sharing of feelings become primary as the individual applies the accom-

4.19 Pictorial Family Genogram

plishments of previous stages to present circumstances. With purpose, competency, and the ability to both give and take, the dependency of earlier years has transformed into a desire to produce. At this stage, the client benefits from both a review of progress made and a chance to express the myriad feelings that closure creates.

In Figure 4.20 the directive given was twofold so that the entire group

4.20 Accomplishment

had a chance to examine its feelings. The group was instructed to "draw something that you would like to give to [name of member leaving] to help him be successful." Conversely, the graduating client was instructed to "create something that symbolizes your feelings of leaving this group of people."

On the left side of Figure 4.20, one peer provided the graduating client with a signpost for success labeled "patience." On the right side, the graduating member correlated his accomplishments to a mission, an undertaking that was akin to a job. His bold statement "and I am out to do it" symbolizes his determination to continue to care for himself and to remain a productive member of the community. After the task concluded, the group presented the graduate with the completed projects, while his drawing was displayed in the group room on a wall designated for comings and goings.

Unfortunately, not all departures represent a sense of achievement. Figure 4.21 represents the departure of an elderly male who was diagnosed with terminal cancer and scheduled to leave to receive medical care. The group, faced with the news, responded with emotions that ranged from denial, fear, and sadness to attempts to "enliven" the situation through jokes and stories. It was apparent that the members were attempting to take care of their friend, yet the intensity of feelings overwhelmed their ability to provide comfort. Because of this, I presented the group with precut pictures and words, rather than drawing materials, to provide containment for the multitude of feelings that required expression. The directive was to "create an image that celebrates your spirituality in times of stress, something calm and reassuring," and as the focus shifted to the process of creating the group's emotional tone turned serene. This interval allowed the members to discuss the disparate pieces in a personal manner, focusing on themselves, their thoughts, and feelings.

After completing the individual pages, the group was instructed to "combine your illustrations on a larger board so they form one cohesive im-

4.21 The Group Bids Farewell

age." The goal of this directive was to symbolically integrate each individual expression into a union with others, as a functioning member of a larger community where care and production provides support. In the end the group presented the poster to the departing member as a transitional object of hope, regard, and encouragement.

Art therapy directives provide a comprehensive approach to emergent issues, but the categorizing of directives as interventions can address the unique developmental needs of the individual to promote the development of a mature identity. With this in mind, Appendix F offers the clinician a list of sample directives divided into the five categories discussed in this chapter: introductory, feelings expression, problem solving, insight and self-disclosure, and closure.

Summary

The objective of this chapter was to introduce the clinician to a range of directives that focused on the maturing individual's ability to move beyond egocentricity toward social reciprocity. To this end, interventions were embedded within the framework of Erikson's psychosocial stages in order to illustrate the process of growth and maturity. However, I must stress that directives do not need to conform to these principles. In fact, art therapy interventions frequently arise from an individual's verbal statements during the session, and it is the therapist's responsibility to decide whether the use of directives will build upon the client's verbal statements or will be decided prior to the therapeutic hour to accommodate transitional stages.

Ultimately, the decisive factor when choosing a directive should be the comprehensive needs of the client. As a form of intervention, directives enhance the growth process as well as offering support where ego functioning is present but tenuous. This distinction is an important consideration for any clinician to understand, for it is the social trust formed and developed through the curative involvement of therapist and client that creates intimacy. And it is this intimacy that paves the way for insight as the ego is able to endure resultant environmental conflict.

As a basis for communication, art therapy directives encourage symbolic and creative representations, stimulate verbal expression, offer a controlled situation to explore and practice new modes of thinking, and provide an outlet for unconscious thoughts and feelings.

In short, art has the power to serve both expressive and interpretive functions of development. With an emphasis on integration and identity formation, directives can heighten the interaction between the individual and his or her environment as mature thinking develops.

PART III

THE PRACTICE OF ART THERAPY

Individual Therapy

Three Cases Revealed

Just as well-designed directives can heighten and strengthen the interaction between the self and the environment, directives also offer an opportunity for the therapist and client to relate to one another. And nowhere is the intensity of a relationship both formed and tested as within the individual therapeutic hour. A one-to-one interaction predicated upon trust, with a focus on intrapsychic and interpersonal stresses, can create an intimate relationship that can produce both change and identification. However, no discussion on individual therapy, especially with the difficult client, is complete without a look at transference reactions.

Freud's original theory of transference has been used "for the past century . . . for understanding the parallels between the patient's experience of the relationship with the therapist and the patient's significant early parental relationships" (Luborsky et al., 1993, p. 326). The therapeutic interpersonal relationship becomes primary as the client works through repetitious and often maladaptive patterns of relating to others. In verbal therapy it is imperative that therapist and client identify and discuss transference reactions (countertransference included) in order to work toward healthier conceptualizations, feelings, and behaviors. Unfortunately, patients often resist such exploration.

Because transference is often intensely exaggerated, unconscious, and repetitive and serves as a resistant or defensive operation, exploration can be complicated. For if the feelings, thoughts, and behaviors are designed to protect and ultimately are unconscious, then a therapist's observations can easily be dismissed, denied, or intellectualized. It is at this juncture that the process of art therapy can intervene in the resistance of here-and-now trans-ference reactions. As stated earlier, the art production is permanent and designed for all to see, and it can offer a gateway to the unconscious represen-tations that impede present interpersonal relationships. Yet it also serves another purpose—the art production offers a transitional object onto which transference feelings (both positive and negative) can be displaced as the in-dividual resolves conflicts, retreats from dependency, and moves toward mastery.

Of the depiction of transference in art therapy Margaret Naumburg (1953) has stated:

> In art therapy, patients frequently create pictorial images which deal with the "transference" relation. . . . Unconscious caricature and mockery of revered parent figures may sometimes break through in bold and startling por-traits. . . . In the process of therapy, with the release of such hostile parental images, the patient frequently deflects the resentment against his parents away from the therapist and into his own symbolic art. . . . When these long-repressed and forbidden feelings are projected into pictures, the patient be-gins to glimpse the intensity of the actual conflict. (p. 8)

Equally, transference reactions are both aided and accelerated by the art productions. The artist of Figures 1.10–1.16 was a shame-based, highly im-pulsive adolescent male who would taunt and antagonize peers and adults until he was "rejected." In this manner he repeated the familial dynamics of approach and avoidance. Nowhere was this negative transference more prominent than within the individual therapy hour.

All of his early conflicts were displaced onto the newly important people in his life. As traditional verbal exploration was proving unsuccessful, art therapy (plasticene clay) was introduced to offer an outlet for the repetition compulsion that drove all his relationships. In the end, the use of symbolic objects that he created and manipulated in a safe and structured environ-ment allowed him to form a meaningful attachment while constructing new positive identifications.

In this chapter I discuss three case histories. The first is a severely ego-regressed adult whose desire for closeness (both physical and emotional) was countered only by his fear of a recapitulation of the familial relation-ship that was perceived as rejecting and lonely. The second is the case of a 38-year-old recidivistic, schizophrenic male, who, after 20 years, finally stabilized on his medication and sought therapy. The third revolves around a resistant teenager who exhibited homicidal ideation and was charged with assault and battery when he threatened a younger peer at school by holding a glass shard to his neck.

As with all case histories within this book, the information concerning therapy and clinical matters is factual. However, the client's personal information, including names (where applicable), dates, and places, has been replaced to retain confidentiality.

Case Study 5.1

This case study concerns a client we will call John. His clinical background follows.

Clinical Background

The client is a married 56-year-old who has lived half of his life in institutions. He is a short, nondescript man who walks with a rigid posture and no arm movement. His facial expression is immobile. John speaks in a soft manner, yet when he is allowed to talk uninterrupted his voice modulation will increase to a rapid pace.

Born in the Midwest, he dropped out of high school, left his family home, and migrated to the west coast. He worked as a retail salesman until enlisting in the armed services at the age of majority. He was honorably discharged 1 year later and by the following year was arrested on his first charge of disorderly conduct and soliciting lewd acts.

As the years passed, John would be convicted of two more sexual crimes and sent to jail and prison, and ultimately he would find a home in the state hospital system. Here he would remain, as his chronic schizophrenia, characterized by loose associations and active delusions, precluded his release into the community. The details of John's final conviction include lewd and lascivious acts with a 3-year-old whom he was babysitting. When the police arrived John stated, "my wife quit going to church and showing me love. She was probably upset with me because I am a Christian."

In early childhood, John was described as a lonely and detached boy who "never played with other children. Nothing bothers John. Things just roll off his back like water off a duck." His parents were married at the age of 17, and this union remains intact. They had three children: Besides John, the oldest, there is a sister and a second son, who was favored by the females in the home. It has been stated that John was terribly jealous of the relationship between his younger brother and sister and often said he wished his brother had never been born. Additionally, John's mother has stated, "John didn't care much about religion, he just tolerated it. But his brother and sister loved it and went everywhere together."

Throughout John's adolescence he viewed his mother as controlling and was frightened of his father's temper. In a conversation with his mother she described John as "having a bad habit of lying. He tells people about the kind of life he really wants to lead or would have liked to have led in the past. For instance, he told me he wished he had been born on a farm." His mother further stated, "John's father is very skilled at being able to make things. I have felt in the last 2 years that John has that talent. In fact, I see more things all the time where John is more like his father in his abilities. John is so much like his father. If his father could tell a lie in the place of a truth he often did it to make himself look better and bigger to me."

I first noticed John standing at the end of a corridor preaching to the light fixtures. There he stood, his face upturned, arms gesticulating, his back to the rest of the hospital community while he recited a jumble of fragmented numbers he attributed to his invented scripture.

My first contact with John was in a group art therapy session to which he had been assigned. In group session, not unlike his hallway activities, John continued to speak in a grossly disorganized and often incoherent manner. Figure 5.1 is his first drawing. The group was instructed to divide their papers into three and "in the first space draw where you came from, in the center where you are now, and in the last space where you are going."

During the feedback stage, John described his sections (which he delineated by folding his paper) in the following manner: (1) "where he came from" he simply identified as a log cabin in the Ozarks; (2) "where he is now" was the center image, an institutionalized building standing before "bland mountains"; and (3) "where he is going" was given much energy and time as John launched into his delusional belief that since he was 5 years old he and his father had been circuit preachers. The two traveled the mountainous area of the Ozarks providing sermons to a group of devoted parishioners.

The group members listened to John's inconsistent and often illogical connections without confrontation, but the wish-fulfilling fantasies that frame primary process thinking did not escape my notice. In this, his first polarity directive, John had summed up his intense emotional need to repeat the familial relationship through the use of projected anger. In this case it served as the basis for his grandiose delusions and distortions of reality.

If we couple John's verbal statements with what we know of his history, it is of particular interest that he has incorporated his father into his delusional subsystem. Freud (1947) has stated that "the father complex and belief in God, has shown us that the personal God is psychologically nothing but an exalted father" (p. 98). Equally, Arieti (1955) seems to have summed up John's formative years and his subsequent retreat into grandiose delusions in the following passage:

5.1 Log Cabin in the Ozarks

In the belief and practice of religion he will try to get the comfort which he could not find elsewhere. Religion and God are the good parents, whom he substitutes for the bad parents. They are the parents who accept even the inadequate and worthless children. The patient is unwilling to submit to the authority of his parents, but may respect the authority of God. He is not able to relate to people, but is able to develop some kind of relatedness to God. People don't give love, but God does. (p. 71)

Thus, John's delusional beliefs served as a protective setting, a rescuer for the meek, a sanctuary for the rejected—an improved reality where John is competent, esteemed, and revered. In this world, instead of fearing his father, he worked side by side with him to offer unconditional acceptance and love to those in need. Instead of shunning religious ideas, as he did in his youth, he embraces the security of the church and thus garners the companionship of his siblings and the approval of his mother. In this world, external reality is regressively distorted, denied, and projected through grandiose beliefs.

Roughly 1 week following the completion of Figure 5.1 John was assigned to my caseload. I met with him for the next 9 months in both individual and group therapy sessions.

The Sessions

From the beginning, it was evident that John's propensity to decompensate increased when he was faced with interpersonal insecurity and anxieties. He sought relief through the delusions, which did not waver. As Arieti (1955) has stated, "delusional life is reality for a patient, not pretension" (p. 340). Even when he was presented with factual information, John's fixed false beliefs persisted. One such belief revolved around his instant offense. In our first session I casually asked why he had been sent to prison. His initial reaction was apathy; with a shrug of the shoulders he said he had no idea of the crime. As we sat quietly he wove a story that began, "security will come and release me once they've gone through my paperwork. I don't know what's taking them so long." He continued to tell how his "people" had sent him to a hospital at the age of 10. After 2 years of his family's fervently praying, his wife brought him his military uniform and he simply walked out. He is now a five-star general and has been wrongly accused and convicted.

The injustices that John described, as carried out by his "people" and authority in general, established a theme that would persist throughout his treatment: (1) security (and the need to feel wanted); (2) rescue (and its hope); and (3) the loss of love (both sexual and emotional) and concomitant loneliness.

In the first month of therapy I used collages to relieve John's anxiety as he coped with the intensity of the reciprocal, interactive process of individual therapy. Working with collage afforded him the "closeness," both physical and emotional, of a safe and nonthreatening interaction that required nothing more than his presence. To increase his feeling of security and assuage his anxiety, I placed no demands on him. Figure 5.2, which he titled "Children of Love," is a typical example of his work within this first month.

John returned numerous times to the collage box that contained images of children, and in Figure 5.2 children again predominate. His explanations ranged from the concrete—"that's a 3-year-old in a tree"—to the wish fulfillment of the upper left-hand corner, "that's a family at home, hugging, talking, and showing love," to his description of the fire beneath as "mountains and lights with a city background."

5.2 Children of Love

Just as his verbal statements shed light on his thought processes, the images he selected pointed toward John's desire for affection, love, and companionship while at the same time expressing his fear of interpersonal relations. The center image of the ever-watchful domestic cat looms above a disconnected family system and beside the fires (and lust) that light up the majority of John's delusional subsystem (the imaginary world where he is respected, regarded, and wanted). Additionally, his verbal fascination with the bottom right-hand image (the 3-year-old boy in the tree) appeared to symbolize his crime.

Throughout John's art the repetition of the illustration of a child within this age range is evident. As with his other work (both individually and within the group), his propensity to return to the family constellation, with its early childhood concerns of belonging and admiration, coupled with infantile sexuality expressions pointed toward the need for John to create in a medium that would allow relevant exploration of the past while providing depth to his experiences.

To this end, I chose the tactile medium of plasticene clay. "The differences between enclosures on the paper and objects in the world remain vast. Objects actually occupy three dimensions, have tangibility, depth, and solidity, and lend themselves to a plethora of actions and interactions" (Gardner, 1980, p. 59). For John, who lived in a world of personal symbols, diffuse boundaries, and social isolation, I felt that the act of creating his own protected environment with the physicality of the clay (refer to Table 1.3, Piaget's stages of preconceptual to intuitive thought) would be as important as the ego-enhancing act of building (recall his mother's early comments, "John's father is very skilled at being able to make things. I have felt in the last 2 years that John has that talent").

For the next 2 months John worked with plasticene clay and found objects to create his protected environment. In the initial sessions I introduced the media and instructed John to "make a family." Figure 5.3 depicts the mother (far left), a 3-year-old daughter (center), and the father (right side). John paid particular attention to the mother character as he added jewelry, eye pupils, and the brown on the face that represents lipstick. As he worked he stated, "beauty is in the eye of the beholder." For the father figure he requested a clay "tool" to work on the facial detailing. Other than these two comments he added nothing further to the session, and I requested nothing further.

In subsequent sessions I asked John, "what does this family need?" This question relates to John Buck's (1948) HTP technique. As part of the post-drawing inquiry, Buck recommends posing the question, "what does that _____ need the most?" This question both allows the client to respond symbolically and affords the clinician insight into personal meaning and issues.

John's symbolic reply was to surround his family with material objects. In

5.3 John's Family

Figure 5.4 these objects consist of a picnic table and bench, swimming pool, slide, swing set, and recreational toys. For the family he made a jump rope for the mother, a ball for the daughter, and a red croquet mallet for the father (see disk to view in color).

As you look at Figure 5.4, examine the articles that John created and give special attention to the croquet mallet. The accoutrements were mainly red, with the phallically engorged mallet symbolically representing both a power symbol and John's conflict. This personal symbol (golf and croquet utilized interchangeably) appeared often in John's verbal comments and art productions. Prior to this directive he had created a collage wherein a father and 4-year-old boy were depicted together in an attic; the two were getting ready to go to "the children's golf course." This comment thus takes on a greater meaning when combined with the pictorial representation of Figure 5.4.

As the project continued and John became familiar with the repetitious directives and tasks, he took more initiative. Soon he was creating objects, experimenting with media, decorating, and detailing without any intervention. Thus, the dependency issues that John normally presented slowly abated as the gradual expansion of his own personality was given sway. At this juncture, I viewed my role as that of the "good parent": providing sup-

5.4 John's Playthings

port where John's functioning was tenuous while offering him both acceptance and kindness. In short, I endeavored to enhance his adaptive functioning (by utilizing countertransference of the good parent) while offering a vehicle for his emotional expression regarding his early familial relationships (transference situation).

However, it is interesting that it took John numerous sessions to build a house in response to the question "what does this family need?" And when this house was built (Figure 5.5) it contained none of the detailing that he had applied to the characters and their playthings.

The house, with its symbolic representation of familial dynamics in John's case, lies bare. If we refer to Appendix C and apply interpretation to the formal items, the small door, unidimensional roof (he had created many roofs that were triangular shaped in group three-dimensional projects), absent chimney, and low-hanging windows point toward feelings of emotional constriction, distance, and the projection of these feelings both toward and from his family.

This significance becomes even more pronounced when we look at the completed project (Figure 5.6), where significant detailing is found in the shrubbery, pathways, and flowers. The need to structure the environment is

5.5 The House That John Built

often a need for emotional protection through the development of ego-defensive barriers.

John had created his "background" for the family, providing them with a bounty of recreational items, yet the house seemed an afterthought, a necessary "evil" that was undertaken out of necessity rather than enjoyment. At this stage John pronounced his project complete, and I asked him to tell me "what was going on." He said that the father (which he stated was him) wanted to play golf with his family and he was in the process of calling them together. They were a happy family, and the father never went to school, as he was a preacher (with his father), which is where he met his wife (who volunteered for the church).

In John's brief story we see the amalgamation of delusion, symbolism, and reality. He holds fast to being a preacher with his father yet reports accurately his meeting his wife in a church. Additionally, he appears to be utilizing the theme of golf or croquet to represent his sexuality and concomitant need for love, whether it is through intimacy or molestation.

In subsequent sessions I provided a wide range of media choices and allowed John to choose among them as his needs dictated. He did not return to any three-dimensional objects. Not surprisingly, his drawings continued to express his fixed false beliefs. However, in one session as he drew his repetitious "church in the Ozarks" he made a superfluous comment that led me to believe that his insight was growing.

5.6 Completed Clay Project

Figure 5.7 illustrates what John called "Omish Land of Love." As he drew, he first focused on the trees, which were a theme that had arisen recently. As he turned his attention to the church, I expected him to return to his fantasy, but that day he did not. Instead, he pointed to the church and said, "It's a false front. On the left is a jackrabbit that only comes out for attention."

I wish that I could add that this insight developed further and allowed him to communicate through language rather than symbolic activity. Unfortunately, the schizophrenic's regression is insidious and pervasive. The feelings of vulnerability and anxiety are countered only by the fantasy productions that lend order and structure to a world that tends to overwhelm the schizophrenic's fragile sense of self. In successive sessions John's insight faded as his delusional mind-set took precedence.

As he oscillated between delusional functioning and moments of reality-based thought processing, I decided to introduce an ego-modifying directive into the session.

John had grown accustomed to deciding on the direction of the therapeutic hour and was taken aback at my suggestion for a topic. However, our relationship was such that in short order he drew as I had requested. John's response to the directive "draw why you are here," included 4 distinct pictures of places he had been. The first was of a church symbolized by a triangular roof sitting atop a square; tentatively attached is a church bell

5.7 Omish Land of Love

212

tower. The next drawing was of a rectangular shaped car and titled ("in car"), the last two renderings were merely squares titled "prison" and "hospital." Overall, each miniscule form item was devoid of detailing; reduced to simplistic shapes the years of John's life had been represented in metaphor. In describing his art production he was as concrete and linear as the completed picture; he pointed at the church on the left and spoke of being transferred in a car to prison and eventually being placed in the hospital. However, the comment that resonates with John's feelings, fears, anxieties, and defensive functioning came toward the end. As we spoke further and I interspersed facts to flesh out John's timeline he stated, "I don't want to remember. Tears and strife, tears and strife."

In John's disorganized world, which he had sorted out through his delusional beliefs, the demonstration of factual accounts produced a reality-based anxiety rather than one of detachment or impassiveness—an important, albeit subtle, gain. For the remainder of our time together I kept the focus of therapy on the here-and-now, which I hoped would help him to find a role within the community and expand his social sphere.

Thus, whenever John resorted to delusional functioning to counter his anxiety, I introduced a here-and-now directive. Figure 5.8 is his response to my request for "a drawing of something that happened in the last 5 days." I countered his attempts to circumvent the directive, and he eventually drew a garden that he only sees out his window. After discussing his drawing, we

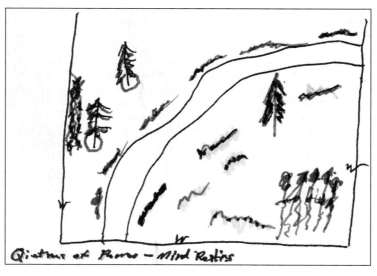

5.8 Quietness of Flowers—Mind Resting

went to the garden and toured it so that John would not just be a passive observer within his world but an active participant.

As the drawings and tours continued, John began to gather flowers to present to select staff members. He inquired into working with the Horticultural Club to "take care of the garden," learned the proper names of trees and flowers, and at times projected his basic problems onto the various flowers. In one such session he found a single blossom among a grouping of sunflowers and stated, "Here I am just trying to survive." Additionally, John's artwork (in individual and group meetings) had turned toward the drawing of trees as they sprouted and grew (Figure 5.9 offers a representative example).

From a metaphorical standpoint, "trees seem to be especially suited as projection carriers for the human process of individuation. . . . In its rising it must stand, withstand, and stand firm, just as we" (Kast, 1989, p. 114). And John's interest in "life" and growth held hope for his desire to connect to that which was reality based, even if only for a short while.

With John taking on increased responsibility for his own therapy, his interactions within the milieu showed improvement. He no longer preached to the light fixtures; instead, he saved that for the dayroom, where he had a dynamic audience. His episodes of regression appeared to lessen as he asserted himself verbally. As his interpersonal relationships grew, he attended

5.9 *Trees of Love*

an increased number of groups, although he was fond of saying that group providers "try to squeeze everything out of you."

One day, as we toured the garden, John evidenced difficulty maneuvering the stairs. With minimal questions John spoke of a long-standing "heartburn" feeling. Once we returned from our session I instructed him to speak with the nurses, and I watched, from a distance, as he followed through on my request. A series of tests revealed that John was extremely ill and would have to be transferred to a medical facility. For this reason, our last sessions focused on closure and the creation of a transitional object as John adapted to changing circumstances. His final project was a garden mural (Figure 5.10), which we worked on together by gluing collage images of flowers and trees. In this way John could take his beloved garden with him, and hopefully the comfort that he derived there would transpose into his new environment.

If therapy had continued, my path for John would have been toward the further management and understanding of his psychotic symptomology, continued interaction within the environment, and supportive living management skills. Ultimately, the connection that we were able to achieve began with understanding and compassion as I allowed him to assert himself, feel wanted, and branch out of his dependent role. In short, I utilized my

5.10 Closure Mural

countertransference toward the end of the good parent—something John had desired in his youth. Regrettably, his inherited biological disorder, combined with his anxiety, confusion, and stress, transferred into the fixed false beliefs of today, the private symbols that allowed John to dream while awake.

Case Study 5.2

This case involves a 38-year-old, married male whom I will call Dion.

Clinical Background

Dion had a history of substance abuse since the age of 13 and paranoid schizophrenia since the age of 18. With a remorseful and often apprehensive affect, he moved about in a restless manner. His eagerness to apply himself was overshadowed only by his intense need to rectify his past mistakes. This scenario took many forms, one of which was his desire to involve himself in every available activity, much to the detriment of realistic planning. The defense of undoing appeared in his repetitive verbal comment "I'm paying my tab," which refers to expiative undoing or the annulment of prior acts. Furthermore, his history of substance abuse and his recollections, memories, and discussions often revealed what Laughlin (1970) refers to as the "Hangover Paradox," which, simply stated, means that atonement is often found within the pain and physicality of the morning-after hangover.

For these reasons, Dion's motivation toward erasure prohibited his ability to problem solve, visualize consequences, surmount issues related to guilt, and effectively free himself from his dependency reactions. At this juncture, my main treatment goal for Dion was awareness. Unlike John (in case study 5.1), Dion was stabilized on his medication, voluntarily seeking treatment interventions, and capable of processing the insight.

Dion's childhood was stable yet chaotic. He belonged to a family of four boys (including Dion) and three girls, and since both parents worked, they left the older children to raise the younger children. Dion was the fourth of six children, and his sibling relationships were strained even in childhood. Presently, his brothers are either battling drug abuse issues through recovery or actively using. Of his sisters, the oldest "is just like mom, she babies me," while his younger sister is "the only one I can talk to. She's honest and straightforward. We talk monthly on the phone."

His parents' marriage remained intact until his mother passed away 6 years prior to our meeting. When asked to describe his mother he stated,

"She was always there . . . a strong woman. . . . She showed me a lot of love. She knew she was a codependent." He would go on to relate stories of how his mother infantalized him even into adulthood. By comparison, he described his father as "a loving man . . . tough as nails. He knows I'm ill; my mother never accepted that."

I met Dion after an anger management class that he was attending. During this particular session, the group had been discussing the offenses that had placed them within the criminal justice system. For Dion this was a charge of spousal abuse. The essence of the offense is that he held his wife captive for over 1 hour, alternately having her read from the Bible and beating her about the face and body. Figure 5.11 is his depiction of his wife running from the ordeal after she managed to escape.

Dion met his wife the same year his mother passed away. At the time he was stabilized on his antipsychotic medication, and they married very soon after. At the time of the birth of their first child Dion suddenly stopped taking his medication, and within 7 months his delusional thinking was so severe that his paranoid mindset returned and he assaulted his wife. He was jailed for 8 months, returned to his medication regime, and released on probation with a restraining order for a period of 1 year. Upon his release he attempted to see his wife, but his wife enforced the order, and he returned to

5.11 Running from the Crime

custody to serve out his sentence. During our initial interview Dion recalled his delusional symptoms and stated, "I thought I could move a house by laying a hand on it."

As I noted in Chapter 3, I generally begin individual sessions by completing an art projective assessment. The assessment I chose for Dion was the 8CRT. I decided upon this procedure due to the 8CRT's inherent ability to identify modes of coping and to illustrate a projected self-concept.

Page 1 of Figure 5.12 illustrates an oversized (aggressive) female figure who stands in the center of the page. Her head is enlarged (opposite sex viewed as smarter or possessing greater authority) and sits directly upon her shoulders (regressive). Her teeth are accentuated (aggressiveness), and there is an accent on the nostrils (primitive aggression). Her fingers are drawn in two distinct styles: The left hand is enclosed by a loop (wish to suppress aggressive impulse), while the right hand appears spikelike (paranoid, hostile). A series of four buttons (dependency issues—normal to age 7–8) is drawn on the shirt, and the figure has long, thin legs (striving for autonomy).

Page 2 is essentially the same drawing (superimposition) as page 1, yet this male is less intrusive. His body and head appear smaller in size. His eyes are drawn incompletely, with the pupil omitted from the left, giving it a bizarre quality. This figure, however, retains its feet only from the preceding drawing (lack of independence, complete only with female), while the hair is drawn in anxious swirls (infantile sexual drives).

Page 3 is another male with tears steaming down his face, hands borrowed from the preceding drawing (helplessness, withdrawal, guilt), and a concave mouth (oral dependence infantile).

The figure in page 4 is smiling, and the buttons reappear; the fingers become smaller and spiked (primitive aggression).

Page 5 has no relationship to any of the prior drawings and shows a child with reaching hands (regression). It is drawn to the left of the paper and has reinforced fingers (guilt indicators), while the use of shape rather than detailing predominates (primitive style, regressed).

Page 6 returns to the figure of a man with a single-lined mouth (tension, shutting the mouth against something), pinpoint eyes (desire to see as little as possible), no feet (lack of independence, withdrawal), spiked fingers, and a single row of buttons. Additionally, the nose is completed in a "V" style, with the accent on the nostrils removed.

Page 7 is a superimposition of page 6, whereby the man's legs are elongated (striving for autonomy), his shoes are detailed (heels), and a moustache and beard appear (masculine symbols).

Page 8, the final image, though superimposed, bears no relationship to any of the preceding drawings. The hair is omitted (lack of virility, mas-

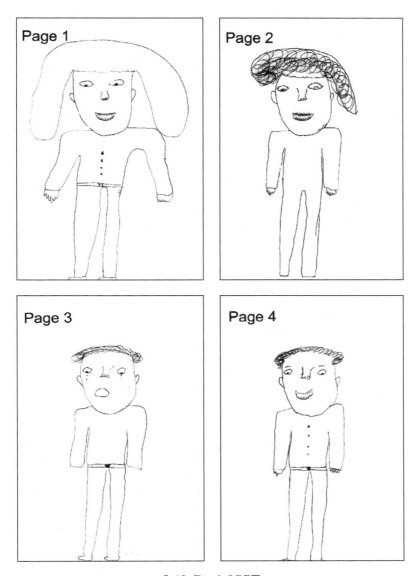

5.12 *Dion's 8CRT*

culinity), there are no pupils (avoidant style of perceiving reality), and there is no nose or detailing within the face. The body has patterned (rationalizes) and perseverative shading (refuge in safety and confinement), while the figure overall is thicker, with large shoulders (preoccupied with need for strength) and trunk (unsatisfied drives).

From a quantitative perspective Dion drew the abundance of figures in

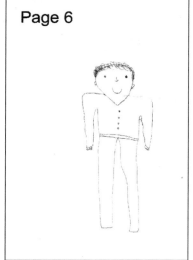

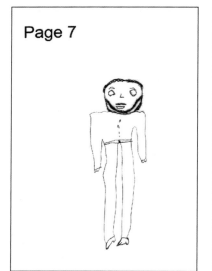

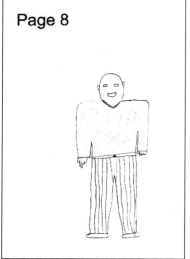

5.12 (continued)

the style of a 9-year-old with a general schema, but not one that is rigid. However, this low-level detailing (in clothing particularly) is indicative of a younger style, as are his long strokes and general lack of shading. Thus, when assessing his drawings, any exaggeration, exclusion, or significant change in schema (like the discrete renderings in pages 5 and 6) takes on greater importance, as younger children tend to draw for emotional effect (Lowenfeld & Brittain, 1982).

Additionally, his drawings begin exceedingly large and scale down to a normal height by page 6. This could be due to his test-taking anxiety coupled with poorly developed inner controls. It is also important to point out that Dion did not shade any of the figures until he reached page 8. A muscular, powerful-appearing man, this figure is accentuated in the body (seat of basic needs and drives), yet the facial detailing is without the characteristics that express social needs and responsiveness—an internal conflict that preoccupied Dion throughout our year-long therapy.

Overall, the symbolic abundance of ideas points toward Dion's aggressive impulses and a sincere wish to suppress these overwhelming feelings and thoughts. In this way, much of his focus is centered on masculinity and the need for strength. However, his dependency issues (especially on mother figures and females in general) create a desire for autonomy and a feeling of helplessness and guilt. If we look at page 3, a tearful, hopeless projection of the self turns into an aggressively smiling projection (page 4) but ultimately returns to a dependent child reaching out for emotional satisfaction in regression.

On the whole, Dion's symptomology suggests what Barton and Kovan (1978) described:

> In adult psychoses, particularly acute schizophrenic episodes, panic occurs which appears to be fusion panic. Ego boundaries are lost and there is an emergence into the adult's ego of this psychic state of fusion which was carried over in the mental apparatus from the earliest life stage. The self tends to be lost in a flood of perception: annihilation fears and engulfment fears result. . . . Omnipotent feelings can occur. . . . The acutely psychotic patient may feel all-powerful and present with random hyperactivity . . . manifested as disruptive and assaultive motor responses. (p. 236)

For these reasons, my therapeutic approach with Dion was twofold. Dion had been stabilized on his medication regime for one and a half years, yet his adaptive defenses remained primitive (recall his major defense of undoing to relieve anxiety). Therefore, my interventions would entail exploration of the past (to promote developmental mastery) as well as the present (to promote insight and awareness) coupled with the ability to cope with life stressors through problem-solving techniques.

The Sessions

Following the completion of the 8CRT, Dion arrived at our next session visibly upset over a conversation with a staff member. His fists clenched into unyielding balls, he sat beside me with tightened lips. A simple "you look upset, would you like to talk about it?" sufficed to unleash a flurry of assumptions ("he's trying to keep me down") and dismissive comments ("he's just an idiot so he'll never understand"), and finally abrupt limit setting ("I give up"). Because Dion was involved in our anger management group, whose course material was compiled from McKay, Rogers, and McKay's (1989) *When Anger Hurts* self-help book, I focused on modifying Dion's behavior by altering his aversive chains.

In this case I utilized an art therapy exercise designed to provide insight and awareness. I gave him a sheet of paper, kept one for myself, and instructed Dion that he was going to be the leader of this communication-driven exercise. I asked him to choose five simple items ("something so simple, a child could understand") for his "master" drawing and keep them a secret. As we sat with our backs to one another, I directed him to draw four of the five items he had chosen and, as he compiled his drawing, to give specific verbal directions to me (the follower). In the end, when we compared our drawings, they should be identical.

However, before we matched our drawings I asked Dion how close in appearance he imagined they would be. He responded, "Identical. I picked easy things and was clear in how to draw them."

Figure 5.13 illustrates the finished exercise. On the left is Dion's rendering, while mine is on the right. The similarities are not striking. Beyond the clouds and sun, little else in my drawing resembles the "master" drawing. The mountains completely baffled me, as did the geometric shapes, which apparently represented lightning bolts. Although we processed the exercise based on its formal and structural qualities, it took little verbiage for Dion to appreciate that misunderstanding occurs even when we believe that our communication is clear and concise.

In the months that followed, I instituted directives designed to promote enhanced communication and problem solving in the here-and-now. As

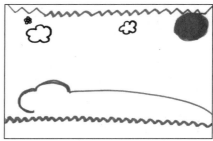

5.13 Something a Child Could Understand

Dion gained self-control and successfully navigated through issues related to conflict resolution and feelings expression, it was time to explore his internalized memories, thoughts, and doubts.

In the ensuing sessions I broke down the developmental stages of Erikson and at separate times instructed Dion to "draw yourself as an infant, child, adolescent, young adult, and mid-adult." Figure 5.14 illustrates his first drawing in the series.

Here Dion has recreated a loving and warm family environment. A picnic, free of siblings, shows interaction between the figures; there is comfort in the symbiotic transparency of the infant Dion and his mother, with a sense of trust and strength in the father's broad shoulders. However, as we move away from the family constellation, the environment becomes increasingly anxious. The apprehensive line quality coupled with short, sketchy strokes adds a sense of trepidation within the outer world.

Dion next drew himself as an 8-year-old (left side of Figure 5.15) as an increasingly social and active child. He rides his bike on a city street with a group of friends, a shared activity that widens his social circle and strengthens his sense of competency and industry. In contrast, the right side of Figure 5.15 is Dion at the age of 14; gone are the details of the larger commu-

5.14 Dion as an Infant

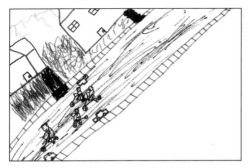 

5.15 Dion at 8 and 14

nity. Instead, a home stands barren while Dion greets two teenaged friends. In this drawing we can not only see but feel the affectual differences.

In these three renderings, Dion has offered us a look within the debilitating and enveloping illness of schizophrenia. The 2-year-old (Figure 5.14) was content in its dependency, and the 8-year-old reveled in new experiences, while the 14-year-old fears the encroaching challenges of adulthood and begins a steady retreat into the self.

In the last two drawings of the series (Figure 5.16) he is 23 years old and in county jail on the left side, and on the right he is 30 years old and in prison. In the second picture the only other person in Dion's immediate world is his bunkmate, who is asleep on the cot (far right). Dion spent an

5.16 Dion at 23 and 30

5.17 *Man under Construction*

inordinate amount of time describing the effects of medication. He indicated that while he was incarcerated he frequently refused treatment because "I didn't want to be a bump on the log."

At this point in Dion's therapy it became increasingly clear that his life effectively ended when his mental illness took over in his late teens. As the drawings illustrate, he had not mastered the tasks necessary to move from a child's sense of dependency to an adult's sense of competency. The confusion that accompanies adolescence was exacerbated by an illness that generates detachment over productiveness. Instead of finding success within his relationships, his work, and social interaction, he found success within his delusional beliefs. He could move houses by laying a hand on them—why would someone with that "power" desire the drudgery and responsibility that attended daily living?

To prepare Dion for a future where responsibility, action, and reality issues outweighed the lure of an omnipotent delusional power (which he could call upon by refusing his medication), our focus centered on the growth of the self as a being separate from the dependency upon a "family unit" (his biological family, the hospital staff, etc.).

After months of art directives designed to strengthen his ego and expand his coping capacities, Dion announced, "I don't really know how to do life." This superfluous statement summed up Dion's developmental existence and

5.18 Dion's Crushing Powerlessness

poignantly articulated his growing awareness. It was time to challenge the disease that had fixated him within adolescence for mastery. Figure 5.17 was his response to the directive "draw you now."

Interestingly, the drawing style and the title that Dion gave to this image communicate his feelings faithfully. The figure is connected by dots that serve to reinforce the body wall. This is generally interpreted as a need to contain and delineate the ego boundaries. For this reason, the reinforcement of the body wall barriers parallels that of human functioning, as "the ego not only mediates between the individual and the environment but also mediates internal conflict among various aspects of the personality" (Goldstein, 1984, p. xv). It is in this image that Dion is able to reconcile unconscious feelings with determined statements and thoughts. In talking about his drawing he stated, "I know it's good, but it's hard and painful to learn new things."

As our work on strengthening problem-solving capabilities continued, Dion's verbal statements began to center on the word "powerless." In group therapy sessions and activities, and throughout the facility whenever a conflict arose, you could be certain he would revert to the idea of powerlessness to describe his situation. Individual sessions were no different: As we explored his early adolescence, withdrawal and retreat became his manner of coping with environmental stressors as outside support systems gave

5.19 Practice Makes Perfect

way to his growing mental illness. Figure 5.18 illustrates Dion's Crushing Powerlessness.

Note that both the driver of the crane and the individual being flattened are projections of Dion. Throughout the discussion Dion processed the figure under the ball as himself: "When I'm powerless I'm all curled up, shrunken." Yet his depiction of himself "in the driver's seat" pointed toward a perception of the future. Utilizing this metaphor became an important reminder for Dion both verbally and symbolically. It was no longer the dropping ball that held the power, but the person in charge; an individual could control environmental events in countless ways. This insight allowed Dion to take action, to become an individual with a sense of self that was not intertwined with his identity of the past (the outcast, the crazy one, the one who was isolative and withdrawn).

By the 11th month Dion was taking an increasingly assertive role in the direction of therapy. Much of his discussion focused on formulating realistic plans for the future. The typical adolescent question of "Who am I?" took on a central role in Dion's life as a distinct and unique personality emerged. His struggles toward development persisted, as Figure 5.19 attests. In this drawing he has combined his past (at the age of 8) achievement of learning to swim with the process of learning new skills as an adult (in this case, jumping rope).

This simplistic rendering held much hope for Dion on a multiplicity of levels. If we recall his earlier works, the environments had a tendency to appear chaotic and anxious. His drawings showed roads slanting upward and trees looming ominously overhead, with a paucity of social interaction and learning. Here an organized environment surrounds Dion, and he is not alone. The social contact in addition to the attainment of knowledge finds him as a cooperating community member.

In our final month of therapy I thought it would be important for Dion to review the entirety of his artwork. He had, in many respects, illustrated a time line of not only fixation in childhood dependency and isolation but a progression toward adult affiliation and competency. In all, Dion had completed a total of 65 drawings, which we reviewed in chronological order. A powerful intervention that often clarifies observation, this process allowed him the opportunity to witness the unfolding of his progression while viewing the artwork as both observer and participant.

Throughout the review his reflections ranged over his feelings ("I blamed them [friends] for moving away. I hated them for that"), his thoughts ("I may not be that [a therapist]; maybe I'll be a sponsor, I can help others that way"), and his relationship with me over the course of our sessions (the ego ideal—the desire to be a therapist—that he no longer found essential as he acquired his own ego identity).

It was to be an arduous journey for Dion to develop not only the awareness necessary to overcome his defense of undoing (a magical means of survival) but also the strength to persevere toward increased production and care. The abandonment of dependency, the focus on the self as a person within a larger community, and the knowledge that he was not powerless but instead capable and industrious, imparted a sense of esteem and regard.

It is my belief that the artwork not only allowed Dion to practice new skills in a safe environment but also provided an outlet for his unconscious defensive functioning. For over 20 years he had suffered the illness of schizophrenia, had found solace in the fantasy of his delusions, and had endlessly repeated maladaptive coping skills in an attempt to shape his environment. And now, in his late 30s, with medication stabilization, Dion recognized that purely communicative therapy was failing him. He had requested to work in an evocative manner, one that offered a symbolic approach to social relationships. As a result, the therapeutic hour allowed Dion to express pent-up emotions and feelings without verbalization, provided opportunities to strengthen his sense of reality of the world, disrupted adaptive regression, allowed him to navigate through the developmental stages at his own pace, and ultimately laid the groundwork for autonomous functioning.

Case Study 5.3

This case review concerns a 13-year-old male whom we will call Randy.

Clinical Background

Randy had a significant history of homicidal ideation. In the year that we were to meet he had been hospitalized three times for making threats; he was placed within the juvenile justice system when he held a glass shard to the throat of another child while in school. Diagnosed with Conduct Disorder and considered to be a budding sociopath, he was initially placed in a series of group homes, from which he was removed due to increasingly aggressive and incorrigible behaviors.

Randy's social relationships alternated between defiance and apathy. With a controlled affect he would scan his environment in a hypervigilant manner. This ever-watchful attitude often preceded a condescending, dominating, and intrusive interaction, especially if he felt threatened in any manner. These peer conflicts became increasingly dangerous, especially when coupled with his poor judgment. Thus, an irritable mood could quickly turn cruel; a guarded attitude could result in days of isolation.

Randy was raised in a home where his brothers and sisters (all sired by different fathers) were left to fend for themselves. Both parents were addicted to crack cocaine, which left the oldest (10-year-old) sibling to provide the necessary care for the younger children (Randy was the fourth of five). At the age of 4 Randy was being repeatedly physically abused by his biological father; by the age of 7 he and his siblings were being left alone for days at a time. It was then that Child Protective Services was contacted and all of the children were removed from the home.

Over the next several years the siblings would be separated and Randy would have no contact with his biological parents. The only individual he desired contact with was his oldest half-brother. Randy rarely spoke of his childhood, preferring to bury those memories deep within his psyche. However, if pressed he would simply say, "It was a hell hole."

Unfortunately, he was unable to conceal his past as well as he would have liked, and he often had night terrors, from which he would awaken in a state of panic. He described these dreams in vague terms, saying only "I saw people dying" or "they were going to hell."

In all, Randy was not merely a child resistant to exploration: He was an individual who was incapable of expressing his emotions in any way other than through the defensive functioning of projecting his aggressive feelings and then reverting to dependency reactions. His behaviors hid maladaptive capacities, internalized perceptions of childhood stress with ensuing paranoid feelings, and the loss of trust in himself and the larger environment.

In an effort to identify and change the symbolic constructs that Randy was determined, though ill equipped, to conceal, I instituted evocative therapy. I felt that if he could not communicate his fears verbally, then a symbolic intervention focused on the unconscious would prove helpful.

> Psychodynamic therapies stress the importance of the unconscious. Symptoms are seen as external manifestations of internal disturbances that usually cannot be reached by conscious efforts. In the Freudian context, clients are led back to traumatic incidents in early childhood for the purpose of bringing those experiences into the conscious mind. In cognitive terms the client is helped to gain new interpretations of those events. (Goetze, 2001, p. 29)

In this case treatment focused on developing insight, providing catharsis, and strengthening the ego, as well as replacing Randy's distorted negative view of himself, the future, and his world. This combination of psychodynamic therapy and cognitive behavioral theory was a way to intervene within the dysfunctional belief system that had permeated not merely his thoughts and emotions but his very sense of self.

To this end, I employed Richard Gardner's (1986) mutual storytelling technique. This method allows the client to express conflict-laden feelings in a safely disguised form, and "from the stories children tell, the therapist is able to gain invaluable insights into their inner conflicts, frustrations, and defenses" (Gardner, 1986, p. 17).

Much as fairy tales, myths, and fables aid the developing personality, the mutual storytelling technique communicates solutions through healthy adaptations. A study on children's fantasies as revealed through storytelling identified eight main themes: "aggression, death, hurt or misfortune, morality, nutrition, dress, sociability, and crying" (Gardner, 1986, p. 181). Of these eight themes the majority correlated to Randy's early childhood developmental issues and his present silent assumptions. His internalized sense of self, of being the misfit whom the world had shut out, screamed for an interpersonal attachment that could restrain the destructiveness of an environment filled with deprivation and abandonment.

With this in mind, my role as an active participant was to become as important to the therapeutic process as was Randy's projection of his internalized self. What Randy required was a return to the significant relationships of his childhood with an adult that could reparent, offer support, reinforce his infantile gains, and offer hope over despair and self-control over impulsivity.

Thus, the mutual storytelling technique, with its combination of evocative and communicative therapy, was the tool that would provide the necessary shared planning, problem solving, and reciprocal interactions in a symbolic structure that was not anxiety producing. In the method's purest form, the client is initially made comfortable with the documentary process (tape recording or videotaping) by first being interviewed. In this phase the client is asked simple questions about him- or herself to decrease anxiety.

Once he or she shows a measure of comfort, the client is formally introduced to the "audience" and can then offer a story. While the client is telling his or her tale, the therapist notes the prominent issues as well as the symbolizing elements within the characters. When the client's narrative is complete, the therapist then chooses the salient theme and retells the story (utilizing the same characters and names), providing supplementary alternatives for healthier adjustments.

In the mutual storytelling technique the therapist acts as the master of ceremonies, offering guidance where ego strength is tenuous as well as "maternal" care in the form of approval and attention. In this way meaning is given to the child's existence. If we were to metaphorically examine the elements of this technique through developmental stage theory, then the pairing of the initial story and the therapist's reciprocal story could be said to parallel the earliest stages of social trust.

The Sessions

Because we were incorporating art therapy into the mainly verbal method of the mutual storytelling technique, it was necessary to introduce Randy to the process in steps. Randy was no stranger to the art room (refer to Figures I.2 and I.3 for Randy's completed masks), and having shown competency in his drawing and painting he felt immediately comfortable in this area. For this reason we used the art room rather than an office. Although he had not ventured into clay work before, he showed minimal anxiety with the medium. Initially, he wanted to use clay molds rather than creating the characters spontaneously; to assuage his apprehension, I provided one mold (of faces).

Prior to the narrative, Randy was instructed to create clay characters for his story. Once these were completed he created the environment (an island) where the characters lived. I purposefully selected an island, rather than other settings, for Randy to symbolically associate the feelings of childhood survival and abandonment with the harshness of solitary endurance that an island conjures. I should add that while creating his characters Randy was increasingly animated. He spontaneously shared their names and gave them distinct personalities. Additionally, when it was time to recite his story (although this was almost 4 weeks later), Randy retained all of the characters' names and biographical information as initially presented.

After completing the art work, Randy told this story:

Therapist: Welcome to "Master Theater," where we have Randy who is going to tell us a story today. Hi, Randy. What is it you are going to tell a story about today? And who are the main characters?

Randy: It's about how to solve problems and conflicts. The main characters are Ug and Thug, and an elephant, bear, monkey, turtle, and dragon [see Figure 5.20].

Therapist: Ladies and gentlemen, I present to you our storyteller.

Randy: There's a person named Ug who has a problem with Thug. Ug lives on Paradise Island [see Figure 5.21], and Thug went after Ug because he thought that Ug had all the gold on Paradise Island, but when he got there he figured out that all Ug wanted to do was just live by himself. He also found out there was no gold. So he started fighting with Ug and he got onto Ug's boat and learned that there was no gold on the entire island, and there has never been any gold. So Thug apologized to Ug and to the elephant and they were friends.

Therapist: So he apologized to the elephant? What did the elephant do?

Randy: Thug had hurt the elephant badly because he tried to get the bear to kill the elephant. But he couldn't and the elephant accepted the apology and they were friends. And they lived happily ever after on the island.

Therapist: Could you explain the boat further?

5.20 Ug, Thug, and the Rest of Paradise Island

Randy: It's the cruise ship that takes Ug, and now Thug, to Paradise Island from the mainland. It's just a magical boat [see Figure 5.21, upper
right corner]. It's got a bear on the back that steers it, and it runs on
the wind. It's got all these little people that maintain it, and the dragon
keeps the little people in order.

Therapist: Could you explain these two faces? [See Figure 5.21, bottom
right side on the island.]

Randy: Those are the spirit faces, they give advice. They give good advice
at the time you need it to everybody that asks them. This over here is
the fire that always burns. Like you touch something to it and it starts
it on fire.

Therapist: Could you tell us about the monkey?

Randy: This monkey was with his family and they had a whole bunch of
brothers and sisters. He was a misfit because he was hurt and smaller
than the others. So they told him "you need to leave." So he was just
walking around the mainland dying. Ug found him and brought him
to Paradise Island.

Therapist: You mentioned a bear; what about the bear?

Randy: The bear's parents are brown bears, but he was a polar bear, and
so the Paradise Island climate is just right for everybody and he is

5.21 *Paradise Island*

233

living there right now because he couldn't get a plane ticket to Antarctica. So he has to live there.

Therapist: Did I forget to ask about anyone or anything?

Randy: The turtle is just a big, huge turtle that Ug found and brought him to the island on his boat. He was drowning in a net. So now he just kicks back. This here is the sand spit of misfortune [see Figure 5.21 just behind the two faces]. You get caught in the sand spit and the sand spit will ask you three questions about your life, and if you're not honest about it, it will eat you up. This is Ug's cave [found in Figure 5.21 at the left rear]; it looks small, but once you get inside and crawl down it opens up into a big, old huge thing. This over here is the hole to the center of the world [found in Figure 5.21 just in front of the boat], you get caught in there and it sucks you down. If you get sucked down there you just stay there forever and ever with the bad people. The ship can go over that. The island is for everybody who is a misfit, or who thinks they are a misfit. They can just think about the island and all the people who are having fun there and have a place to go in their head. They can just kick back and relax and do what they want to.

Therapist: Well, that was an excellent story. What is the moral of the story?

Randy: That every misfit has a place in life even though he doesn't think he does. There is somebody who will help them, but they need to get up and work and try to find it.

Therapist: You also told a story within a story about Thug and the gold, what is the moral in that story?

Randy: You need to talk and trust people sometimes even when you know they might be lying to you because it could get you killed, or hurt, physically or mentally, if you don't.

In Randy's story the theme of misfits takes precedence. Each character on Paradise Island can be said to symbolize Randy at different stages of his life. Ug is Randy in the present ("all Ug wanted to do was live by himself") as well as the idealized personality ("Ug found him [monkey] and brought him to Paradise Island" [Ug as a competent rescuer]). Additionally, Thug with his ever-present knife represents evil, something feared. His relationships parallel the aggressive characteristics of Randy's interactions, as well as the abusive familial relations. The monkey seems to represent Randy in his hurt, infantile state as the smaller entity in the family unit who is cast aside. The bear, another cast-aside entity, appears to correlate to Randy's removal from his home ("The bear's parents are brown bears, but he was a polar bear, and so the Paradise Island climate is just right for everybody . . . so he has to live there"). Interestingly, magical components in his story are either out of reach (boat), evil (hole to the center of the world), or based upon strictly superego manifestations (the spirit faces and the sand spit).

Overall, Paradise Island has been populated with those who have been cast aside from the mainland, a group of misfits where Ug has found a measure of self-esteem and regard. Unfortunately, the "guidance" that is available is not being utilized and instead sits idle awaiting counsel. Instead, the group is content to "just kick back and relax and do what they want to" on an island based upon inner desires and primitive impulses.

In response to Randy's story the following narrative was related:

Therapist: Once upon a time there was a young man named Ug who came to the island because he wanted to escape the mainland. The mainland was evil where a lot of bad things happened to Ug. He decided he had enough of that, and he built his own ship and sailed the magical ship far away into the sea beyond all signs of land. He came upon an island that was not on any map and he named it Paradise Island. Ug was living happily and built a hut and lived alone with the animals who treated him nicely, until one day this guy named Thug came on the island who said he was there to get him. Ug was surprised and professed his innocence. Thug stated, "You've stolen my gold and that's why you ran to this island and hid." Ug continued to profess his innocence, but Thug didn't believe him. Thug tried to get at Ug, but he couldn't because Ug was being protected by the friendly bear. The bear was very powerful, as powerful as any brown bear. This bear was Ug's protector. Ug ran toward the ship while Thug was busy and he accidentally slipped into the quicksand. As he was sinking, the elephant came by and rescued Ug, who ran to the ship and was now protected by the dragon. He did not know what to do until the monkey came to him and told him to go work out the problem with Thug. Ug then went to the wise turtle, who explained to Ug that he needed to show Thug that he had no need for gold as they were very rich on the island. All the animals, with Ug, went to confront Thug and explained it to him as the turtle had said. Thug still didn't believe him because he was a very angry person. As Thug chased Ug he tripped and was hit on the head with a coconut. While he was sleeping, he dreamed that two good spirits came to him and begged him to change his ways and apologize. Thug desperately wanted to change, and he dropped the knife in his hand and apologized to the others. Now that Thug lived on the land the animals helped Ug by making him a larger home [see Figure 5.22], above the ground, and making him better

5.22 *Ug's New Home*

clothing. The two became good friends, and they lived happily ever after.

Randy: What about the misfits?

Therapist: Anyone can come, but they can only come in peace. That is why Ug now lives above the ground. He is not fearful any longer.

Randy: What's the moral of your story?

Therapist: Go to others to protect you and resolve your conflicts without violence.

This story depicts Ug as being competent through action ("he built his own ship") rather than resorting to isolation in order to escape the abusive relationship. Moreover, the bear (a symbol of Randy's inferiority) is friendly and "as powerful as any brown bear," while the animals, far from being slothful outcasts, work together in unity. In this retelling Ug seeks counsel from the wise and venerated superego symbols, but he must complete the task for himself by mustering courage and strength. The story indicates that one accomplishes goals not by wishing, daydreaming, or hoping, but through action.

Therefore, the theme in this story revolves around cooperation and the sharing of oneself with others, all skills necessary to navigate the stage of

5.23 The Island of Guidance

latency and adolescence. This is an important point to stress in order to counteract Randy's misfit feelings that lead toward aggression or isolation. Additionally, Randy had continued to experience sporadic nightmares that encompassed visions of harbingers of death. Although solving conflicts through magical means is not realistic, the dream sequence that Thug experiences, in all its care and friendliness, was added to communicate to Randy that sleep can facilitate healing.

Throughout the retelling of his story Randy listened in awe. He appeared fascinated with the process of creating (both verbally and kinesthetically) and found special interest in listening to the tape of the session. This entire project took 4 weeks to complete (3 to create the setting and 1 to tell the stories). Due to his connection to the process, I initiated a sequel to the Paradise Island project. Figure 5.23 depicts the Island of Guidance.

> *Therapist:* Welcome back. I am here with our storyteller, Randy, and we are going to tell a sequel to our last story, "Paradise Island." So, without further ado, our storyteller will tell us briefly about the characters on the Island of Guidance.
>
> *Randy:* This brown tower [Figure 5.23] is the Rock of Hope that tells if

5.24 Bob, the Monster Terrell, and John

you have any hope or where to seek guidance. The blue ball on top points to guidance. The characters [see Figure 5.24] are Bob in the blue cape, John in the poncho, and Terell, who is a monster. This is the bridge of guidance. The raft is coated in gold and is blessed by God. If the ball points to it, it's supposed to lead them to knowledge, and it will take them to the person who can seek knowledge.

Therapist: I introduce to you Randy with his story of the Island of Guidance.

Randy: The story begins with a monster that comes from beneath, and he was condemned by a higher power when he was little. What the higher power did was put a rope around him saying that the only way he can remove the rope, which took away his happiness, was to find the guidance he needed to succeed. He was clever and smart and waited until someone came along to show him the guidance. Finally he heard of the Island of Guidance and he went to seek the truth. When he arrived he first tried to trick them [Bob and John], but they were wise to his ways. Then he tried to force them, but they were wise to his ways and they hid on Paradise Island and were protected by Ug and Thug who hid them. Terrell's time was almost up and he would have to go back beneath the sea and he started begging them to take off the rope. He said he didn't want to stay down where he was because it wasn't a nice place. He then asked them nicely and they pointed him to the guidance. He climbed the rope and was told that he needed to apologize for what he did and not to do it again. Then he got the rope off of him and he too became very wise in the ways of others and started helping them.

Therapist: How did he get the rope off?

Randy: When he found the guidance he needed, he thought it in his head and the rope lost what it was supposed to do, you know, take away his happiness, and it fell off.

Therapist: You said when he first came to the island people were afraid of him?

Randy: Yes, when he first came he was trying to trick them and they thought he was a sly monster. It was like when Thug first came to Paradise Island thinking that Ug had gold.

Therapist: What is the moral of the story?

Randy: Instead of trying to abuse people and getting what you want, try to ask them.

In the sequel Randy now begins to identify with a "monster" who through no fault of his own was condemned at a young age. If we interpret this story from a developmental point of view, Randy has taken us from the stage of infantile hopes (waiting for another to meet needs) to that of adolescence, with its models of leadership. As we walk through the story we see Randy's infantile hopes of care and nurturance only assuaged when Terrell the monster "went to seek the truth." This autonomous attitude forced him to initiate a search; however, his response remained primitive, and he attempted first to deceive and, when that did not work, then to bully the benevolent superego symbols (Bob and John, who are the only beings to possess the molded faces—perhaps an unconscious representation that such goodness cannot be manufactured from our own hands). This regression gives way to humility as he speaks to the wise counsel about his anxiety-laden fears. Terrell is then seen climbing the rope (industry) and in receiving guidance is able to help others through care and trustworthiness.

With this interpretation the following story was told:

Therapist: Once upon a time there was a man named Ug who lived on Paradise Island who had a misunderstanding with Thug a long time ago, but they resolved their differences and they are now friends. They work well together and have built a house. They find out that there are problems on a neighboring island, and soon Terrell shows up at Paradise Island, and he is vexed with all types of problems. Someone had cast a spell on him when he was very young. Terrell came to Paradise Island to bully and trick Ug and Thug, but the power of friendship was too strong for anyone to harm them and they saw through his anger. So Ug and Thug sent Terrell to the Island of Guidance to get help, and they built a bridge that provided shelter and light for his trip. Terrell went to the Island of Guidance and he was scared and frightened. But once he arrived he noticed the caring and gentle expressions of the wise men and he spoke with them. They told him to climb the rope, but it was very difficult. It took him a long time to reach the top, but he never gave up. Once there, the blue ball revealed his inner secrets and showed him a true reflection of himself. He was not a monster. In the process the rope around him uncoiled [note that at this point Randy began to uncoil the rope]. He also trimmed his claws, as they were unnecessary. Then Terrell and the wise men, Thug and Ug, lived happily ever after.

Randy: What is the moral of the story?

Therapist: The moral is that no one is a misfit who is willing to look at the truth.

In this retelling, the story combines the misfit theme with a thrust toward cooperation, but it also presents Ug and Thug as competent guides who take care of not only one another but others in pain. Compared to Randy's, this story offers a healthier adaptation, as it involves action by all the characters, protagonists and antagonists. Once Terrell (the lost youth condemned) found the strength to seek help and support, he was offered a true reflection of himself: He was not a monster. As Randy enters the fantasy play and uncoils the ropes (Figure 5.25), he is symbolically allowing happiness to envelop not merely Terrell but himself. This metaphorical gesture is significant because Randy takes action against his past rather than passively reliving the experiences.

Both projects combined (Figure 5.26; see disk to view in color) took over 8 weeks to complete, and during this time Randy's behavior in the environment improved. His peer relationships were less strained, and he experi-

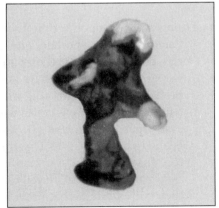

5.25 Terrell Before and After

5.26 Randy's Projects Combined

enced a significant decrease in the amount of nightmares. Prior to working evocatively, Randy had spent much of his time attempting to change the environment; his punitive retaliations caused further rejection and intensified his internalized sense of himself as a "monster." The symbolic abundance of ideas pointed toward Randy's traumatic experiences in the safe forum of symbolism. With every story and subsequent retelling, Randy allowed himself to identify with the characters he had created as well as internalizing their awareness, insight, problem solving, and affiliation. In the fantasy of play he was hero and villain, rescuer and child. Through the method of the mutual storytelling technique, he shared his suffering and opened the door for corrective healing of his experiences.

In the end, I believe that the use of storytelling allowed Randy the initial release of the fundamental problems that both confounded and occupied his thoughts.

CHAPTER

6

Group Therapy Illustrated

To this point we have focused upon the individual and the relationship between client and therapist. I hope that the instances provided made clear that the manner in which we relate and solve problems is established within earlier periods of our lives. These past memories, behaviors, and feelings define the individual and his or her place within the world. As we turn our focus to the group therapy hour, the microcosm of individual therapy becomes a macrocosm of characterological issues. From the moment the individual enters the group circle he or she assumes the roles, behaviors, and responses of a lifetime to meet the growing stressors of the moment. Consequently, these behavioral exchanges convey an enormous amount of information for the psychodynamic therapist.

For the purposes of this chapter we will be incorporating the therapeutic techniques of art therapy with the theoretical foundations of Irvin Yalom. In this way, the interactions within the group center on interpersonal learning through the expression of the here-and-now experience. Although the focus of this chapter is the client and his or her relationship to the environment, do not think for one moment that the group leader has it easy. That which is important in the individual hour (transference reactions) is equally important in the group therapy hour, for the leader of any group must come to terms with his or her own issues, strengths, and weaknesses in order to be effective. Thus, it is imperative that the clinician's needs and expectations are not projected onto the group.

Similarly, you must explore your comfort level surrounding feelings discussion, angry reactions, and frustration with defiance or dependency issues to provide a corrective interpersonal experience.

Additionally, the group leader must decide upon a framework for the hour, for, unlike individual therapy, an unstructured group can turn rebellious as anxiety rises and old patterns of interpersonal relationships come into play. This tendency is especially pronounced when you are working with the difficult client. However, the incorporation of art therapy significantly eases the process of group interaction. Art therapy's inherent qualities provide the necessary levels of task introduction, completion, and discussion, together with an opportunity to speak, review, and offer feedback on an equal basis.

In reviewing the structure as it has been outlined, let's begin with task introduction. When working with an art production, this would be the implementation of the art directive. As stated in Chapter 4, the clinician can choose to preassign directives based upon the long-term objectives or develop an agenda based upon the needs at the moment. In any event, the use of directives, both verbal and pictorial, has distinct purposes, which Jay Haley (1976) has outlined:

> First, the main goal of therapy is to get people to behave differently and so to have different subjective experiences. Directives are a way of making those changes happen. Second, directives are used to intensify the relationship with the therapist. By telling people what to do, a therapist becomes involved in the action. . . . Third, directives are used to gather information. (p. 56)

Although Haley was referring to verbal directives rather than pictorial ones, this quote remains relevant to a discussion of the introduction of art therapy interventions into the therapeutic hour. As we saw in prior chapters, art therapy not only affords the individual an opportunity to practice new ways of behaving in a safe environment but also provides opportunities for assessment as well as the forging of a relationship, both individually and collectively. In addition, the metaphorical quality of the art production allows the client to express unconscious responses without the confrontation that verbal insight would engender.

When we evaluate the structure of group therapy based upon task completion, we see that the application of an evocative therapy inherently draws each member into the process by concentrating their attention upon the directive. Within the concreteness of the task every client, regardless of diagnosis, ability, or age, can participate, accomplish, and experience competency. Even in difficulty the client can receive support, encouragement, and the kindness of staff and his or her peers to work through a problem toward success.

Figure 6.1 provides an example (see disk to view in color). This drawing

6.1 Raven Mountain

was completed by a significantly depressed adult male. This rendering most likely stirs nothing special within the viewer. It certainly does not stand out as a milestone in treatment, yet it is exactly that. For a period of 5 months this adult male symbolically rendered his social isolation through the monochromatic hue of a black marker on a white page. These drawings, in stark contrast to his peers' often brightly colored renderings, symbolized an interpersonal separation that was also behaviorally evidenced outside of the group therapy hour.

Yet on this day, and each subsequent day thereafter, this gentleman accented his monochromatic drawing with color (inside the sun, around the tree foliage). Thus, Figure 6.1 was a milestone in his progression toward a group identity or what Yalom (1985) termed "universality." Yalom notes that when universality is absent, isolation prevents the individual from experiencing intimate relationships. This narrow frame of reference removes the client from the give and take of daily living, where instead of affiliation and feelings of "membership" there is division and a sense of alienation.

As important as Figure 6.1 was, it was not the only therapeutic factor signifying change that occurred in that group. The addition of color was not an independent idea. A group member sitting near this client initiated contact of his own volition with the artist of Raven Mountain and prompted him toward the addition of color. This spontaneous, altruistic exchange and its resultant consequences met with acceptance, praise, and pride of accomplishment for both members. In fact, this gesture and the ensuing recognition created a foundation toward group cohesiveness and socialization.

As Yalom (1985) stated, "universality, like other therapeutic factors, cannot be appreciated separately. As patients perceive their similarity to others and share their deepest concerns, they benefit further from the accompanying catharsis and from ultimate acceptance . . . by other members" (p. 9).

Consequently, this brings us to the final task of group, the discussion phase. Although I have focused largely on the completion of the directive, it is imperative that the group leader ascertain the proper amount of time required for a verbal review of the art work. The symbolic and oral expression by each member provides invaluable insight into the client's instinctive self. A self that is often controlled during mere verbal expression can be revealed through the creative and kinesthetic undertaking of the artwork. As a result, the process of sharing becomes a uniquely personal and integrating experience. Keep in mind, however, that "the role of the therapist is to create the right atmosphere and facilitate and catalyze the therapeutic process so that the group will not become simply a social gathering" (Kymissis & Halperin, 1996, p. 31).

In this chapter I describe three types of structured exercises that promote interpersonal learning: (1) the here-and-now interaction, (2) empathy, and (3) self-disclosure. These categories of interpersonal learning have been summarized from Yalom's (1983, 1985) influential work on group therapy and have been adapted to fit an evocative framework.

The Here-and-Now Interaction

In working with the difficult-to-treat client, an interpersonal process group becomes an essential component for therapeutic change. For it is within the group that interpersonal difficulties surface, maladaptive interactions are identified, and feedback can be provided. Thus, the group's focus is not upon the history of individual members but instead upon the here-and-now interactions that drive their repetitious patterns of behavior. In short, the immediate events in the group members' lives provide the direction, while the exploration of the group members' interactions provides the impetus for change. It is imperative that both factors be present, for, without the transactional processes among and between the clients, the learning will not be generalized.

Incorporating art therapy into Yalom's therapeutic strategies is an effective method for achieving both goals. When you incorporate an evocative therapy, such as art, into the process you make a powerful tool supreme, for not only do you have the verbal interactions, but you also have a permanent record in the form of the artwork to refer to and explore. This transitional object is present for all to see and encourages members not merely to interact but to examine those interactions both as participants and as observers.

Often work with the residential client or inpatient group is criticized because many view these clients as incapable, incorrigible, unwilling, disinclined, or all of these things. Yet I believe that, for just those reasons, group therapy must facilitate interaction that cultivates and fosters interpersonal learning. These individuals frequently spend hours in one another's company, and the therapeutic ward milieu provides a multitude of encounters. Thus, the group setting can assist in the development of realistic interpersonal goals, promote group leadership skills, and nurture new resolutions.

By way of example a group of adult males were paired and instructed to "find two ways in which the two of you are alike and two ways in which you are different [Yalom, 1983, p. 298]. When you are done, draw your responses." In this exercise each pair had four distinct tasks to complete: (1) to verbally interact, (2) to render the discussion symbolically, (3) to discuss their differences and similarities with the rest of the group members, and (4) to illuminate the process.

If you recall the individual case history on John (Chapter 5), this grossly disorganized, lonely, and detached male was involved in individual and group therapy to address his many issues. John was one half of the pair that we will focus on in this discussion. His companion was a 20-year-old developmentally delayed male with a significant history of substance abuse, passivity, and social isolation, whom I will call Martin. During the first stage of the directive John, instead of asking questions, blurted out a description of Martin that was wholly inaccurate. He decided that Martin was a Catholic preacher, much like his delusion about himself. Martin, on the other hand, wanting to abide by the rules of the directive (much as a 9-year-old would), attempted with composed redirection to gather information from John. John was not to be swayed from his fantasy productions, however, so Martin's responses moved from initial calm to frustrated anger, then to humorous acquiescence, and finally to withdrawal.

When the group was instructed to begin the drawing phase, Martin marked off two squares for John and two for himself. This act of boundary making provided Martin the distance he required and provided John with a structured base to ground his fantasy productions. Additionally, it allowed Martin to move from a paired identity to one that was more comfortable, an individual identity.

As the group moved into the discussion phase, John again resorted to imaginary descriptions that frustrated Martin as he attempted to correct John's delusion.

In the final stage the group undertook the examination of the here-and-now behavior that had just occurred. It is during this phase of the group process that interpersonal learning is fostered. For this reason, I began by asking the pair processing questions about their verbal and nonverbal communication. These questions ranged from "who didn't understand someone's attempt to communicate?" to "what went wrong in the communication attempt?" These clarifying questions allowed Martin to express his feelings of dissatisfaction about John's weak listening skills. Although John said little in this portion, the other group members were allowed the opportunity to comment and process relationship issues, not in the heat of anger but in a respectful give-and-take of opinions and observations. In the end, the implication about John's relationships with others was an accurate one: He preached to his partner much as he would to a congregation. Reciprocity was not evident, as John preferred to moralize rather than taking notice of others in his environment. After some time, John was able to state, "I'm not a listener, and a listener is a good friend."

The group also processed Martin's patterns of behavior during the exercise through questions such as "how did you feel when you asked for something and got refused or rejected?" and "what signs or body language did you give that told John how you were feeling?" These inquiries moved the focus from John to the self and forced Martin to look personally and exclusively at the impact of his own behavior.

In Figure 6.2 we see another group responding to the directive "After separating your paper into three sections, draw a wish for yourself, a wish for someone in the group, and a wish for the group as a whole." I gave this directive to help the group transition from a self-absorbed and often dependent manner of relating to one that focused on relationships outside of the self.

Figure 6.2 typifies the conflicting emotional wishes of many clients. The wish to change coupled with the feeling that change is an insurmountable obstacle produces fantastical wishes that become much more fulfilling than reality. In this case the client wished for a pot of gold; with each word his verbal explanation gained intensity as he imagined the multitude of purchases he was going to bestow upon those in his life. The verbal dialogue filled the room with such a sense of pride, mingled with power, that every group member was immediately drawn into the fantasy.

Inside the image: "A POT of GolD", "Feeding", "AND", "Go BACK TOO THe WiTh A New Ou...", "COMMUNITY"

6.2 My Three Wishes

At this juncture, the members became highly involved and interactive, yet it was the examination of the process that afforded the group the most important step toward change—clarification. In this vein, I shifted focus away from the sheer enjoyment of whimsy and toward an emphasis on re-sponsibility and the present behavior that interfered with their hopes and desires. Thus, I encouraged them to see the pot of gold as the prestige, re-spect, and freedom that money affords. The processing questions in this session revolved around the issue "how does it feel to daydream about un-limited admiration, self-esteem, and independence?"

It was only in the following group meeting that the group members were able to process the third section of each rendering. In this session I placed importance on the opposition of autonomy and dependency reactions, or what Yalom described this way: "To attain what I really want, I must change" (1985, p. 176). In this phase of the group process we explored the dependency of institutionalized living, discussed the group members' com-monalities and differences, and managed the maladaptive interactions.

In the end, I used the verbiage of the drawing as the question about change: "What is a new outlook on life that you have adopted?"

The last example from this same group of males is illustrated in Figure 6.3. For this session the group was offered copious amounts of plasticene clay and a single piece of white cardboard and instructed to "create a group

6.3 Members of a Larger Whole

sculpture." I gave no further comments and instead watched the group navigate the task, not merely as individuals but as members of a larger whole.

As with all here-and-now interactions, the primary focus is the immediate relationships and interactions of the group members. In combining this approach with art therapy, one creates a visual experience that has the ability to break through the well-honed verbal defenses acquired over a lifetime. In this way, each individual's three-dimensional work revealed his or her internal concerns, issues, and needs before feedback and discussion even began.

One male with significant organic deficits metaphorically illustrated his need for structure and support as he spent the majority of the group session forming a foundation out of his clay. When his peers pointed out to him that the cardboard paper would be the base, he abandoned the underpinning he had so carefully worked on and created the walls for the house.

Another member, a chronic schizophrenic, formed the fencing that runs the length of the project, symbolizing his need for boundaries that function to contain as well as protect. A regressive schizophrenic fashioned three bears and placed them in front of the home, while a developmentally delayed young adult superfluously fantasized about living with Goldilocks and cooking meals together.

The leader of the group produced the items meant for transportation, while the coleader anxiously instructed others in the finishing of the details. Ultimately, he focused his attention on the house's roof and the profuse smoke that metaphorically symbolized his inner tension.

I took these observations into consideration and wove them into the dialogue to foster illumination of the process. Consequently, my questions revolved around how the group made decisions ("who were the leaders of the group project today?" and "who can you hide behind in group when you prefer to withdraw?"), their tendency to defer judgment to others ("were you satisfied with the judgments of others?" and "how did you feel about being told what to do?"), and the personal symbols that emerged in the three-dimensional creations ("how important is it for you to have clear, concise instructions to build upon?"; "how do you close yourself off to others in this group?"; and "how do you protect yourself when you feel lonely, anxious, or trapped?").

In a case in which I worked with female preteens and adolescents the initial project began as individual pursuits (simplistic cooperative tasks) and ended one and one half months later with my directing them to take all of their two- and three-dimensional items and create "a group sculpture." As Landgarten (1981) stated, "working towards large group work in stages lessens group anxiety and assists group cohesiveness" (p. 306).

For ease of interpretation I have chosen to focus on one child's verbal and nonverbal productions. This 13-year-old client (whom I will call Sarah) has a tendency to express herself through fantasy production and obsessional rumination. When frustrated, she exhibits aggressive outbursts that are accompanied by infantile traits such as baby talk and tantrums. Sarah's social relationships are marred by her passive-dependency: She disregards the personal boundaries of others in her childlike self-absorption.

Sarah had been a frequent participant in my art therapy groups and thus was familiar with the framework of task introduction, completion, and feedback. However, the processing of the here-and-now interactions was relatively new to all of the girls; therefore, I made a conscious effort to ease their anxiety about the intensified communications.

One of the first directives I gave was a pass-around assignment (refer to Chapter 4 for specific information). The group members were inherently familiar with this exercise, and it was one they enjoyed. Figure 6.4 is Sarah's completed production, which she titled "The Maze."

Sarah was the only group member who asked others what they wanted on their initial board, which included crumpled tissue paper, feathers, pom-poms, and markers. Although others freely copied her technique of crumpling the tissue paper before applying it, they singled Sarah out for ridicule when her title mimicked another's. This form of communication was one that Sarah was ultimately comfortable with, as the scenario pro-

6.4 The Maze

vided her with attention and the opportunity to play the discouraged victim or flamboyant innocent.

Figure 6.5, the result of the second directive of the larger group project, was basically a free drawing in which they were instructed to "create anything you wish that complements your first art piece." In this assignment Sarah again provided the momentum for imitation, as the other members covertly followed her lead. However, as Sarah drew a self-portrait and added her dream boyfriend, Harry Potter, these internal fantasy productions became overwhelming, and she began to mutter her desires aloud. When her peers derided her verbalizations, she began to furiously add items to her drawing.

She began by adding a series of five clouds, and then to the left of the self-portrait she drew two more suns. Again, Sarah's vulnerability is tangible. Her invented realities (whether fantastical, behaviorally isolative, or verbally affected) provided an escape from her ineffective attempts to cope with social interaction, pressures, and conflicts.

When we began to process the here-and-now interactions (with questions like, "can you think of an example when you judged someone in group today?" and "how did you express your anxiety when frustrated or ner-

6.5 I'm Going to Marry Harry Potter

vous?"), many of the group members were stunned. Discussions on their immediate communication had not been managed with such depth, and the group began to grow restless. As a way to integrate what they had experienced and to offer support for the group's effort, I asked the members to complete the following sentence: "Today I was proud of _____." This unaccompanied declaration offered an opportunity to both state and receive an admiring comment and provided closure to the formal group discussion. Sarah's sentence completion was "Today I was proud of me!"

The third directive in the series was to "choose a three-dimensional object and decorate it in any way you wish."

Figure 6.6, the resulting art production (see disk to view in color), offers the reader an example of a process that Kramer (1971) termed chaotic or emotional discharge. Kramer describes this regressive use of the art materials as "spilling, splashing, pounding; destructive behavior leading to loss of control" (p. 54).

Prior to the completion of these boxes, Sarah had entered the group session in a restless mood. It took her many moments to settle into her seat and even longer to begin the project. She initially chose the box on the left and painted it in the brightest pink available. After she swept the color across the box, immersed in the process, she added green polka dots, which

6.6 Sarah's Boxes

escalated her enjoyment. Her peers watched cautiously as the paint took on a life of its own. It sloshed out and around her project as her excitement spiraled upward until she abandoned the paint brush and began to smear the colors into one mass of brownish black.

In short order this regression had become part of Sarah's obsessional rumination. The only thing to return her to a state of calm would be the removal of the paint supplies. This tangible intervention served to calm Sarah's frenzied behavior, and I offered her markers and the choice of a second box. She chose a clear plastic container (right side of Figure 6.6) and swirled a variety of colors onto all sides. As her motions gained momentum, she again reverted into a chaotic loss of control, and since the marker ink would not dry on the plastic surface of her box, she touched the box to the tip of her nose (leaving a dot) and placed her fingertips on strategic parts of her face and arms.

By now, Sarah had become the center of attention. Some of the girls stared in dismay; others laughed, which served as encouragement; and others berated her for her immaturity. These reactions did little to contain Sarah's anxiety and instead provided reinforcement for her continued regression. I removed the second box and instructed her to clean up her area and wash her hands and face. This shift from self-absorption to performing concrete and tangible tasks offered Sarah the time she needed to coalesce, return to the group, and join the discussion phase.

However, rather than focusing the discussion on Sarah's metaphorical communication—something she would have no doubt enjoyed, as any attention is good attention—I elected to ameliorate the anxiety by focusing on relationship goals. Consequently, I asked each group member to respond to a closure directive in an orderly fashion. The directives were "Name one thing you are going to work on so that you can improve your relationships in future groups" and "Name one thing that you accomplished in group that was good." In response to these directives Sarah stated that she would be "less silly" and "I cleaned up the mess I made."

The following week I planned the exercise carefully. Through the implementation of structured directives and media, I intentionally provided boundaries that I hoped would contain any residual anxiety. Additionally, before beginning group I asked each member to repeat her relationship goal of the previous week and charged each with working toward that objective in this group.

In this session the directive was to draw three lines on the cardboard tube (Figure 6.7). Then, one step at a time, I instructed them to add two

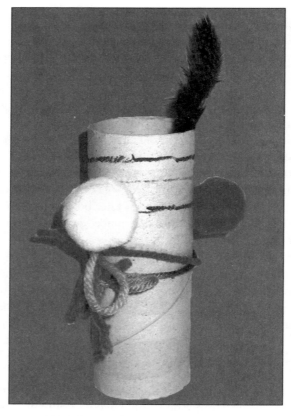

6.7 What a Difference a Directive Makes

254

pom-poms, one feather, and two strings, and to write their name. If you compare Figure 6.7 with Figure 6.6, the differences are profound.

Although less expressive than Sarah's prior creation, Figure 6.7 indicates a level of organization and group interaction that was constructive both pictorially and verbally. In the feedback stage of the group Sarah's peers praised, and thus reinforced, behavior that was not regressive. Through the groups verbal statements Sarah was able to find a measure of self-esteem and regard through belonging to a larger group.

In the last directive before the group was to combine all the projects, the girls were directed to "draw a wish." This simple directive brought a squeak of delight from the majority of girls, who immediately began illustrating their wedding day. Figure 6.8, Sarah's project, depicts Sarah as a princess.

Throughout the discussion Sarah attempted to enter into the fantasy of the drawings rather than the reality of the present. Each time she reverted to these infantile productions I posed questions about the value of effective communication and contributing through cooperative interactions. By accentuating the here-and-now these process-oriented statements underscored the reasons for Sarah's failed relations and offered her the opportunity for a corrective experience.

6.8 Draw a Wish

In the final stage of this project I gave the members all of their art productions and instructed them to work cooperatively to make a sculpture. I then left the group with the task of making group decisions through listening, leading, and collaboration.

It took quite a while for them to begin. They sat quietly looking at the box, then looking at each other, then scrutinizing the media I had supplied, then looking at each other again. Eventually, one member took her pom-pommed pass-around assignment and attached it to the box. This then began a flurry of activity, in which Sarah followed suit until she felt comfortable enough to branch out and create the inside of the project (left side of Figure 6.9).

In complete silence the group members moved around the room as they constructed the outside of Figure 6.9 (right side) by enlarging the walls and adding felt, colored yarn, and more drawings.

When they were satisfied with their work, they took their seats and gazed at the once-disparate creations that now formed their group sculpture. To complete the process I asked them to decide upon a title. Sarah was the first to offer one—"The House"—which the group rejected out of hand even though the members had identified the items on the inside as a television, table, shower, and so on. Sarah attempted to promote her title by again clarifying the contents both inside and outside, but to no avail.

As the girls struggled with the collaborative effort of making a group decision, Sarah listened attentively and then offered the title of "The Haunted Mansion." The group accepted this title, and we moved into the here-and-now discussion.

The first question I posed was "who was the leader during this group?" Without hesitation Sarah yelled, "Me!" and then attempted to verbally justify her statement, which completely disregarded the roles of her peers.

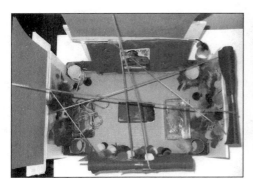 

6.9 *Inside and Outside the Haunted Mansion*

With input from the group she corrected and amended her comment by noting that she had been a follower in the beginning but took the lead to title the project.

As this group proceeded, Sarah's interactions focused less on the self and more on reciprocal identification. This progress, the beginning stages of group identity, marked a nodal point of change, as all members to varying degrees began the process of mutuality.

Empathy

When using structured exercises toward empathic understanding, it is integral that the client's subjective here-and-now experience allow him or her not merely familiarity but also a means to get in touch with the personal identification of another. This awareness of feelings, emotions, and behavior spans the self and broadens into the larger community of group insight.

In working with the low-functioning client, Michael Monfils (1985) has outlined three philosophical constructs as they relate to a theme-centered group. The first principle "promotes the autonomy and separateness of each individual but also emphasizes the fact that group members need one another and are connected" (p. 178). The second concept concerns a triangle of connections. In this triangle, "the 'I' represents each individual person. . . . The 'We' stands for the consciousness of the group members of the fact that they are a group, and the 'It' is the theme or focus" (p. 178). The last formulation is what he calls the "globe." Simply stated, this is the structure of the group, including everything from time and place of meeting to the outlined objectives.

In my work with the difficult-to-treat client I have found these theoretical beliefs to be invaluable. A low-functioning client tends to focus on the immediate needs of the self and in so doing forgoes the awareness, acknowledgement, and needs of others within his or her circle. In this manner, the client gains neither empathy nor insight.

In the following example a group of residentially placed teenage males met in an open group setting for 1 hour a week. This group comprised a variety of diagnoses, with the majority falling within the Pervasive Developmental Disorder category concomitant with mild to moderate mental retardation. These young men lived together, attended school together, took their meals together, and in so doing spent nearly every waking hour together. Additionally, their cognitive disabilities and low self-esteem produced a one-sided empathy that ignored the feelings of others and consisted mainly of simplistic responses to process-centered exploration.

If we refer to the three philosophical constructs outlined by Monfils and apply them to art therapy directives, the straightforwardness of the pass-around directive embraces the first two flawlessly: Each member interacts autonomously (by first working on his or her project separately), and the subsequent passing of the artwork epitomizes their connection to one another. Moreover, every step of the art production allows each individual to focus on the self—and on the interactions in and among the group members—and provides the impetus for the processing of the here-and-now interactions.

As an example, consider the pass-around project I instituted involving collage imagery and paper plates. Each group member was to choose a collage image and glue it to the paper plate. After this was completed I instructed members to pass the plate to their right and to keep doing so (at predetermined times) until their original image was in front of them.

Figure 6.10 shows a completed project by one of the group members. This low-functioning client chose the panda bear image, and other members within the group framed the picture by coloring the rim, accenting it

6.10 A Lack of Empathy

258

with a single line, and placing colored marks within this boundary. However, as it reached the fifth member of the group (an infantalized and angry youth placed out of the home for the first time, whom I will call Tony), this member maliciously scribbled over the collage image. As no rebuff was forthcoming, he anxiously awaited the next project, and on this one he wrote derogatory epithets. At this juncture the group took notice and began a retaliatory confrontation. It was only upon Tony's leaving the group that the verbal processing of respect, feelings expression, and trust could be explored.

However, it is important to note that Tony's imagery (what he chose and drew individually) provided a secondary level to the discussion. In reviewing his image I believed it metaphorically described his deep sense of loss, fear, and feelings of entrapment (see Figure 6.11).

Figure 6.11 is Tony's image of a spider caught in an exaggerated web (see disk to view in color). By the time Tony had passed his plate there was very little room left for others to interact. They were consequently relegated to reinforcing the spider's trap by adding circles of color. What a fearful and lonely symbol for a frightened and friendless boy.

When Tony returned to the group, timid and apologetic, the discussion focused on empathy, not merely for how Tony had defaced others' art (and therefore lost trust) but for the feelings of loneliness that all individuals feel

6.11 Tony's Caught in a Web

when removed from the security and familiarity of their homes. Through the symbolism of Tony's plate, and the subsequent interpretation, the feedback became central as the group members explored the possible fear behind Tony's anger in a mutual partnership. The importance of a mutual understanding cannot be overstated, as it is the very foundation on which objective empathic awareness is based.

One of the benefits of utilizing art therapy within the therapeutic hour is that it allows members to practice new ways of behaving in a safe and supportive atmosphere. To take advantage of this, I often link directives from one week to the next in an attempt to reinforce goals and strengthen the skills reviewed in the prior group meeting.

Accordingly, in the following group session I gave the same members a sheet of paper with predrawn black boxes. I instructed them to draw anything they wished inside the square. As they passed the artwork, I further informed them that no one was allowed to cross the boundary of the black box. In this session, unlike the previous one, Tony respected the space, feelings, and emotions of others on both a symbolic and a conscious level.

Unfortunately, Tony was not so lucky. On the second pass the victim of his earlier defacing attained revenge by drawing a circle within Tony's square. When Tony verbally protested, another peer calmly intervened and offered him a second sheet of paper (see Figure 6.12).

Tony immediately drew his initials (digitally changed) inside the box

6.12 This Is My Box

and emphasized these by encasing them within concentric squares. In so doing he symbolically asserted his sense of self while defending the space as purely his. The peer who offered Tony a second sheet of paper provided him with a constructive response to a situational stressor.

This manner of peer-to-peer interaction serves to advance the client's interpersonal learning as group members acknowledge and become concerned with one another's feelings and thoughts.

When the objective is feelings oriented, in this case empathic identification, the use of a tangible medium such as plasticene clay frequently proves beneficial. The process of creating in a three-dimensional form offers the artist a deeper level of accomplishment, because the experience of working with a physical medium requires intellectual thought, sheds light on the unconscious, and provides kinetic relief.

In a group session with high-functioning adolescent females I adapted Yalom's (1983) verbal exercise into an art therapy directive. I instructed the group to make a clay animal that represented the self and, when this was complete, to create another clay animal for the person sitting on their right. Yalom notes that "it is important to explain this exercise carefully so that the members fully understand that they are to choose on the basis not of physical resemblance, but of some trait of the animal which is similar to a trait of the person" (p. 297).

One client, the scapegoat of the group, fashioned a penguin as an image of the self and conversely created a black cat for the member to her right (see Figure 6.13). In the discussion phase she commented that the penguin characterized her since "penguins don't mind the cold," while the black cat symbolized the member to her right "because you don't want to mess with her."

6.13 Me and You

In another clay exercise, this time with adult males, I instructed the group to "make a gift out of clay and present it to someone within the group."

One young adult presented the American flag (Figure 6.14) to one of his peers and stated, "Jimmy makes beautiful things, and in case we have to add this to another project I want him to do it."

In each of these cases (Figures 6.13 and 6.14) the objects created offered a symbol of the instinctual self and provided further illumination of the unconscious. Accordingly, for the female who created the penguin, this personal symbol and her resultant verbal statement "penguins don't mind the cold" constituted a metaphor for her peer's "coldness" and her ensuing protective need to insulate herself. For all the peers, this expression, coupled with an interactive process that was largely centered on anxiety, gave impetus to planned directives that focused on acceptance, feeling motivation, and cooperation.

In this vein, it was integral for these females to experience and explore their anxiety (rather than distracting themselves through attack) in response to member-to-member interactions.

In contrast to the personal metaphor of the penguin, the flag, in Figure 6.14, has a rich history of symbolism and, in addition to being purely a personal symbol, is in many respects universal as a representation of group allegiance, honor, and independence (Matthews, 1986). Thus, its creation and presentation held numerous levels of meaning, both personal and collective. It was therefore important to process and discuss the image on a deeper level than the creator's statement ("Jimmy makes beautiful things, and in case we have to add this to another project I want him to do it").

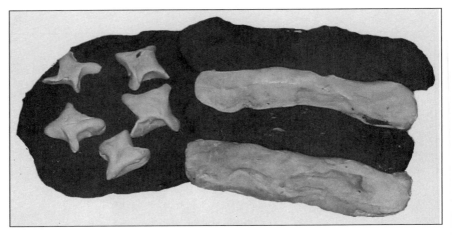

6.14 A Gift of Fidelity

The group discussion began with individual interpretations of the flag (mainly surrounding honor and pride), but soon the complexity of emotion shifted from principled hopes to inertia. This symbolic process eventually ended with the artist saying, "All my life I've lived like this. It's too late now. I messed up." The group nodded in agreement.

Within this union of despair lay the seeds for future groups—personal growth. As with other directives in this chapter, Yalom's (1983) sentence completion tasks provide an excellent foundation upon which art therapy projects can be based. In this case, the group was struggling with significant life issues surrounding a sense of competency offset by the comfort and lethargy of dependency. Thus, I gave the group directives focused on personal change in the hope that these topics would motivate the clients not only to interact but to take action against the fears that threatened to overwhelm their fragile sense of self.

One personal change directive I offered the group was to draw "the differences between your personality now and your personality five years ago" (Yalom, 1983, p. 299). The responses to this directive were as varied as the members in the group. However, it was the drawings completed by two actively recovering alcoholics (Figures 6.15 and 6.16) that encapsulated the group members' feelings.

The right side of Figure 6.15 highlights this client's lifelong struggle with

6.15 Passed Out in the Parking Lot

263

alcoholism. This drawing illustrates the complexity of emotions concerning his drinking—from the confidence gained (and now lost) in social situations to the distress associated with blackouts and multiple arrests. The client had recently begun to discuss and accept the problems associated with his heavy drinking. As a consequence, the left side of Figure 6.15 depicts the positive steps he had taken as he set his future goals and prepared for change.

In much the same manner, Figure 6.16 symbolically communicates the memories, thoughts, and feelings of another male who expresses the destructive impact of his past (hopelessness and violence) with an idealistic optimism that sheer willpower will produce freedom (butterfly and birds in upper left).

These two art tasks produced the greater part of feedback as the group members actively processed the vicissitudes of change, motivation, and daily living. In these discussions personal growth was identified by the group members as a desired goal but one out of reach as fear and apathy again overtook the group consciousness.

In response to these pervasive emotional struggles I adapted another directive from Yalom (1983) and instructed the group to draw "a change you would like to make but don't think you can." In this session the pictorial re-

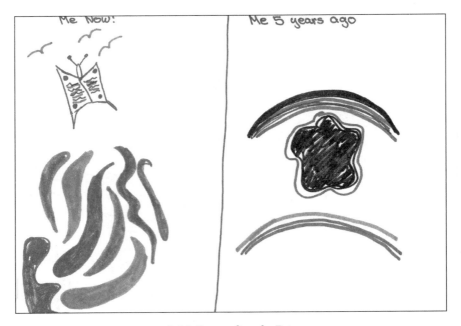

6.16 Reconciling the Pain

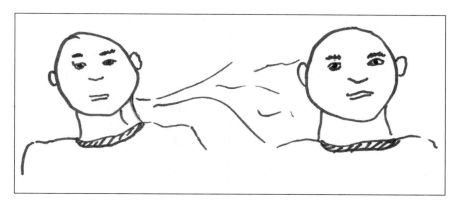

6.17 Organic Deficits

sponse that garnered the most shared affect was an illustration of mental illness (Figure 6.17). This figure was completed by a young adult who suffered from auditory hallucinations secondary to a traumatic head injury.

Due to profound cognitive disturbances, his impaired executive functioning capabilities (planning and organizing) and significant memory impairments often impeded his participation in group sessions. He would frequently require numerous sheets of paper, forget the directive, or perseverate on a single detail. However, on this day his drawing (Figure 6.17) facilitated an open interaction by exploring an issue that affected everyone—the insidious nature of mental illness.

In the discussion that followed, group members shared issues related to their lifelong struggle to attain symptom relief. For some, medication provided liberation from their delusional and often disorganized symptoms; for others, medication negated that which made them special and unique (see Figure 6.18); and for the artist of Figure 6.17 medication simply proved ineffective.

Ultimately, for this group member the artwork paved the way to a shared feelings expression that would have been nearly impossible to initiate verbally. Additionally, it allowed his peers to empathize with, appreciate, and accept another's perspective through a supportive interpersonal experience.

Self-Disclosure

In the last structured exercise we will review, self-disclosure is the foundation upon which interpersonal interactions between group members rest. Yalom (1985) specifies that "the self-disclosure may involve past or current events in one's life, fantasy or dream material, hopes or aspirations for the future, and current feelings toward other individuals" (p. 360).

As with any art therapy interaction, the active leader stance produces total group communication, from the individual creation to the process-illuminating questions; focus on a group-centered model is always foremost. For this individual and collective group investment promotes a sense of community, understanding, and intimacy, which we hope will be generalized into the larger environment.

Figure 6.18 is an example of a disclosure that produced both group understanding and reality-based discussions surrounding fixed false beliefs. Recall Figure 6.1. This depressed adult had a propensity to render his drawings in black, devoid of adequate detailing. Additionally, he only found success or glory through his delusional religious beliefs. Thus, his mood-incongruent psychotic features and his symbolic renderings afforded him a

6.18 *Happy Times*

sense of integrity, which paradoxically kept him isolated and protected from the reality of daily living.

The art therapy directive for Figure 6.18 was to "draw a significant or important event." Although this gentleman, whom I will call Alan, regularly attended group sessions, his usual pattern was to follow the instructions but remain quiet during the feedback stage. However, on this day not only did he complete the assignment, but he requested a second sheet of paper; writing on both sides, he described his "Happy Times."

Alan's story was as follows:

> A long time ago I was homeless and doing without a lot. This one day I started walking from a donut shop—I walked miles and miles on the East road out of town where there was nothing but lemon groves. There was no houses, just a hiway. After a walk of about ten miles I came upon a golf course with a college next to it. I needed a drink of water real bad. It was a Saturday I'll never forget. I entered the college and tried to get a drink of water but the water was shut off. I walked out the road of the college and I heard a voice from the sky. I looked up and saw the face of our Lord. To think our Lord cared and spoke to me. I was ever grateful and the rest of the day was beautiful.

When it was time to discuss his drawing, not only did he read his text, but he elaborated upon the events of the day as his peers asked questions. Alan stated that an apostle, sent by the Lord, appeared in a convenience store and gave him both money and food. With each response Alan became increasingly animated as he revealed feelings and emotions related to a sense of affiliation and love that affected him deeply.

Because Alan was usually reluctant to share with his peers, we discussed this act of self-disclosure not in terms of the subject matter (seeing a vision of the Lord) but in terms of the underlying emotions that each group member could relate to and explore—the need to be acknowledged, treasured, and accepted unconditionally.

Conversely, too much self-disclosure can generate distance among group members that works against intimacy and relational healing. For this reason, an individual who exhibits poor boundaries may never feel part of the larger whole if his or her attempts to improve interpersonal relations are thwarted by alienating behaviors or symptoms.

Figure 6.19 offers an example of such a dynamic. Although the completed drawing may appear innocuous, it typified the larger issues that plagued this teenager (who will be called Sally). The search for friendship and affiliation is never more intense than in the stage of adolescence, and Sally's exclusion from her larger group of peers was merciless. Her intense

6.19 From Your Best, Best Friend

desire for an intimate friendship immediately set her apart, and thus Sally took any affirmation offered by a peer as a sign of fidelity.

In one group Sally disclosed an intimate secret and received a supportive reaction from her peers. Sadly, this single success set in motion a series of indiscriminate self-disclosures that both burdened the group process and further isolated this client. Once this pattern had begun, the management of recovery spiraled downward, and regardless of the directive her renderings focused on "best friends," with each drawing being presented to select members of the group. As these were ill received (often left behind at the end of the session or thrown away as group members exited), she experienced feelings of shame. As Yalom has stated, "the high discloser is then placed in a position of such great vulnerability in the group that he or she often chooses to flee" (1985, p. 366). For this female the stress became unbearable, and she eventually retreated into the safety and confinement of her mental illness.

I contend that, as with all psychotic thought processing, the delusions are never far from the individual's internal truths. Thus, these disorganized and often nonsensical admissions can offer us a plethora of information when we pay attention to them. Sally completed Figure 6.20 roughly three weeks after completing Figure 6.19. As stated, she had been slowly decom-

6.20 *No Smoking*

pensating and, due to the nature of her illness, the stress of the member-to-member interaction and the ensuing rebuffs were too much for her fragile sense of self.

She completed Figure 6.20 in response to the directive "Draw something that is important to you." While Sally's peers were completing drawings of their families, boyfriends, and desired weddings, Sally was writing out a dialogue between a father and mother. The drawing focused on a pregnant woman who is protecting her unborn child from the secondhand smoke of the father. Sally whispered the mother's written comments ("you are not going to kill my baby") aloud and only paused when a helicopter flew overhead, at which point she said, "Helicopters save. They rescue people."

Although Sally's rendering was disorganized and chaotic, central to the response to "draw something that is important to you" was a theme of hope and despair found within protection, loss, respect for others, and an assertiveness of will that Sally possessed but was only able to express symbolically. For these reasons, I integrated this symbolic communication into the discussion and feedback.

Additionally, it was clear that the group was counterproductive to Sally's needs, and the ultimate self-disclosure of the drawing was her metaphorical request for protection and safety from the threatening elements in her environment. As a result, with Sally's involvement, she was provided a psychopharmacological review and placed in a group setting that could support her needs, decrease her isolation, and offer an experience of success.

When dealing with the difficult-to-treat client, incorporating self-disclosure directives is an invaluable tool in interpersonal learning and interaction. A directive that I particularly enjoy centers on issues related to comfort, care, and safety. When an individual is deprived of what Maslow (1970) termed the lower needs (i.e., safety needs based on stability and consistency), humans often choose to defend themselves through cruelty. Thus, if we are to work toward the objectives of belonging, competency, and esteem, the path often begins with security.

Figure 6.21 is a response to a polarity directive that was created by a high-functioning adult male with a diagnosis of Bipolar II Disorder. The directive was "Separate your paper into two. On the left side draw your quiet and safe place in the community. On the right draw your safe place while living here." On the left side this male drew a scene filled with fond memories: a country lake to which he made annual outings with friends. The right side of the image represents the library where he could read in solitude. Taken at face value, these responses appear to be uncomplicated. However, when asked where he was in the drawing (on the left side) he replied, "I'm walking around the cabin." When asked what he was doing inside the cabin, there was an interminable pause before he replied, "I'm walking around with a fake smile on, like I'm happy, but really I'm confused and sad. Just wandering around."

6.21 Just Wandering Around

At this juncture, both of the drawings took on a very different sentiment. This male had no safe place; even in idyllic surroundings his feelings of isolation, alienation, and insecurity were profoundly devastating.

In another example of a self-disclosure directive based on safety and security, Figure 6.22 shows the response of an adolescent male who, along with his group members, was given a sheet of paper predrawn with an empty room and instructed: "Think about a room that is safe and comfortable. It can be a real place or imaginary. Draw your room."

One of the first things this young male did in Figure 6.22 was to reinforce the door frame and place a horizontal strip across the door itself. Only after this was completed did he begin drawing the remainder of the image. In the discussion phase he wove a story in which his safe room was filled with four football fields of cars, which were all organized by type. Recalling the time spent on fortifying his doorway, I asked about the horizontal strip. It was at this point that he described an elaborate security system that required a password both when one entered and when one left. The other group members were enraptured with his description, and "ooh's" and "ahh's" were clearly audible.

As he was the only client to add safety measures in such a concrete manner, I took this addition as a demonstration of his intense need to control

6.22 A Football Field of Cars

his environment coupled with significant mistrust. For that reason, during the process of illumination my questions focused on trusting and the expression of feelings (e.g., "Can you give us examples of when you trusted someone in this group?" and "Is mistrust a common feeling in your life?").

Our final example, Figure 6.23 was completed by a 12-year-old female in response to the same directive as in Figure 6.22.

This client had recently been separated from her biological and extended family due to multiple deaths. In Figure 6.23 she recreated a trip to Las Vegas made when the family was intact. Her most vivid recollection was the time spent at the hotel pool, which she rendered to the right of the page. While relating the memory, her affect visibly shifted from pleasurable reminiscence to grief-stricken pain. Group members acknowledged this genuine emotion in the most empathic manner possible: They listened. And while she spoke she spontaneously drew a second image (Figure 6.24), a rainbow-colored heaven rendered in light, sweeping strokes. However, her feelings of loss intensified into a silent, aggressive mourning. She expressed this anger of loss by gathering a variety of markers and swiftly bringing them down on the page, effectively covering the heavens with the grief of her suffering.

The vulnerability she expressed in her self-disclosure was instrumental in creating a greater group understanding and acceptance of her often conflictual emotions of grief. Thus, this revelation provided a release for the

6.23 Las Vegas

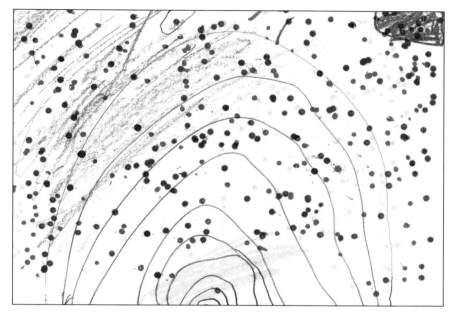

6.24 Rainbow Heaven

overwhelming feelings of anger and loss and also offered her a forum where acknowledgment and compassion overcame isolation and friendless misery.

Appendix G offers the clinician a list of sample directives divided into the types of structured exercises we have discussed: here-and-now interventions, empathy, personal change, and self-disclosure. These directives have been compiled or adapted from Yalom (1983, pp. 291–299), Cain and Jolliff (1997), and my own practice.

7

Two's Company, Three's a Crowd?
Family Therapy Directives

Whenever we speak of therapy we are truly speaking of communication. Whether it is individual, group, or family therapy, the interaction between others, both verbal and nonverbal, is paramount. Just as the here-and-now experience of group therapy provides a gauge of maladaptive responses, family therapy offers the clinician a glimpse into the influences that shaped the individual and his or her pervasive patterns of interpersonal functioning.

In short, family therapy focuses on the collective interpersonal experiences of the individual. Thus, the therapist views the individual's problems in relation to the family as a system. Whether the objectives are to uncover dysfunctional interactional patterns (Framo, 1992), develop increased adaptive functioning skills (Minuchin, 1974), develop healthy communication patterns (Satir, 1983), or differentiate the self (Bowen, 1985), the basic goal of family therapy is based not on intrapsychic content alone but instead on interpersonal process.

> Family therapists . . . believe that the dominant forces in personality development are located externally in current interactions in the family system. This is the fundamental premise of family therapy as an orientation: that people are products of their social context, and that any attempt to understand them must include an appreciation of their families. (Nichols, 1984, p. 80)

With this in mind, it is time to turn from the traditional verbal family therapy, with its multitude of approaches, to family art therapy. Hanna Kwiatkowska (1978) is often referred to as the originator of family art therapy. Through her extensive research with the National Institute of Mental Health, she developed three family art techniques. These consisted of art therapy directives combined with traditional verbal therapy, family art therapy as the primary treatment choice, and a family assessment comprising six distinct art tasks. Kwiatkowska said of these techniques:

> The families' spontaneous art productions were intended to help family members and therapists to better understand the problems in the family, to clarify family members' roles and perceptions of each other, and to constitute a therapeutically useful mode of expression and communication. (1978, p. 8)

On this basis she worked with the entire family toward the resolution of shared problems. Unfortunately, this collaborative approach, which included each member of the family regardless of age, is frequently overlooked in favor of traditional verbal family therapy. By way of example, Korner and Brown's study (cited in Lund, Zimmerman, & Haddock, 2002) surveyed 173 therapists and found that 40% never included children in family therapy sessions, while 31% invited children yet did not include them as participants.

According to sources cited in Lund et al. (2002) this condition is due to a multiplicity of reasons ranging from the inherent difficulties in engaging children in the therapeutic process to a family's diversity in developmental levels, stages, and abilities. Because of this diversity, the incorporation of the entire family unit produces, out of necessity, interventions that require both cognitive and emotional considerations. With these considerations in mind, the interactive experience of art therapy and its inherent emotional expression allow symbolic communication between parents and children regardless of age or ability. Consequently, "when the two disciplines, family therapy and art therapy, are integrated into family art therapy, they do so sharing theoretical frameworks of personality development, family systems, and the art therapy process" (Arrington, 2001, p. 4).

As with group therapy, the use of art media provides an opportunity for the clinician to watch as the familial dynamics unfold not merely on a verbal level but in a way that reveals the unconscious motivations, behaviors, and feelings that make up the family interactional patterns. And this symbolic communication, from a psychodynamic framework, is the focus of this chapter. Derivatives of the psychoanalytic school, dynamically oriented family art therapists are interested in both internal processes and interactional ones and place an emphasis on understanding and working with the unconscious mind.

However, no discussion of psychodynamic family therapy is complete without a dialogue focused on transference reactions as agents of understanding and change. In my practice I use an analysis of the transference from a here-and-now perspective. In this way, the patient-therapist relationship becomes an integral aspect of therapy, not through scrutiny only of infantile conflict but through clients' pervasive maladaptive relational patterns (Bauer, 1993).

By way of illustration, I provide Figure 7.1. This rendering is an adaptation of the Non-Verbal Family Art Task (Landgarten, 1987), in which the entire family draws on a single sheet of paper at predetermined times. In this case the family consisted of a single mother and her preteen daughter. The daughter, whom I will call Frances, had been referred to out-of-home placement due to increasingly aggressive, intrusive, and impulsive behaviors.

My first individual meetings with Frances were met with loud resistance quickly followed by temper tantrums. I knew that she had been involved in therapy for many years and often utilized coping strategies of aggressive isolation when she felt she was under scrutiny. Therefore, my approach was to

7.1 *Monkey in the Middle*

validate the anxiety by commenting aloud on our relationship, effectively bringing the acting-out behavior into a conscious realm where we could explore it.

Roughly 1 month after beginning individual therapy, Frances was able to attend to the sessions without regression. However, I did not begin family art therapy sessions until 3 months later because it was important to build a strong therapeutic alliance based upon process illumination, containment, and ego-enhancing directives to develop awareness.

In our first family session I instituted a Family Mural Drawing (Figure 7.1). Throughout the task, Frances frequently made comments like "Don't look" or "Don't watch me." Additionally, the first form item she placed on the mural was the sign that reads "Do Not Enter," while the last form item she completed was the monkey in the chair. Frances's form items are gathered into the center of the mural, while her mother's drawings surround them in a metaphor of protection and enmeshment.

As with other art therapy techniques, a family mural drawing allows the participants to be both contributor and observer. This provides the therapeutic hour with rich clinical material that in many ways is incontrovertible. This symbolic communication metaphorically parallels the interactional patterns of the entire family. Moreover, the artwork's permanency lends itself particularly well to interpreting transference reactions, as the artwork provides a tangible object that gives meaning to the experience as well as the interpretation. In these ways, the family art mural provides the mental health clinician with both interrelational examples and intrapsychic concerns that are often disguised in purely verbal communication.

As you refer to Figure 7.1, bear in mind that the mother's drawings surround her daughter's as a depiction of maternal overprotection. However, pay particular attention to the figures on the left side (drawn by the mother to represent the mother-daughter dyad). Frances's facial characteristics appear blithely secure, while the mother, clutching her daughter's hand, looks on with an expression of reflexive hostility and disapproval.

During the discussion phase, Frances identified the "monkey in the middle" as me. Although this representation of the therapist could easily be a realistic perception based upon numerous other therapists, helping professionals, and counselors in this young child's life, it is the "Do Not Enter" sign that conveys the conflict-laden anxiety as it moves from the familial home to the therapist. With her temper tantrums, her exclamations of "Don't look at me," and her outright pictorial statements of "Do not enter," Frances figuratively communicated the criticism that she both expected and feared. As Butler and Strupp (1993) have noted, "the interpersonal problems that emerge with the therapist are assumed to be similar in form to the chronic, maladaptive interpersonal patterns that underlie the patient's difficulties in living, expressed as symptoms such as anxiety and depression" (p. 195).

In response to Frances's statement that the "monkey in the middle" was me, I approached the mural as it hung on the wall and said, "So that's me? Frances, could it be that you're worried that if I did enter, I'd find things to be critical of? Maybe about you? Or your mom?"

Although the only answer I received was a resounding, "Oh, Lisa!" followed by incessant jumping and hopping about the room, the transference from an interpersonal and transactional perspective was a crucial component for continued exploration of overwhelming feelings of anxiety, discomfort, and fear for the entire family constellation.

Paired Communication Drawing

Overall, psychodynamic family art therapy unites symbolic communication with concepts related to transference reactions, the interpretation of individual as well as shared defenses, issues related to maturation, resistance, responses to inner conflict, and unconscious motivations. The process of communication can be enhanced by the implementation of art therapy directives as the family works toward productive ways of interacting. As Haley (1976) notes,

> The first and primary idea is that change occurs when the therapist joins the ongoing system and changes it by the ways he or she participates within it. When dealing with a governed, homeostatic system that is maintained by repeating sequences of behavior, the therapist changes those sequences by shifting the ways people respond to each other because of the ways they must respond to the therapist. (pp. 125–126)

In the following case example an emphasis upon the intrapsychic as well as familial interactional patterns of relating proved essential. This family consisted of a teenaged male (who we will call Gregory), his preteen brother, and a mother and father from two diverse cultures. His mother, who had traditional East Asian values, viewed her role as subservient to those of the father and her children (McGoldrick, Pearce, & Giordano, 1982). The father, an Anglo-Saxon, dictated the rules, as his authoritative role was not challenged.

In this situation the father utilized rigidity and overcontrol in an effort to keep his children compliant; when developmental issues took the forefront and Gregory reached adolescence, the father viewed Gregory's normal quest for identity as insolence. At this point the familial attachments disintegrated, and Gregory distanced himself from his family. In time his rebellion turned dangerous, as his drug use led to criminal pursuits and assaultive behaviors.

Gregory was adjudicated on his crimes and sent to residential placement for individual, group, and family therapy. In one of his first sessions he was introduced to the art room and took an immediate interest in the sand tray.

Figure 7.2, though calm in appearance, offers a glimpse into Gregory's intense aggression as the defense mechanism of displacement is employed (see disk to view in color). The sand tray, much like art therapy, gives expression to nonverbal emotional issues in a symbolic form that guards the individual from anxiety-laden conflict.

In Gregory's tray he has illustrated both enjoyment and loathing. The front of the tray symbolizes freedom (motorcycle), escape (palm trees), and a partially buried serpent (far left side), which I interpreted as representing the destructive forces that threaten from within. The back of the tray contains what Gregory described as his father watching sports on television (which was the only activity that continued to unite the two) and a graveyard (right rear), which he was reluctant to discuss. I then asked him about the praying mantis (left rear), which is situated very close to the father symbol. In an uncharacteristic explanation Gregory spoke at length about how praying mantises fight and kill their opponents with deadly accuracy.

While discussing the prowess of the praying mantis, Gregory never

7.2 Dad and the Praying Mantis

made the unconscious conscious; the praying mantis remained the acceptable repository for his fear, anger, and emotional conflicts. Additionally, this substitution was not confined to the art room or the miniatures. Gregory's interpersonal relationships were fraught with resentment as the intensity of his animosity shifted from the father to less intrusive victims.

In the early stages of family therapy I utilized quiet listening and clarification to establish a safe environment that would foster insight and growth. Gregory's symptomatic behavior began to reflect the problems surrounding the marital dyad as issues related to complementarity (Nichols, 1984) and projective identification (Klein, 1946) came to the forefront. This unconscious interactive process was maintaining the family's dysfunction.

At this juncture I instituted a paired communication drawing. The basic structure of this exercise pairs the family constellation into even teams. Often I will direct specific family members to draw with each other; however, select situations call for a less directive approach and in these cases I allow the individuals to decide for themselves. Once pairs have formed, the partners sit back to back with equal supplies (e.g., same-sized paper, same number and color of markers). After each pair appoints a leader, I direct them to think of a drawing they would like to complete. Through verbal communication the leaders help their partners to render an exact duplicate.

If you recall the case review on Dion, in Chapter 5, this technique was illustrated through his rendering of Figure 5.13. The paired communication drawing can be utilized in a multiplicity of ways and with any number of people. If you are in a group setting, or if the family has an uneven number of participants, one individual can take on the role of leader while the remainder of the group members form a horseshoe with their backs turned away from one another. As with the majority of art therapy directives, the mental health professional is hindered only by a lack of creativity. Thus, you can employ numerous variations on this technique to maximize any number of goals or objectives. This family's finished artwork appears in Figure 7.3.

Due to this family's dysfunctional interaction patterns, their invisible loyalties (Boszormenyi-Nagy & Spark, 1973), and regressive coping styles, I opted to determine the teams. I paired the mother (upper left of Figure 7.3) with her younger son (lower left of Figure 7.3) and the father (upper right of Figure 7.3) with Gregory (lower right of Figure 7.3).

As is evident from the completed drawings, the parents—the leaders of this communication-driven exercise—did not accomplish the goal of an exact rendering. The differences begin with the physical direction of the

7.3 Family Paired Communication Drawing #1

paper and end with the size and placement of the form items. In the feedback stage of this directive the family's spontaneous comments focused on these tangible, visual, and clearly noticeable differences.

Although these obvious signs engendered a spirited discussion, as I noted in Chapter 6, without illumination of the process the session will not be generalized because the interrelationships will be ignored. For this reason, I initiated a commentary on the interaction, which was fraught with conflict, power, and control issues.

Of further note is that while the mother was directing her son, he not only abandoned the task when he did not understand her direction but was verbally cruel and judgmental, blaming his difficulty on her inadequacies. Similarly, the father, while giving instructions to Gregory, became frustrated with Gregory's questions and responded in a manner that was noticeably vague and distancing.

In an effort to clarify, confront, and interpret I directed the discussion by asking the family which suggestions the partners had listened to and which ones they ignored. I followed this question by asking all the family members if they had listened the same way today as they generally did. The responses to both questions ranged from indifference and disregard (manifestation of transference by the younger son and father) to self-justification (a sense of cultural obligation on the mother's part) and reproach toward both his father and brother (defensive functioning by Gregory).

Figure 7.4 illustrates this family's second attempt at the exercise. This came about because the younger son made the brusque comment that if he had been the leader the results would have been better. Consequently, the father unexpectedly decided to give his son his wish, and the children thus became the leaders.

The left side of Figure 7.4 illustrates the younger son's final image (leader on top) and his mother's rendering below. To the right is Gregory's lead drawing (top) with his father's located beneath. Beyond the placement of the paper (which was perfect in both cases), the younger son did not produce an improved response, as he once again became frustrated and suddenly discarded the project while attempting to describe the vertical and horizontal lines. Equally, the father's aggravation became increasingly apparent as Gregory was describing the diamond shape that connected to the outer lines. Unaccustomed to following another's direction, his situation worsened by confusion and a lack of understanding, the father reacted by abandoning the effort through a palpable lack of emotional response.

In this brief case example, the technique of art therapy allowed each family member to divulge his or her underlying conflicts from a here-and-now perspective as the artwork provided a template for the transference re-

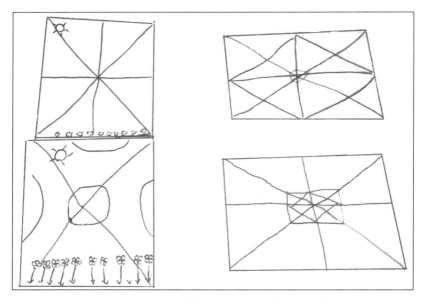

7.4 Family Paired Communication Drawing #2

actions to surface. In this way, I could explore the familial dynamics from both within and without, while the artwork assisted in developing an observing ego as emotions were not split off but instead clarified through the use of concrete directives, identification of motives, and the process of working through.

Additionally, if one believes, as Nichols (1984) has stated, that "family members reveal repressed images of past family relationships in their current interactions with family members" (p. 207), then the artwork and ensuing communication indicate past projections as well as the projective identification of the present. Thus, the resistance expressed through scapegoating of select family members (illustrated in Figures 7.3 and 7.4) reveals interactional patterns that are mutually reenacted and subsequently passed on to new generations.

Family Mural Drawing

In the field of family art therapy the family mural drawing is, in my opinion, a most impressive technique: Not only does it provide the mental health professional with a visual reference of a family's coping strategies and individual ego defenses, but it also illuminates the interpersonal, as well as the intrapsychic, aspects of the here-and-now relationship.

Jay Haley (1976) speaks of a family system in which sequences of behavior are often elaborately performed and therefore overlooked by therapists because "our cognitive attention spans seem to have difficulty with such sequences" (p. 112). In response to this problem he advocates videotaping the session in order to observe the interaction in a systematic manner.

By and large, the family mural drawing emphasizes a family's communication and captures the interactions with a permanence comparable to video: Both the product and the process of therapy can be explored, the sequential patterns of behavior clarified, and individual as well as joint protective defenses revealed.

The technique of the family mural drawing (as it will be called for the purposes of this book) exists in many variations. One popular procedure is the collaborative drawing technique (Smith, 1985). Often used in the initial sessions with a family, it is a structured nonverbal art task in which each family member takes consecutive turns drawing on a sheet of 12" × 18" paper with crayons. As each member completes his or her drawing, the time limit for each turn is gradually reduced from 30 seconds to 3 seconds, thereby increasing the task's intensity.

Correspondingly, Helen Landgarten (1987) outlines three distinct diagnostic procedures for working from a family systems perspective. The one most closely resembling the family mural drawing is the nonverbal family art task. The family is given a 12" × 18" sheet of paper. Each member is instructed to choose one marker that he or she will use throughout the exercise and takes turns drawing in silence. Unlike the collaborative drawing technique, there is no time limit; once the family members have completed the drawing, they are allowed to speak in order to title the rendering.

In contrast, the family mural drawing utilizes a sheet of 36" × 24" butcher paper that is secured to a wall. In this way the family members must approach the wall to take their consecutive turns. Unlike the collaborative drawing technique, in which the paper is on a table and the member moves to a chair to draw, using oversized paper and attaching it to a wall allows each member to watch the progression of the completed family mural drawing. Additionally, like Landgarten's technique the family mural drawing uses markers, rather than crayons, because a broad-tip marker can be handled adequately by small children and does not infantalize the older members of the family as a crayon would.

Regardless of the name, each of these techniques offers a wealth of information for the assessment of family interaction and when utilized metaphorically can provide direction for future therapeutic interventions and an increased understanding of the family functioning that defines the system.

Before we review case illustrations, the directives for the family mural drawing are as follows:

- "You are going to create a family mural. This is a nonverbal exercise, and everyone will get an even number of turns."
- Provide a basket of markers whose colors are not duplicated. Instruct each person to select one marker to use throughout the entire task.
- After they have selected markers, instruct the family to decide in what order the members will take their turns.
- Direct the first person to walk up to the paper (36" × 24") that is secured to a wall and inform the family, "Feel free to draw anything you wish. However, please do not use numbers, letters, or words. When you are done, have a seat so the next person can begin. Continue to take turns, and I'll tell you when you each have one turn left. Remember there is no talking during this exercise. Begin whenever you're ready."
- When the family has taken the prescribed number of turns (at least two

and generally no more than four), tell them, "As a family I would like you to title your drawing. You can talk for this portion of the exercise."

• After the drawing has been titled, discuss the completed family mural with a focus on illuminating the process.

Typically, a family, or select members of a family, will ask for clarification of the directives. When this is the case it is prudent to simply repeat the instructions until they understand the task rather than providing them with picture ideas. Often families will exhibit extreme difficulty in the early stages, and decisions such as who will draw first or how to pick a color will prove cumbersome. Although it may be tempting, the therapist should not intervene with the family's decision-making process. Additionally, many families will ignore the nonverbal component of the exercise and will speak with one another, either covertly or overtly. Again, it is important to confront these behaviors and restate the directives, as each of these actions typifies the family interactional process, symbolizes the internal processes of the individual, and illustrates transference reactions in the here-and-now.

Equally, while the family is completing the exercise, the therapist must pay close attention to the process. Give special attention to every nuance of the family's involvement. From the decision-making procedures of who will draw first or last, to color choice and titling, each selection is indicative of a family's patterns. Moreover, the completed art production yields a plethora of information as you note who worked cooperatively or independently, who respected the form items, and who disregarded the space of others.

In all, the completed family mural drawing provides a permanent record of the characteristics of the familial relationships and offers a visual aid for exploring the ensuing dynamics.

Case Study 7.1

A teenaged male whom we will call William and his mother attended family therapy due to William's extensive substance abuse history, which resulted in a recent probation violation and placement in out-of-home care. The 8CRT was administered to William (see Figure 3.10) during his initial interview. In that session he presented with an elevated and grandiose mood. However, the results of this projective test yielded dependency reactions and nurturance needs that created feelings of vulnerability. He responded to this vulnerability by avoiding emotional attachments and thus shutting out the overwhelming feelings through antagonism, substance abuse, antisocial relationships, and ultimately the defense of reaction formation.

Although William's parents had been separated for many years, they maintained an amicable relationship and were highly involved with their son. However, in this first family art therapy session William's mother arrived unaccompanied. Since I had requested that all family members attend, I noted the father's absence as significant, both as a pretext of resistance and as a factor in the family's problem.

In a private interview the mother related William's long-standing behavioral problems and opposition to rules and authority, and she summarized the difficulties by stating, "Maybe I was too hard on him." Throughout the interview she never mentioned William's substance abuse issues; only when I pointed out her resistance and questioned her directly did her discussion turn to her family of origin. She relayed a maternal and paternal familial history of alcoholism, her ex-husband's struggle with dependency, and eventually William's similar dependency, regarding which she stated that William had told her something about his drug use but she couldn't remember anything specific. At this juncture it was abundantly clear that she was employing the defensive functioning of secondary repression (Laughlin, 1970). As such, William's mother was expelling the anxiety-provoking feelings from conscious awareness as a pattern of coping with interpersonal strife.

Once William joined the session he outlined his goal for family therapy, which was to improve his communication with his mother. His mother stated that she wanted to decrease her enabling qualities and naïveté. At this point I instituted the directives for the family mural drawing.

Figure 7.5 is their completed rendering. As I gave the instructions, William quickly chose a color and walked to the mural paper without consulting his mother. His drawings occupy the uppermost portion of the mural, while his mother worked her renderings underneath and around his. With each successive turn William surreptitiously monitored his mother's progress while outwardly acting uninterested. This interaction mirrored his relationship with me, which was indicative of his maladaptive pattern of relating and the dependent bonds he was striving to refute.

In turn, William's mother compensated for his antagonistic renderings by applying themes that signified familial unity and devotion. Similar to the affect she exhibited in our verbal interview, these illustrations reflected her unconscious need to present Ferreira's family myth (cited in Nichols, 1984) of harmony and repeated codependent patterns in the hopes of reaching a resolution.

7.5 William and His Mother Struggle

With the completion of the drawing and the subsequent directive to title the exercise, each sat impassively. As the silence lengthened, eventually William's mother offered the title of "Power Struggle." With emblematic detachment, William added the title to the completed mural.

As noted earlier, it is important to allow the family to complete the decision-making process without interference. The use of silence allows the family to manage the here-and-now relationship without interruption or assistance from the therapist's questions or statements and these interactional struggles provide the mental health clinician with information with which to form his or her interpretations (Nichols, 1984).

Overall, the clinical approach, starting from the here-and-now of the session, is to develop with the family an understanding of the nature and origins of their current interactional difficulties. Accordingly, interpretations are relegated to the completed family mural drawing and the resultant verbal and nonverbal exchanges.

When beginning the process illumination, I prefer to offer the family an open-ended question or request such as "Who would like to tell me what they thought?" or "So, tell me what's going on."

In this case I put the latter question to the family, to which William quickly replied, "It's the invasion of the mini-mullet men trying to invade my truck." William's mother looked at me and stated, "I feel like I'm in the middle of an argument. I did peace. He did war."

William's face registered a slight smile.

At this point I interpreted both the art production and the subsequent verbal exchange as follows: "Throughout our meeting today you've spoken of both your family's and son's habit of disagreeing and arguing. Now you outline that you feel like you've been in a war. It would appear to me that you tend to deny your own needs, and therefore the battles are never won, and that's why William chooses to go to war with you. He acquires your undivided motherly attention but never truly feels secure because his needs are not met either."

William's smile was no longer visible.

In reply, his mother discussed issues related to generational substance abuse and her struggle to simply survive in a dysfunctional and maladaptive family system.

If we refer to the family's stated goals from the beginning of the session, we can see that it was important for William's mother to decrease her enabling qualities and naïveté not merely through education but through an understanding and conscious awareness of how her repression of emotionally charged material reflected her present manner of relating. Likewise, William sought more than improved communication with his mother; unconsciously he cried out for a parental relationship that he could both cling to and release (Erikson's autonomy versus shame and doubt developmental stage) as he moved from dependency and self-destructive relationships (including his substance abuse) to a sense of self predicated on the power of the will and competency.

In this case it was therefore important to look toward the internal processes as well as looking within the interactional ones. From this perspective the here-and-now interpersonal relations could be explored toward the goal of insight, communication, and productive methods of contact.

Case Study 7.2

For the purposes of this final section I do not discuss the family mural drawing as a session review but instead focus on providing the clinician with an analysis of the final product. To that end, I apply each individual's symbolic communication to the larger context of the family's social system.

The Harrisons were an intact family with two teenaged boys. The older son, Larry, was placed in a residential treatment facility due to an attempted theft during which he threatened a security guard. His younger brother, Jeffrey, had recently been referred to outpatient therapy for explosive bouts of rage following periods of guarded withdrawal. These siblings, though outwardly projecting two very different personalities (Jeffrey quiet and reserved, Larry loud and uncompromising), shared a need to conceal their orally aggressive feelings.

By way of example, their father had lost a high-paying job some months earlier, and this loss had brought about numerous lifestyle changes. However, these changes were not open for discussion. The family members suppressed their shame, while at the same time the family as a whole harbored unexpressed resentment against Mr. Harrison for losing his job.

In this case Larry, playing his role of the irrepressible and disobedient child, disguised his aggression through verbal sarcasm and distrust aimed at his father, while Jeffrey defended against his anxiety by retreating from interpersonal relationships through an obsequious demeanor. However, his hostility lay just beneath the surface and was often projected onto his older sibling.

Mrs. Harrison was equally distressed over the recent loss, as she was accustomed to both receiving and offering love through the transfer of material objects. This was the pattern of nurturance in her family of origin and one she expected from her husband and replicated with her sons. However, as the family savings were dwindling, this was no longer feasible; thus, her interpersonal relationships suffered, because she did not know how to please without offering a gift of substance.

Conversely, Mr. Harrison's calm acquiescence contradicted the intensity of his feelings: He channeled emotional conflicts into intellectualized control. Much like his younger son, Mr. Harrison presented with a guarded demeanor, preferring to protect uncomfortable feelings through containment.

Following an initial interview I presented the directives for the family mural drawing. Figure 7.6 illustrates the Harrisons' completed artwork (see disk to view in color).

Mrs. Harrison (upper center) and Larry (lower center) used the center of the mural, while the outside paper walls held Mr. Harrison's renderings (left side and middle right), with Jeffrey occupying the upper and lower right side of the paper. Assessed on an individual basis, each family member dominated his or her compartmentalized and unconsciously sanctioned-off space, which characteristically delineated common feelings of isolation. However, when working from a psychodynamic model, one must consider the family unit as a whole; an examination of how these individual personalities blend becomes vital when examining the interpersonal dynamics.

In Figure 7.6 this "coming together" was noted on a horizontal plane; the interpersonal distance shows a combination of anxiety and reproach.

7.6 Collaborative

Place your hand over the lower half of Figure 7.6 and note the visceral response the upper portion evokes. For me it was one of unsettled turbulence, a tempestuous feeling of foreboding that was matched only by the intensity of the lower half of the drawing. This portion, rendered completely under water, metaphorically illustrates the dark depths of the unconscious. The emotional impact of the bottom half of this drawing, dominated by Larry and his father, symbolizes feelings of passive acquiescence, powerlessness, danger, and aggressiveness.

In its totality, the art production metaphorically pointed toward this family's long-standing pattern of concealing their true emotions, thoughts, and feelings in order to maintain outward appearances, while their individual concerns and needs remained either suppressed or disguised as family members employed maladaptive models of relating.

Additionally, the symbolic separation of each member's drawings replicated this family's ineffective interactional process. I will examine each drawing individually, because the pictorial communication of the family mural drawing imparts both individual and interpersonal concerns.

As has already been stated, Mrs. Harrison was having grave difficulties adapting to the changing circumstances and inherent stresses within the family system. The materialistic considerations of her childhood had joined with the unconscious expectation that her husband would provide her with the same care and protection that her own family had. However, she outwardly denied the conflict that her husband's unemployment had produced in accordance with the family's tendency of emotional suppression.

In Figure 7.7 she has rendered a bleak and depressing environment

where a winter tree is surrounded by a brooding skyline. The heavy line pressure throughout her form items suggests an inner tension, while the aggressive shading found at the bottom right of Figure 7.7 draws a boundary between Larry's submerged attack and Jeffrey's encroaching storm. Additionally, the tree, often viewed as a symbol of the self in relation to the environment (Buck, 1966), has been rendered with exposed branches and a trauma scar.

Therefore, the drawing taken as a whole may correspond to feelings of depressive apprehension from Mrs. Harrison's inability to manage life's vicissitudes without the comfort of past introjects. Thus, we may view her turning away from the individual needs of others as a defensive reaction against the manifestation of her own internal dependency needs, since her old patterns of coping and the confidence she usually receives from others have been disrupted by the uncertainty of recent events.

Just beneath his mother's renderings, Larry has illustrated a destructive and fearful landscape where a vulnerable swimmer is confronted by not one but two hazards (Figure 7.8). This primitive scene, reminiscent of annihilation fears with its two menacing predators, calls to mind a panic that produces a duality of affect. Thus, if we look at Figure 7.8 as a metaphorical expression, the ocean may be a symbol "of dynamic forces and of tran-

7.7 Desolate

7.8 Fight or Flight

sitional states between the stable . . . and the formless" (Cirlot, 1971, p. 241). Cirlot notes that "the ocean . . . denotes an ambivalent situation. As the begetter of monsters, it is the abysmal abode . . . the chaotic source which still brings forth base entities ill-fitted to life" (pp. 241–242). Moreover, only the electric eel with its intrinsic defensive protection appears undisturbed as it resides blithely in the quagmire of the unconscious.

For Larry, the acknowledgment of the self as defenseless and defeated, as it is depicted pictorially, is a wholly unacceptable feeling. In this fashion, his defensive attitude in life may reside within the intrapsychic dynamics found in fear. As Kast (1989) has stated, "the emotion inherent to the victim is fear, and fear easily turns into aggression. Thus, fear and aggression are both merged in guilt" (p. 159). Accordingly, rather than being at odds with his identity, Larry projected reproach for defensive purposes. In an effort to maintain a sense of self, he placed his feelings of frustration, anger, and anxiety squarely on the shoulders of his father.

Further completing the picture of the impassive "bad object," to the right of Larry's predator is a submarine drawn by Mr. Harrison (see Figure 7.9). In this drawing a prominent periscope monitors the chaos from behind safe confines, yet it provides little protection or aid for Larry's defenseless self.

Beyond Mr. Harrison's submarine Jeffrey has rendered heavily shaded clouds, patterned flames, and a driving downpour, which he termed "acid

7.9 Acid Rain

rain." Thus, Jeffrey's drawing (Figure 7.9) symbolically discharges a caustic force upon each family member's illustration. Not unlike his own temperament, Jeffrey's aggression was superficially disguised as his infantile attachments clashed with a desire for differentiation of the self from his family. At the bottom of this drawing a hacky sack rests upon the ocean floor. Separated and emboldened, it embodies the interest that provided Jeffrey with necessary feelings of competency and enjoyment. His hacky sack prowess earned accolades from his peers; this individual pursuit was altogether his.

Figure 7.10 represents Mr. Harrison's final additions to the completed mural. His drawings in total comprise the sun reflected onto the water, the ocean's edge, and a scrutinizing submarine monitoring the commotion from a well-defended position. As an observer, who not unlike his wife created a boundary around Larry's primitive ocean, he exhibits defensive functioning, which is observable when we look at his form items as representations of intrapsychic processes.

As discussed earlier, Mr. Harrison's ongoing unemployment was kept as a shameful secret, the guilt and pain causing him to don a well-defended suit of protective covering—either through a recitation of events that was

7.10 My Two Suns

intellectualized or, as in Figure 7.9, symbolically presented through the shielding of the submarine. Additionally, the sun is often representative of parental love, a sign of an all-seeing power (Tresidder, 2000), and in Figure 7.10 Mr. Harrison also presents it as a reflection on the frenzied ocean. The fear and anger found within the son's rendering are manifested in the opposing tendency of the father's resistance-intellectualization (Laughlin, 1970) as the need for contemplative mental considerations and emotional insulation take precedence over outward expressions of care and support.

In the language of symbolism the Harrisons' mural drawing was less a collaboration, as the title would lead one to expect, than an imbalance: The severed connections signified the familial relationships and the family members' dysfunctional reactions to each other's behaviors. These metaphoric images shed light on their defensive functioning, while the visual experience offered permanence for further clarification.

As the family members worked through the avoided emotional conflicts, the unconscious symbolizing process of the artwork would prove beneficial in eliciting perceptions about both themselves and others. The structured exercise of the family mural drawing, and any subsequent therapeutic interpretations or metaphors, provides an opportunity to challenge individual and family views and creates an empathic and nonthreatening holding environment.

Concurrently, the process analysis of Figures 7.6–7.10 can focus on the larger relationship and provide a foundation for true collaboration. Along these lines, the therapist could pose questions to Mr. Harrison in this manner: "Where in this mural would you place yourself if you left the confines of the submarine? How would you feel leaving its protection?" Likewise, the acid rain, viewed as a symbol of unexpressed anger and rage, could be the subject of a question to each family member: "What would happen if the acid rain were to encroach on only your section of the drawing? Or if it fell from paper edge to paper edge? Who would survive? Who would fall apart? How would individual family members handle such destruction and devastation? If each drop of acid rain held a secret/had something to say, what would it be?"

The mural's use of barriers (i.e., submarine, acid rain, ocean perimeters, brooding skylines, predatory marine life) can also prompt evaluation. With each stressor (unemployment, residential placement) the family's sense of security had been threatened, triggering maladaptive defenses (depressive symptomology, aggression, and detachment). Therefore, family members engaged regressive coping patterns—rigid boundaries and projective mechanisms—to ease feelings of anxiety. Thus, utilizing the artwork the clinician could interpret this family's rigid interactional process and raise the question "What would it be like without these barriers?" to explore whether the family members consider such defensive measures necessary in their interpersonal situations.

In the end, the structured directives of art therapy afford the mental health clinician an opportunity to explore both internal defensive functioning and the ensuing interactional processes. These metaphorical images can render the unconscious conscious and thus can lead to healthier forms of relating. For this reason, verbal and symbolic communications are more than an illustration of the psyche: Interpreted, they are projections of our yearnings, our instinctual needs, and the opposing tendencies that influence our present interpersonal relationships.

Structural Aspects
Quantitative Analysis

I. Proportion/size
   A. Large drawings: grandiose feelings, poorly developed inner controls
   B. Small drawings: timid, shy, withdrawn, insecure
   C. Height of figure
      1. Over 8 inches high: self overemphasis and environment underemphasis; impulsive, possibly aggressive; excessive fantasy if drawing is controlled
      2. 5–8 inches high: normal height of figures
      3. Under 5 inches high: environment experienced as overwhelming and self as inadequate; avoidance and withdrawal from environmental stimulation; regressed; infantile tendencies

II. Placement: Figures placed other than in center reveal limitation in individual's ability to cope with his or her environment or attempted avoidance.
   A. Figure placed on *right* side of page (from viewer's perspective): self-oriented, introversion, prefers intellectual satisfaction over emotional satisfaction; inhibition; delays gratification; overconcerned with environment and future
   B. Figure placed on *left* side of page (from viewer's perspective): environment oriented; extroversion; seeks immediate and emotional satisfaction; impulsive, overconcern with self and past

C. Figure placed on left side of page and coupled with reinforced lines outlining the figure: possible defense mechanism of isolation

D. Drawing high on the paper: high standards of achievement; seeks satisfaction in fantasy; keeps self aloof and relatively inaccessible; anxiety and insecurity in coping with environmental stressors

E. Drawing placed in upper left-hand corner (quadrant of regression or never was; normal in young children): possible defense mechanism of regression; psychosis, organicity, poor concept maturation, desire to return to safety of past to avoid pain in present

F. Drawing low on the paper: insecurity, inadequacy, depression of mood; oriented toward the concrete; feelings of helplessness; nonaction

G. Drawing placed in lower right-hand corner: unusual quadrant

H. Drawing centered on the page: self-directed; feelings of security

I. Using bottom edge of page as ground line: insecure; feelings of inadequacy

J. Paper chopping (lines run over edge of the page): lowered ability to orient self in the environment; disturbed relationship in the interaction between the individual and the environment
   1. House
      a. Room: unpleasant association with the room "chopped"
      b. Top: pathological need to seek satisfaction in fantasy
   2. Tree
      a. Top: seeks satisfaction in fantasy
   3. Person
      a. Legs/feet: feeling of helpless immobility in environment
      b. Head: pathological need to seek satisfaction in fantasy
   4. Toward *left* margin: fixation on past, fear of the future
   5. Toward *right* margin: desire to escape into future and get away from past
   6. Tendency toward paper chopping (lines come within one quarter inch of page but not over): problems with reality testing but less pathological than paper chopping

K. Figure slanted 15 degrees: instability, mental imbalance

III. Line quality: the "wall" between the body and the environment; reflects the degree of barrier, vulnerability, insulation of the client
   A. Impairment in motor control: possible organicity

B. Pressure
   1. Heavy
      Apprehensive
      a. If throughout entire drawing: possible organicity, inner tension, possible aggression
      b. If in one detail: a fixation; hostility against the detail drawn
      c. Peripheral lines of an object: attempting to maintain ego identity
   2. Light/faint: timid, uncertain, self-effacing; fearfulness, depression
      a. If in one or select details only: reluctance to express that detail
   3. Varied pressure: moody and unstable behavior
C. Strokes
   1. Fragmented: uncertain, anxious
   2. Long strokes: apprehensive; requires support and reassurance
   3. Average length: one quarter to three quarters inches long
   4. Short strokes/sketchy lines: anxiety, impulsivity
   5. Well-controlled, free-flowing: good adjustment
   6. Jagged (sharp edges): aggression that is difficult to contain
D. Reinforcement of items: indicative of anxiety regarding the individual's functioning in the environment

IV. Shading
   A. Aggressive: cathexis, concealment
   B. Patterned: rationalizes; reduces shock in that area of conflict
   C. Perseveration: organicity, refuge in safety and confinement, low IQ
   D. Healthy: produced quickly, lightly, with random strokes
   E. Unhealthy: unwarranted use of time, excessive force; over-meticulous; inferior control and reinforcement

V. Use of color: Attention should be paid to excessive use of any one color.
   A. Variety of colors: well adjusted
   B. Few colors, if any: constricted, emotionally shy, reserved, emotionally unstable
   C. Expansive use: inability to exercise self-control and restraint over emotional impulses

D. Norms
   1. House: three to five colors
   2. Tree: Two to three colors
   3. Person: Three to five colors
E. Color output
   1. Emphatic intensity: emphasis on a particular item; normal
   2. Tensional intensity: repeated reinforcement of a color; anxious individual
   3. Clash intensity: use of inharmonious color combinations; profound disturbance; immature, regressive, possibly psychotic
   4. Pressure intensity: improperly modulated, involuntarily heavy pressure; organicity, central nervous system pathology

VI. Drawing opposite sex first: strong attachment to or dependency on parent or person of the opposite sex; possible sexual identification conflict
   A. By a male: possible difficulty in establishing a masculine identity
   B. By a female: aggressive, striving, desirous to compete with males; rejection of feminine role
   C. Drawn by a male or female: strong attachment to or dependence on parent or other individual of opposite sex

VII. Ground lines and backgrounds: vulnerable to stress; adding these elements reduces the anxiety about one's functioning by structuring the self within the environment; need for support (backgrounds) or a "stage" to exhibit self
   A. Differentiated (detailed, delineated): conflict under control and contained by intellectual defenses
   B. Ambiguous (single lines, sky, drops of rain): anxiety regarding environmental intrusions, poor intellectual defenses
   C. Vague (scribbling or shading for the ground): free-floating anxiety, poor coping

VIII. Opposite-sexed figure larger: opposite sex viewed as more powerful

IX. Emphasis on left side of the figure: feminine identification

X. Excessive, unnecessary detailing/over-symmetrical: possible defense mechanism of compulsion, intellectualization; obsessive-compulsive

XI. Redrawing an entire rendering: threatened by the content and needs to draw a "safer" image

XII. Transparencies: distortions of reality; tenuous reality testing, low IQ; normal in young children
   A. Older children and adults: possible psychosis, thought pattern disturbances, uncontained anxiety

Formal Aspects
Qualitative Analysis of the Person

Essential details:

Head
Trunk
Two legs (unless accounted for [e.g., by figure position or amputation])
Two arms (unless accounted for [e.g., by figure position or amputation])
Two eyes (unless accounted for [e.g., by figure position or amputation])
A nose
A mouth
Two ears (unless accounted for [e.g., by figure position or amputation])

Person: Conscious feelings regarding body image and self-concept

    I. Partial figure: basic discomfort with body image, sense of inadequacy, defense mechanisms of blocking or evasion
       A. Seated or prone: dependency; passive self-concept and mode of interaction; inhibited energy, lack of drive

   II. Head: expressive of social needs and responsiveness, locus of the self
       A. Large: preoccupation with fantasy life, focus on mental life; wish they were smarter or better able to achieve; organicity
       B. Small: obsessive-compulsive traits, intellectual inadequacy

C. Back to viewer: paranoid or schizoid tendencies; rejection; evasion; avoidance to show or express feelings, impulses, or fantasies; fears a loss of control

D. Enlarged on the opposite sex: opposite sex viewed as smarter or possessing greater authority

E. Malformed: organicity

F. Effeminate features (large eyes and lashes) on male figure by male: homosexual tendency

G. In profile view: fear of commitment; expression of impulses is controlled; avoidance of the environment

H. Profile head with full view of body (usually seen with adolescent boys): social uneasiness, guilt, dishonesty

I. Drawing the head last: disturbance in interpersonal relationships, possible thought disorder

J. Shaded face: seriously disturbed, poor self-concept

K. Smiley face (normal with small children) infantile social behavior

L. Bulge on forehead: emphasis on brain power

III. Hair (anywhere on the body): expression of virility/striving, masculinity, and strength

A. Heavily shaded: anxiety, overthinking, fantasy

B. Long, loose hair on men: sign of freedom

C. Beards/moustaches: masculine symbols, phallic substitutes

D. Hair excitement/chaos: infantile sexual drives

E. Barrettes, bows: efforts at control

IV. Eyes: Normal eye detailing includes two to three of the following items: eyeball, iris or pupil, lashes, eyebrow.

A. Only one item: immature; avoidant style of perceiving reality

B. All four items: hypersensitivity aware of environment, hypercritical

C. Omission: suspect visual hallucinations

D. Small: desire to see as little as possible

E. Hollow sockets: Reluctance to accept stimuli; hostility

F. No pupils: visual processing/learning problems, immaturity (egocentric), possible defense mechanism of regression

G. Sideways glance: suspicion, paranoid tendencies

H. Closed: Shuts out world and needs of others; self-absorption

V. Eyelashes
   A. Long: coquettishness, seductiveness, self-display
   B. Pronounced on a male figure: sexual identification issues

VI. Eyebrows
   A. Trim: disdain
   B. Bushy: uninhibited

VII. Mouth
   A. Overly emphasized: immaturity; oral-aggressive; fixations; overly dependent
   B. Very large: orally erotic; language and/or speech disorder
   C. Omitted: difficulty in relating to others
   D. Concave/orally receptive: oral dependence, infantile
   E. Heavy line slash: verbally aggressive, overcritical; sadistic personality
   F. Heavy but brief mouth: verbal aggression; the anticipated rebuff makes the client withdraw
   G. Single line: tension, shutting the mouth tightly against something
   H. Object in mouth: Oral preoccupation

VIII. Lips
   A. Cupid's bow lips (in concert with heavily cosmetized features): sexually precocious
   B. Inclusion of object (cigarette, pipe, toothpick): oral erotic

IX. Nose
   A. Overemphasis: phallic preoccupation
   B. Nostrils: accent on primitive aggression
   C. Overextended: feelings of impotency

X. Ears
   A. Omission (normal in young children, low IQ in adults): hallucinations, desire to shut out criticism
   B. Overemphasis: sensitive to criticism; auditory hallucinations; paranoid; ear injury or hearing disability
   C. Underemphasis: desire to shut out criticism

XI. Teeth
   A. In profusion/exaggerated: aggressiveness

XII. Tongue: oral concentration on a primitive level, erotic

XIII. Chin
  A. Emphasized on opposite sex: dependency on opposite sex; views opposite sex as stronger
  B. Overemphasis: need for social dominance

XIV. Neck: organ joining control area and impulse, coordination between head and body
  A. Long and thin: schizoid tendencies; schizophrenic; possible defense mechanism of repression
  B. Excessively large: awareness of physical impulses with an effort to control them
  C. Elongated neck: problem with anger management or primitive drive
  D. Omission: regressive; body drives threaten to overwhelm
  E. Short and thick: uninhibited impulse expression

XV. Shoulders: physical power
  A. Unequal: emotionally unstable
  B. Large: preoccupied with the perceived need for strength
  C. Squared: overly defended, hostile toward others
  D. Broad shoulders on female: confusion of physical power and maternal symbol
  E. Drooping: dejection, guilt

XVI. Trunk: seat of basic needs and drives
  A. Round: less aggressive, undeveloped
  B. Exceptionally thin: discontent with the body type possessed by the artist; frailty or weakness; compensation for unwelcome weight
  C. Trunk with angles: masculine
  D. No enclosure to represent the trunk: regressed, primitive, or disorganized individual; immaturity
  E. Small: denial of drives, inferiority
  F. Larger: unsatisfied drives
  G. Navel: nurturance, dependency needs, material issues
  H. Midline stressed (shading, fancy belts, lines, lines down center of body, rows of buttons, etc.): somatic preoccupation, emotional immaturity, feelings of inadequacy, mother dependence, possible defense mechanism of somatic conversion

XVII. Arms and hands: used to change or control surrounding environment; ego development and social adaptation; organs

of relationship; basic emotional contact; symbols of activity
and power; contact with environment

A. Folded over chest: hostile or suspicious
B. Held behind back: wanting to control anger; interpersonal reluctance; evasive
C. Omitted: inadequacy, helplessness, withdrawal, guilt
   1. On opposite sex: rejection by maternal or paternal figure
   2. Armless figure of male drawn by a male: strong sexual drives associated with guilt; wish to be castrated
D. Winglike: schizoid
E. Held tight to body: rigid; fear of aggressive impulses
F. Broad/extended: feeling of strength, power
G. Long
   1. Supported by graphic indication of power: reaching out, ambition
   2. Weak: need for support from others in environment with no active manipulation of it
H. Overly long
   1. In self: overambitious striving, rejection of other individuals; desirous of isolation or withdrawal
   2. In others: a rejecting or threatening person
   3. Weak: nurturance needs
   4. Coupled with prominent hands (female figure): wish for protective maternal figure (drawn by a male)
I. Short: feelings of inadequacy
J. Thin: weakness and futility
K. Muscular (frequent with adolescent males): concerns about masculinity
L. Reaching: desire for affection
M. Dangling at sides: views self as dependent, helpless, insignificant
N. Heavy or shaded on opposite sex: opposite sex is viewed as punishing
O. Large on male figure: assaultiveness
P. Reinforced: assaultiveness

XVIII. Hands
A. In pocket: masturbation or guilt; evasiveness
B. Large hands: compensation for weakness; reaction to some guilty use of hands

C. Hands near genital region: preoccupied with autoerotic practices
 1. Female figure drawn by a male: female regarded as sexually rejecting
D. Raised: subordination
E. Hidden: difficulty with interpersonal relations
F. Fanned out or splayed: compulsive
G. Fanned out or splayed with unarticulated fingers: minimal achievement

XIX. Fingers
A. Long and spikelike: aggressive, hostile, paranoid
B. Enclosed by loop or single dimension (mitten hands): wish to suppress aggressive impulse; repressed aggression; efforts at control
C. Large: hostility, aggressiveness
D. Omitted: inability to make adjustments; guilt, insecurity, difficulty dealing with the environment
E. Fingers without hands (stick fingers): infantile aggression
F. Severely shaded or reinforced fingers: guilt indicators
G. Clenched fist
 1. Arm away from body: rebelliousness close to surface; overt rebellion
 2. Arm pressed against or close to body: inner and repressed rebellion finds expression in symptoms
H. Closed hand: keeping silent about a secret
I. Less than five: helplessness
J. Grape fingers: infantile traits
K. Fingernails: compulsive body image problem, seen in early schizophrenia
L. Fingers look like feathers: schizophrenia

XX. Breasts
A. Overemphasis
 1. Drawn by a male: maternal dependence, oral eroticism
 2. Drawn by a female: exhibitionism, narcissism, possible maternal dependence
B. Low pendant line: mother image representation (strong/dominant)

XXI. Legs: represent contact with the environment
A. Absent: constricted; feelings of constriction; lack of support; immobile; withdrawal

    B. Size difference: mixed feelings regarding independence

    C. Long: striving for autonomy

    D. Short: emotional immobility

    E. Held tightly together: possible sexual maladjustment; tension, rigidity

    F. Pants are transparent (legs show through): homosexual anxiety

    G. Broad-based stance: defiance or need for security

XXII. Feet: degree of interpersonal mobility

    A. Long: striving for security or virility

    B. Tiny: dependency, blunted feelings; effeminate

    C. Omitted: lack of independence, withdrawal

    D. Overdetailing: obsessive traits with strong feminine component

    E. Tiptoe: need for security

    F. Barefoot: humility, poverty

    G. Toes drawn (not on a nude figure): pathological aggressiveness

    H. Pointing in opposite directions: ambivalence

    I. Figure clothed with toes exposed: aggressive tendencies

    J. Dwarf foot (ducklike): infantile, schizophrenic

    K. Feet and legs drawn first: depression

XXIII. Shoe detailing

    A. Eyelets, laces, bow: impotence

XXIV. Joints: faulty and uncertain sense of body integrity, used by psychotic individuals when decompensating to stave off body disorganization, somatic preoccupation

XXV. Stick man: possible organicity

    A. When all are stick figures: reluctance to reveal self; avoidance of risk taking; regression as a defense mechanism; low IQ

    B. One or more but not all: defensiveness, poor relationship with the figure

XXVI. Buttons (oral dependence; count number for possible repetitious numbers (trauma); may be drawn on the individual looked upon for nurturance; normal to age 7) dependency issues; regressive; feelings of inadequacy; affectionally or materially deprived

XXVII. Belt
    A. Overemphasis: sexual preoccupation, overconcern

XXVIII. Pockets: affectional or maternal deprivation, dependency issues; infantile
    A. In adolescent male: virility strivings, which conflict with emotional dependence on the mother

XXIX. Tie: sexual symbol, symbol of sexual adequacy
    A. Long or conspicuous: sexually aggressive; fear of impotence
    B. Flying away from the body: overt sexual aggression, sexual preoccupation

XXX. Trousers
    A. Fly: preoccupied with masturbation

XXXI. Hat (incongruous): regressed, schizoid; infantile sexually while nurturing fantasies of virility

XXXII. Sex organs (in 4–6-year-olds somewhat normal stage): acute body anxiety, poor impulse control

XXXIII. Cigarette, pipes, guns: manifest sexual symbols
    A. If given emphasis: acute sexual preoccupation

XXXIV. Cowboys: desire to be masculine and tough

XXXV. Clowns: poor self-concept, self-deprecating thoughts, feelings of inferiority

XXXVI. Monsters or witches: poor self-concept; feelings of depersonalization; threatening aspects of the psyche
    A. Drawn by a male (witch): overt hostility toward females

XXXVII. Puppet: compliance

XXXVIII. Smiley face: infantile social behavior

XXXIX. Hanging or falling figures: tension and anxiety

XL. Blackening or shading specific body part (preoccupation with that body part): anxiety, issues of sexuality when blacked from waist down

XLI. Distortion, reinforcement, or omission of select parts: conflict relative to that part, possible defense mechanism of repression

Formal Aspects
Qualitative Analysis of the House

Essential details:

> One door
> One window
> One wall
> A roof
> A chimney

House: examines connections regarding home and familial dynamics; a symbol of the human body

Irrelevant: Shrubs, flowers, walkway (equals needing to structure environment; shows feelings of insecurity or need for control in interpersonal contact)

    I. Wall (adequacy of): directly associated with ego strength
       A. Transparent: reality testing impairment
       B. Using paper edge as sidewall line: insecurity (note whether on left or right—see placement)

    II. Drawn on base of paper: basic home or intimate insecurities

    III. Perspective from below: either rejection of home or feelings of an unattainable desirable home life

    IV. Perspective from above: rejection of home situation

V. Fence around house/shrubbery/porch: need for emotional protection, need to erect ego defense barriers

VI. Gutters/rainspouts: suspiciousness with attempt to channel the unpleasant stimuli

VII. Door: accessibility
  A. Above baseline/without steps: interpersonal inaccessibility
  B. Absence: extreme difficulty in allowing accessibility to others
  C. Open: strong need to receive warmth from external world
  D. Very large: overly dependent
  E. Small: reluctant to permit access
  F. With lock or hinges: defensiveness, sensitivity
  G. Highly decorated doorknob: Overconsciousness of function; phallic preoccupation
  H. Home drawn with two doors: provides manner of escape (Is this an existing home or fantasy? Therapist must ask.)

VIII. Walkway
  A. Very long: lessened accessibility
  B. Narrow at house, broad at end: superficially friendly
  C. Well proportioned and leading to doorway: exercises control and tact in contact with others
  D. Long and winding: initially aloof in contacts with others, slow and cautious in making friendships
  E. Incomplete: relative inaccessibility

IX. Windows
  A. Absence of: hostile, withdrawing
  B. Present on ground or absent from upper story: gap between reality and fantasy
  C. Curtains
    1. Partially open or open: controlled interaction with the environment, anxiety manifested as tact in interpersonal relations
    2. Closed: withdrawal needs, reluctance to interact
  D. Bare/no panes: behavior is mostly blunt and direct; oppositional; hostility
  E. Bars on windows: Accurate representation? Therapist must ask. Overdefensive: feelings of imprisonment
  F. Attached to edge of walls: need for support, fear of autonomy and independent action
  G. Reinforced (only): oral fixations, oral character traits

  X. Shutters
      A. Closed: extreme defensiveness and withdrawal
      B. Open: ability to make sensitive interpersonal adjustments

 XI. Roof
      A. Unidimensional (single line connecting two walls): Un-imaginative or emotionally constricted
      B. Overly large: seeks satisfaction in fantasy; low IQ
      C. Overhanging: immersed in fantasy, withdraws from overt inter-personal contact
      D. Reinforced/traced/repeated (only): defense against the threat of fantasy, prepsychotic

 XII. Chimney: symbol of warm, intimate relations; sometimes a phallic symbol
      A. Absence of chimney: lacking psychological warmth; conflicts with significant male figures
      B. Overly large: overemphasis on sexual concerns, exhibitionistic tendencies
      C. Smoke in profusion: inner tension or emotional turbulence in the home situation

XIII. Rooms
      A. Bathroom: elimination and sanitation
      B. Bedroom: intimate interpersonal relationships, desire to with-draw, need to rest
      C. Dining room: satisfaction of oral and nutritional needs
      D. Living room: social intercourse
      E. Kitchen: where food is prepared; oral eroticism, possibly related to strong need for affection
      F. Cellar/basement: unconscious, hidden drives, hidden treasures

Formal Aspects
Qualitative Analysis of the Tree

Essential details:

Trunk
One Branch

Tree: Unconscious feelings of self in the context of the environment; symbolizes life and growth

I. Size
  A. Extremely large tree: aggressive tendencies, need for dominance; feels constricted by and in the environment
  B. Tiny: inferior; feelings of insignificance, oral erotic fixation, need for maternal protection
  C. Keyhole: oppositional tendencies
  D. Christmas tree/decorated (normal around Thanksgiving and Christmas): well-developed narcissism, need for nurturance, regressive tendencies
  E. Dead: significant maladjustment; schizophrenic, depressed; feelings of futility

II. Line quality
  A. Faint lines: feelings of inadequacy
  B. Fine, broken lines: overt anxiety

    C. Shading, excessively dark or reinforced: hostile defenses or aggressive behavior

III. Trunk: Trunk is patient's feeling of basic ego strength.
    A. Composed of just 2 lines for trunk and looped crown: impulsive, variable
    B. Exaggerated emphasis: emotional immaturity

IV. Bark
    A. Easily drawn: well-balanced interactions
    B. Heavily drawn: anxiety
    C. Meticulous: compulsive, overly concerned regarding relationships
    D. Vines/vinelike bark: loss of control, forbidden ideas or needs

V. Roots
    A. Exaggerated emphasis: emotional responses shallow, reasoning limited; poor reality contact, tenuous contact with the ground

VI. Crown
    A. Exaggerated emphasis: inhibited emotionally, analytical
    B. Leaves closely drawn together/meticulous: obsessive-compulsive traits
    C. Leaves falling: fear of losing ability to hide thoughts and feelings
    D. Highly detailed leaves on tree: clinging to nurturance, dependency

VII. Branches: depict ability to derive satisfaction from the environment
    A. Overemphasis on the *right* side: avoidance of emotional satisfaction; looks toward intellectual satisfaction
    B. Overemphasis on *left* side: seeks emotional satisfaction
    C. Branches in absolute symmetry: ambivalence regarding a course of action
    D. Branches' ends not complete: little control over expression of drives
    E. Branches loop and curve in at ends: strong ruminative tendencies, introversion
    F. Branches drop to bottom of picture: trauma
    G. Apples (very common in young children): dependency and oral needs

H. Apples falling from the tree: feelings of rejection
I. One-dimensional branches: possible organicity, impotence, futility, poor ego strength, inadequacy
J. Broken branches: trauma
K. Omitted: withdrawal, lack of interpersonal relations
L. Club- or spearlike with sharp points: hostility, aggression

VIII. Knothole, broken branch, scar: sexual symbolism, trauma
A. Outline reinforced: shock impact greater
B. Circles inside: experience in past and healing
C. Blackened: shame associated with the experience
D. Large: preoccupation with procreation
E. Small animal inside (common in children): ambivalence surrounding childbearing; obsessive guilt

APPENDIX E

Eight-Card Redrawing Test Adapted Scoring Sheet

Factor	1	2	3	4	5	6	7	8
1. Size of figure (use key scores)								
2. Placement (rt, lt, middle)								
3. Placement (top, center, btm)								
4. Perspective (forward, rear, profile, confused)								
5. Symmetry (use key scores)								

(continued)

Factor	1	2	3	4	5	6	7	8
6. Line Closure (use key scores)								
7. Pressure (heavy, light, varied)								
8. Graphic control (use key scores)								
9. Line type (frag, jagged, long, short, average)								
10. Shading (aggressive, patterned, perseveration, healthy)								
11. Detailing (use key scores)								
12. Sex of figures (M/F/Unk.)								
13. Transparencies (number)								
14. Paper chopping (Y/N)								
15. Continuity (use key scores of superimposition, overlap, discrete)								
16. Partial figure drawn (number)								

Superimposition = figures drawn with same body wall, body area, body proportions

Overlap = figures overlap but have no relationship otherwise

Discrete = figures are obviously separated

Key Scores:

>> = Extreme presence

> = Above average in size

A = Average

< = Below average in size

<< = Extremely limited in size

316

Sample Directives

Introductory

1. Draw what you want to convey about yourself.
2. Draw in abstract something that represents you.
3. Draw your initials as large as you can on the page. Using the initials and the design they make, find ideas for pictures. Your ideas can be something real or a design. Once you see the picture, color it in using as much color as you want. You can stay inside or outside of the lines. Title your image.
4. Close your eyes and relax; when you are ready, open your eyes and look at your colors; now let a color pick you and draw on your paper.
5. Draw something you like about yourself (design/representational). Title it.
6. Trace your hand on the paper. Draw a symbol in the hand that represents something friendly about you. Cut it out and glue it on the butcher paper one person at a time.
7. Draw a picture or design into or around the Xeroxed copies of the hands. Cut them out and place on butcher paper.
8. Draw a circle on your paper. Now fill your world.
9. Choose four to five pictures that appeal to you and write down why underneath.

Feelings Expression

1. Draw your present feelings.
2. Draw specific feelings (sadness, anger, love, hate, joy, envy, anxiety).
3. Draw a wish.
4. Draw a specific fear.
5. Draw a dream.
6. Draw a self-portrait.
7. Draw a significant event or situation.
8. Draw an important relationship.
9. Draw someone you hate in all his or her most vile manifestations. (Clinician: Remember this is a self-portrait of disowned parts of self.)
10. Draw with your wrong hand.
11. Draw with your eyes closed.
12. Draw or use clay to make a picture you feel strongly about (a person, place, or thing).
13. Draw pictures of animals that symbolize each member of your family.
14. Create two fantasy animals. These fantasy animals don't have to look like anything you've ever seen before.
15. Draw yourself with people. Draw yourself without people.

Problem Solving

1. Draw a picture of a bridge going from some place to some place.
2. Close your eyes and visualize a chasm, and design a way of crossing it, considering that you have every means at your disposal. Draw the chasm and your solution.
3. Draw your problem as it exists now (draw what the problem looks like). Draw the problem all better (how would it look all better?) What will help the first drawing change into the second drawing? Draw it.
4. Draw how the [*problem*] looks. Draw a character who will comfort the _____ and protect you. Draw a gift that would turn the _____ into something else. How does your _____ look better?
5. Suppose that while you sleep tonight a miracle happens and all of your problems are completely solved. What will be different the next day? What will be better?
6. Make something that shows what you wish you could change.
7. Draw a picture together.

8. Hang up a piece of poster board and have the group choose one picture to place in the center. Have the group members fill in and create a drawing around it.
   Variations: no talk; use 3-D objects instead of markers
9. How are you going to overcome your obstacles?
10. How do you feel when your needs are met? How do you feel when your needs are unmet?
11. Draw your problem and solution.
12. Make a collage of how you feel in this group.
13. Create a group sculpture using one color of clay. Title it.
14. Divide the group into two. Offer multiple items and media. Instruct the group to imagine themselves as a group marooned on an island. Create the situation and the part that each person will play.
15. Listen to a story and recreate it in 3-D.
16. Using the media, create a piece of work that shows how you see the group and your place in it.
17. Working individually, make anything you like by tearing apart paper. Put the pieces together with tape or glue.
    Variation: Place your torn paper with others to make a group sculpture.
18. Make a game: Divide group in half. Have each person make a symbol for the self (game piece) and set a personal goal (treasure). As a team, the group decides on the obstacles for the game (mountains, rivers, monsters, etc.) and creates questions to answer once they reach an obstacle (switch each team's questions when play starts). A sheet of butcher paper and cardboard are given to the entire group, and they create a game board and the 3-D obstacles. As the game begins, each group uses the same game board but responds to the other team's questions when they encounter an obstacle. They move their game pieces individually, and the first person to arrive at an obstacle must wait for the team members to join him or her before answering the question as a group. Once the question is answered properly, the group must decide how to overcome the obstacles and create solutions by using art supplies and building a way around/over. The entire team must reach the treasure at the other end. The only way to succeed is for *all* to reach the goal together.
    Variations: (1) Have questions already prepared; (2) Have the group earn or lose building materials in the quest to surmount obstacles; (3) Give the group building materials at the beginning of the game to use as a team; they must continue to use only these to surmount obstacles.

19. Have each group member draw his or her favorite animal. Members pass the drawing and on another sheet of paper draw a friend for the animal. They pass both drawings and add something to both of the animals. Pass the drawings again and cut them out. The drawings go back to original owner, who adds anything he or she wishes to the cut-out drawings. Provide butcher paper in center of table (or on wall). The group decides how to place all the drawings into a single whole. Title.

Insight and Self-Disclosure

1. Create the face you present to new people you meet on one side of the bag and the face you would like to present on the other side. Variations: (1) The "me" others see and (on other side) the real "me"; (2) how the world sees you/how you see yourself.
2. Use collage to depict family, friends, and others with whom you have left something unsaid. Write what you wish you could say to each of these people.
3. Select and paste pictures of people, then write down what they are thinking and saying.
4. Select a picture that shows how you see yourself.
5. Draw an image that sums up all the things you like about yourself.
6. Have each group member choose collage pictures (can limit number). Working as quickly as possible, make their own picture from the images selected.
7. Decorate the outside of a box showing who you are. On the inside decorate, draw, or use clay to represent what you value.
8. Draw where you came from, where you are now, and where you are going.
9. How do others perceive you? How do you perceive yourself?
10. Draw your most "together" time. Draw your most "un-together" time.
11. Draw a wish for yourself. Draw a wish for someone else in the group. Draw a wish for the group as a whole.
12. Make any kind of object out of clay. Give the piece you made to someone in the group. (Discuss how it felt giving away, getting it, whether you like what you got, etc.)
13. Decorate the four sides of a box with construction paper. On one side draw what peace looks like, on the next draw a trouble, on the third draw trust, and on the last draw anything you please. Title.
14. Give each group member a box and have them decorate the outside

showing "who you are." Have them paint the inside. On index cards represent the following:

(a) Draw a wish for yourself.

(b) Draw a wish for someone else.

(c) Draw a wish for the group as a whole.

(d) Draw something that represents what you value.

(e) Draw a gift you would like to receive.

(f) Draw a gift you would like to give.

(g) Draw a characteristic about yourself you would like to discard.

(h) Draw something you should stay away from.

(i) Free drawing.

(j) Draw something you do not value.

(k) Make a 3-D (clay, paper, etc.) item for the box of anything you wish.

(l) Paste two to three important pictures on the inside walls of the box.

Closure

1. Make three separate drawings: one of you at the beginning of group or before group started; one of you during the group; and one of you presently.

2. Make a drawing that represents another group member at the beginning and ending of the group.

3. Draw a memory of another "leaving" or "ending" in your life.

4. Draw the feelings you have about leaving this group.

5. Draw symbols for what you feel you got out of this group.

6. Draw your future goals beyond this group.

7. Draw what you've liked most about this group, what you've liked least about this group, or one final gift you'd like to give to someone in this group.

8. Draw something that you would like to give to [name of person leaving] to help him or her be successful.

9. Working together, combine your efforts to make a visual tribute to someone who is leaving (or has left).

10. Draw or make something to commemorate your leaving the _____.

11. On a piece of butcher paper draw or paint a large spiral. Along the spiral depict significant life events.

12. Offer each group member a sheet of butcher paper; have them produce a cartoon strip showing significant events in their lives.
    Variation: Write a continuous piece of prose about your life, and select a significant image from your writing and draw it.

13. Draw a gift you would like to give to someone. Draw a gift you would like to receive from someone.
14. Mark off a piece of paper in quarters and draw symbolically: (1) Where do I come from? (2) Where do I want to go? (3) What is in my way?
15. Draw a picture of the past, present, and future.
16. Draw how it was in the past. Draw how it will be in the future.
17. Draw how you say good-bye to a friend.

Sample Group
Processing Directives

Here and Now

1. Who have you cut yourself off from in this group? Draw why or how you have made yourself lonely here.
2. Who in this room do you have good communication with? Who in this room would you like to improve communication with? How could you improve it? Draw one solution to improving your communication.
3. Who in this room would you like to say something to/express something toward? Draw one positive thing you would like to see them keep and one negative thing you would like to see them change.
4. Draw the person in this room that you trust, and write down why. Discuss what trust feels like. After the discussion draw on the back of your paper what trust looks like.
5. Choose three pictures from the collage box that illustrate how you make friends.
6. Draw how it felt to be new in the [new situation] and how it feels now.
7. What have you done to improve the manner in which you are being treated? Draw what you will do after this group to improve your situation.
8. How do you protect yourself when you feel upset/scared/alone? Draw your feelings on the paper.

9. Draw the things you have done to set yourself apart from the group and what you have done to make yourself a part of the group.
10. Who did you follow in this group? Draw how that felt.
11. What did you do with the feelings you had in group today? Draw those feelings.
12. Give each group member a box and have them decorate the outside showing "who you are." Have them paint the inside. On index cards have them represent the following:
    (a) Draw a wish for yourself.
    (b) Draw a wish for someone else.
    (c) Draw a wish for the group as a whole.
    (d) Draw something that represents what you value.
    (e) Draw a gift you would like to receive.
    (f) Draw a gift you would like to give.
    (g) Draw a characteristic about yourself you would like to discard.
    (h) Draw something you should stay away from.
    (i) Free drawing.
    (j) Draw something you do not value.
    (k) Make a 3-D item (clay, paper, etc.) for the box of anything you wish.
    (l) Paste 2 or 3 important pictures on the inside walls of the box.
    Variation: Use clay, construction paper, or the like for directive instead of index cards.
13. Give each group member a piece of paper and divide it in half. Have each member draw on the left side how they feel today. Pair the group members up and have the partners discuss how they feel and why (but do not show their drawings). Have each group member return to the original drawing and on the right side draw how their partner feels. Share as a group.

Empathy

1. Place a series of collage images in the center of the group. Instruct the group members to sort through and select two that they think the group member sitting on their left would most like. Discuss why after the project is completed.
2. Have each member put his or her name on paper and draw two strengths. Have members pass the drawings around the group circle and add to the drawings a strength each sees in the person.
3. Have the members make a gift out of clay for the group member sitting next to them, present the gift, and describe why they made this one in particular.

4. If you could go back in time and change one thing, what would it be? Draw how things might have been different for you if you could change this one thing.

Personal Change

1. On the front of your paper draw at least three things that you want to change. On the back write down why these changes are important to you.
2. Draw at least three things that you like about yourself and don't want to change. On the back of the paper write down why.
3. Draw your most important change.
4. Draw all the changes that you've made since coming to the _____.
5. Draw all the things you worry about when you think of trying to change.
6. Using any of the materials (collage or drawing supplies), illustrate an important change that you've seen someone in the group make.
7. Think about a change that you would like to make but don't think you can. Separate your paper in two. On one side, draw what you think will happen if you do not make this change, and on the other side draw what you think would happen if you did make a change.
8. Draw the obstacle that stops you from changing.
9. Draw two significant differences between your personality now and your personality 5 years ago.
10. Draw a trait belonging to someone else in this group that you would like to have.

Self-Disclosure

1. Draw the most important person in your life.
2. Using the four-sided box provided, decorate the outside using any materials you wish. When this is done, seal the box and cut a slit in the top. On a piece of paper write out or draw one thing about yourself that people would be surprised to know. Discuss the outside of your box and share your secret.
3. Draw the one thing that you enjoy the most.
4. Draw a picture of someone you really miss. Choose three collage images that you think this person would enjoy, and explain why you chose them.
5. Remember a time when it was hard for you to separate from someone. Draw your feelings on the paper. On the back of the paper draw how you handle separation.

6. Draw the last time you got angry, and on the paper write one thing that irritates you. Choose a word from the collage word box that describes how you feel when you are angry.

7. Draw a time when you felt alone on the front of the paper. On the back draw the time when you've felt least alone.

8. Give the group members multiple sheets of paper and divide them in fours. Ask the group member to draw, "Who are you?" Continue to ask them the same directive until they have filled up the front of the paper, then move to the back or on another sheet. Ask the question at least eight times. Discuss.

9. What is one secret (or feeling/thought/fear/worry) you would be willing to share with the group?

10. Draw all the special things in your life.

11. Draw a favorite place you've lived in or visited.

12. Draw what you see when you look in the mirror. Discuss with the group whether they agree with the perception, what they would change and keep about their reflections, and what they learned.

References

Al-Issa, I. (1970). Cross-cultural studies of symptomatology in schizophrenia. In I. Al-Issa & W. Dennis (Eds.), *Cross-cultural studies of behavior* (pp. 494–510). New York: Holt, Rinehart and Winston.

Alter-Muri, S. (2002). Viktor Lowenfeld revisited: A review of Lowenfeld's preschematic, schematic, and gang age stages. *American Journal of Art Therapy, 40*(3), 170–193.

American Psychiatric Association. (1994). *Diagnostic and statistical manual of mental disorders: DSM-IV* (4th ed.). Washington, DC: American Psychiatric Press.

Anderson, H. H. (1951). Human behavior and personality growth. In H. H. Anderson & G. L. Anderson (Eds.), *An introduction to projective techniques* (pp. 3–26). Englewood Cliffs, NJ: Prentice Hall.

Arieti, S. (1955). *Interpretation of schizophrenia*. New York: Robert Brunner.

Arrington, D. B. (2001). *Home is where the art is: An art therapy approach to family therapy*. Springfield, IL: Charles C. Thomas.

Attwood, T. (1998). *Asperger's syndrome: A guide for parents and professionals*. London: Jessica Kingsley.

Barton, H. R., & Kovan, R. A. (1978). Infantile ego states and adult clinical practice. *American Journal of Psychoanalysis, 38*(3), 235–242.

Bauer, G. P. (1993). *The analysis of the transference in the here and now*. Northvale, NJ: Jason Aronson.

Bettelheim, B. (1977). *The uses of enchantment: The meaning and importance of fairy tales*. New York: Vintage Books.

Boszormenyi-Nagy, I., & Spark, G. (1973). *Invisible loyalties: Reciprocity in intergenerational family therapy*. New York: Harper & Row.

Bowen, M. (1985). *Family therapy in clinical practice*. Northvale, NJ: Jason Aronson.

Buck, J. N. (1948). The H-T-P technique: A qualitative and quantitative scoring manual. *Journal of Clinical Psychology, 5*, 1–120.

Buck, J. N. (1964). *The House-Tree-Person (H-T-P) manual supplement*. Los Angeles: Western Psychological Services.

Buck, J. N. (1966). *The House-Tree-Person technique* (Rev. ed.). Los Angeles: Western Psychological Services.

Burns, R. C. (1987). *Kinetic House Tree Person drawings*. New York: Brunner/Mazel.

Burns, R. C., & Kaufman, S. F. (1972a). *Actions, styles, and symbols in Kinetic Family Drawings (K-F-D): An interpretative manual*. New York: Brunner/Mazel.

Burns, R. C., & Kaufman, S. F. (1972b). *Kinetic Family Drawings (K-F-D): An introduction to understanding children through kinetic drawings*. New York: Brunner/Mazel.

Butler, S. F., & Strupp, H. H. (1993). Effects of training experienced dynamic therapists to use a psychotherapy manual. In N. Miller, L. Luborsky, J. Barber, & J. Docherty (Eds.), *Psychodynamic treatment research: A handbook for clinical practice* (pp. 191–210). New York: Basic Books.

Cain, J., & Jolliff, B. (1997). *Teamwork and teamplay*. Dubuque, IA: Kendall/Hunt.

Caligor, L. (1952). The detection of paranoid trends by the Eight-Card Redrawing Test (8CRT). *Journal of Clinical Psychology, 8,* 397–401.

Caligor, L. (1953). Quantification on the Eight Card Redrawing Test (8CRT). *Journal of Clinical Psychology, 9,* 356–361.

Caligor, L. (1957). *A new approach to figure drawing*. Springfield, IL: Charles C. Thomas.

Camara, W. J., Nathan, J. S., & Puente, A. E. (2000). Psychological test usage: Implications in professional psychology. *Professional Psychology: Research and Practice, 31*(2), 141–154.

Carpenter, E. (1920). *Pagan and Christian creeds: Their origin and meaning*. Urbana, IL: Project Gutenberg. www.gutenberg.net/etext/1561.

Chase, S. (Ed.). (1956). *Language, thought and reality: Selected writings of Benjamin Lee Whorf*. Cambridge, MA: MIT Press.

Cirlot, J. E. (1971). *A dictionary of symbols* (J. Sage, Trans.). New York: Philosophical Library.

Cohen, Y. A. (1961). *Social structure and personality*. New York: Holt, Rinehart and Winston.

Collodi, C. (1969). *The adventures of Pinocchio*. New York: MacMillan.

Craddick, R. A. (1980). Behavioral levels. In R. H. Woods (Ed.), *Encyclopedia of clinical assessment* (Vol. 2, pp. 911–918). San Francisco: Jossey-Bass.

DiLeo, J. H. (1973). *Children's drawings as diagnostic aids*. New York: Brunner/Mazel.

DiLeo, J. H. (1983). *Interpreting children's drawings*. New York: Brunner/Mazel.

Erikson, E. H. (1940). Studies in the interpretation of play: Part 1. Clinical observations of play disruption in young children. *Genetic Psychological Monograph, 22,* 557–671.

Erikson, E. H. (1963). *Childhood and society*. New York: W. W. Norton.

Evans, I. H. (1970). *Brewer's dictionary of phrase and fable* (Rev. ed.). New York: Harper & Row.

Feldman, G. C. (1999). Dissociation, repetition-compulsion, and the art of Frida Kahlo. *The Journal of the American Academy of Psychoanalysis, 27*(3), 387–396.

Fiske, J. (1870). *Myth and mythmakers: Old tales and superstitions interpreted by comparative mythology.* Urbana, IL: Project Gutenberg. URL: www.gutenberg.net/etext/1061.

Framo, J. L. (1992). *Family-of-origin therapy: An intergenerational approach.* New York: Brunner/Routledge.

Freud, A. (1946). *The ego and the mechanisms of defense* (Vol. II). Madison, CT: International Universities Press.

Freud, S. (1947). *Leonardo Da Vinci: A study in psychosexuality.* New York: Vintage Books.

Freud, S. (1950). *The interpretation of dreams.* New York: Random House.

Freud, S. (1959). *The standard edition of the complete psychological works of Sigmund Freud* (Vol. XX; J. Strachey, Trans.). London: Hogarth Press.

Freud, S. (1963). *Character and culture.* New York: Collier Books.

Freud, S. (1972). *The psychopathology of everyday life of Sigmund Freud* (A. Tyson, Trans.). New York: W. W. Norton.

Freud, S. (1989). Totem and taboo. In P. Gay (Ed.), *The Freud reader* (pp. 481–514). New York: W. W. Norton.

Gamwell, L., & Wells, R. (Eds.). (1989). *Sigmund Freud and art: His personal collection of antiquities.* Binghamton, NY: State University of New York.

Gardner, H. (1980). *Artful scribbles: The significance of children's drawings.* New York: Basic Books.

Gardner, R. A. (1986). *Therapeutic communication with children: The mutual storytelling technique.* Northvale, NJ: Jason Aronson.

Gesell, A., & Ilg, F. (1940). *The child from five to ten.* New York: Harper & Row.

Gesell, A., Ilg, F., & Ames, L. (1956). *Youth: The years from 10 to 16.* New York: Harper & Row.

Gilbert, J. (1980). *Interpreting psychological test data: Associating personality and behavior with responses to the Bender-Gestalt, Human Figure Drawing, Wechsler Adult Intelligence Scale, and the Rorschach ink blot tests* (Vol. 2). New York: Van Nostrand Reinhold.

Goethe, J. W. (1912). *Faust: A tragedy* (B. Taylor, Trans.). New York: Houghton Mifflin.

Goetze, H. (2001). Metaphorical stories. In H. G. Kaduson & C. E. Schaefer (Eds.), *101 more favorite play therapy techniques* (pp. 29–36). Northvale, NJ: Jason Aronson.

Goldstein, A. P., & Rawn, M. L. (1957). The validity of interpretive signs of aggression in the drawing of the human figure. *Journal of Clinical Psychology, 8*(2), 169–171.

Goldstein, E. G. (1984). *Ego psychology and social work practice.* New York: Free Press.

Goodenough, F. L. (1926). *Measurement of intelligence by drawings.* New York: Harcourt, Brace, & World.

Greenspan, S. I. (1979). Intelligence and Adaptation: An Integration of Psycho-analytic and Piagetian Developmental Psychology. *Psychological Issues*, Vol. 12, No. 3/4, Monograph 47/48. New York: International Universities Press.

Gutheil, E. A. (1951). *The handbook of dream analysis*. New York: Liveright.

Haley, J. (1976). *Problem-solving therapy*. San Francisco: Jossey-Bass.

Hall, C. S. (1954). *A primer of Freudian psychology*. New York: World Publishing.

Hammer, E. F. (1958). *The clinical application of projective drawings*. Springfield, IL: Charles C. Thomas.

Holman, A. M. (1983). *Family assessment: Tools for understanding and intervention*. Beverly Hills, CA: Sage.

Jacobson, W., & Cooper, A. M. (1993). Psychodynamic diagnosis in the era of the current DSMs. In N. Miller, L. Luborsky, J. Barber, & J. Docherty (Eds.), *Psychodynamic treatment research: A handbook for clinical practice* (pp. 109–126). New York: Basic Books.

Jamison, K. R. (1996). *Touched with fire: Manic depressive illness and the artistic temperament*. New York: Free Press.

Jung, C. G., & Kerenyi, C. (1963). *Essays on a science of mythology: The myths of the divine child and the divine maiden*. New York: Harper & Row.

Jung, C. G., VonFranz, M. L., Henderson, J. L., Jacobi, J., & Jaffe, A. (1964). *Man and his symbols*. New York: Doubleday.

Junge, M. (1985). The book about Daddy dying: A preventative art therapy technique to help families deal with the death of a family member. *Art Therapy*, 2(1), 4–10.

Kast, V. (1989). *The dynamics of symbols: Fundamentals of Jungian therapy* (S. Schwarz, Trans.). New York: Fromm International.

Kernberg, O. F. (1975). *Borderline conditions and pathological narcissism*. New York: Jason Aronson.

Kipfer, B. A. (1997). *The order of things: How everything in the world is organized*. New York: Random House.

Klein, M. (1946). Notes on some schizoid mechanisms. *International Journal of Psychoanalysis*, 27, 99–110.

Klepsch, M., & Logie, L. (1982). *Children draw and tell*. New York: Brunner/Mazel.

Knoff, H. M., & Prout, H. T. (1985). *Kinetic drawing system for family and school: A handbook*. Los Angeles: Western Psychological Services.

Kramer, E. (1971). *Art as therapy with children*. New York: Schocken Books.

Kwiatkowska, H. Y. (1978). *Family therapy and evaluation through art*. Springfield, IL: Charles C. Thomas.

Kymissis, M. D., & Halperin, D. A. (Eds.). (1996). *Group therapy with children and adolescents*. Washington, DC: American Psychiatric Press.

Landau, J. (1982). Therapy with families in cultural transition. In M. McGoldrick, J. K. Pearce, & J. Giordano (Eds.), *Ethnicity and family therapy* (pp. 552–573). New York: Guilford Press.

Landgarten, H. (1981). *Clinical art therapy: A comprehensive guide*. New York: Brunner/Mazel.

References

Landgarten, H. (1987). *Family art psychotherapy: A clinical guide and casebook*. New York: Brunner/Routledge.

Laughlin, H. P. (1970). *The ego and its defenses*. New York: Appleton-Century-Crofts.

Levick, M. F. (1983). *They could not talk and so they drew: Children's styles of coping and thinking*. Springfield, IL: Charles C. Thomas.

Lidz, T. (1976). *The person: His and her development throughout the life cycle*. New York: Basic Books.

Lowenfeld, V., & Brittain, W. L. (1982). *Creative and mental growth* (7th ed.). New York: Macmillan.

Luborsky, L., Barber, J. P., Binder, J., Curtis, J., Dahl, H., Horowitz, M., Perry, J. C., Schacht, T., Silberschatz, G., & Teller, V. (1993). Transference-related measures: A new class based on psychotherapy sessions. In N. Miller, L. Luborsky, J. Barber, & J. Docherty (Eds.), *Psychodynamic treatment research: A handbook for clinical practice* (pp. 326–341). New York: Basic Books.

Lund, L. K., Zimmerman, T. S., & Haddock, S. A. (2002). The theory, structure, and techniques for the inclusion of children in family therapy: A literature review. *Journal of Marital and Family Therapy, 28*(4), 445–454.

Machover, K. (1949). *Personality projection in the drawing of the human figure*. Springfield, IL: Charles C. Thomas.

Mahler, M. (1975). *The psychological birth of the human infant: Symbiosis and individuation*. New York: Basic Books.

Maier, H. W. (1978). *Three theories of child development*. New York: Harper & Row.

Malerstein, A. J., & Ahern, M. (1982). *A Piagetian model of character structure*. New York: Human Sciences Press.

Malmquist, C. P. (1985). *Handbook of adolescence*. New York: Jason Aronson.

Maslow, A. (1970). *Motivation and personality* (2nd ed.). New York: Harper & Row.

Matthews, B. (1986). *The Herder dictionary of symbols*. Wilmette, IL: Chiron Publications.

McGoldrick, M., Pearce, J. K., & Giordano, J. (Eds.). (1982). *Ethnicity and family therapy*. New York: Guilford Press.

McKay, M., Rogers, P. D., & McKay, J. (1989). *When anger hurts: Quieting the storm within*. Oakland, CA: New Harbinger Publications.

Meissner, W. W., Mack, J. E., & Semrad, E. K. (1975). Classical psychoanalysis. In Alfred M. Freedman, Harold I. Kaplan, & Benjamin K. Sadock (Eds.), *Comprehensive textbook of psychiatry* (2nd ed., Vol. 1, pp. 482–565). Baltimore: Williams and Wilkins.

Mills, J. C., & Crowley, R. J. (1986). *Therapeutic metaphors for children and the child within*. New York: Brunner/Mazel.

Minuchin, S. (1974). *Families and family therapy*. Cambridge, MA: Harvard University Press.

Monfils, M. (1985). Theme-centered group work with the mentally retarded. *The Journal of Contemporary Social Work, 66*(3), 177–184.

Naumburg, M. (1953). *Psychoneurotic art: Its function in psychotherapy*. New York: Grune & Stratton.

Nichols, M. (1984). *Family therapy: Concepts and methods*. New York: Gardner.

Office of Juvenile Justice and Delinquency Prevention. (1996). *Children in custody: Census of public and private juvenile detention, correctional, and shelter facilities 1994/5*. Washington, DC: Bureau of the Census.

Ogdon, R. O. (1977). *Psychodiagnostics and personality assessment: A handbook* (2nd ed.). Los Angeles: Western Psychological Services.

Opler, M. E. (1959). Family, anxiety, and religion in a community of North India. In Marvin K. Opler (Ed.), *Culture and mental health* (pp. 273–289). New York: Macmillan.

Oster, G. D., & Gould, P. (1987). *Using drawings in assessment and therapy: A guide for mental health professionals*. New York: Brunner/Mazel.

Payne, J. J. (1948). Comments on the analysis of chromatic drawings. In John N. Buck: The H-T-P technique: A qualitative and quantitative scoring manual. *Journal of Clinical Psychology, 5*, 1–120.

Perry, J. C. (1993). Defenses and their effects. In N. Miller, L. Luborsky, J. Barber, & J. Docherty (Eds.), *Psychodynamic treatment research: A handbook for clinical practice* (pp. 274–307). New York: Basic Books.

Piaget, J. (1952). *The origins of intelligence in children*. New York: International Universities Press.

Piaget, J., & Inhelder, B. (1971). *Mental imagery in the child*. New York: Basic Books.

Pinocchio (1986). The Walt Disney Company. New York: Penguin Books.

Reich, W. (1949). *Character analysis*. New York: Orgone Institute.

Reynolds, C. R. (1978). A quick scoring guide to the interpretation of children's Kinetic Family Drawings (KFD). *Psychology in the Schools, 15*, 489–492.

Rubin, J. (1984). *Child art therapy: Understanding and helping children grow through art* (2nd ed.). New York: Wiley.

Russell, B. (1921). *The analysis of mind*. Urbana, IL: Project Gutenberg. URL: www.gutenberg.net/etext/2529.

Sargent, D. A. (1974). Confinement and ego regression: Some consequences of enforced passivity. *International Journal of Psychiatry in Medicine, 5*(2), 143–151.

Sarnoff, C. A. (1987). *Psychotherapeutic strategies in the latency years*. Northvale, NJ: Jason Aronson.

Satir, V. (1983). *Conjoint family therapy* (Rev. ed.). Los Altos, CA: Science and Behavior Books.

Seitz, J. A. (01/18/2002). A cognitive-perceptual analysis of projective tests in children. Retrieved January 18, 2002, from www.york.cuny.edu/seitz/analysis.htm

Shattuck, R. (1996). *Forbidden knowledge: From Prometheus to pornography*. New York: St. Martin's Press.

Siegler, R. S. (1978). *Children's thinking: What develops*. New York: Wiley.

Smith, G. M. (1985). The collaborative drawing technique. *Journal of Personality Assessment, 49*, 582–585.

Souby, A. (1990). *Folktales from around the world: Tales of nature*. Austin, TX: Steck-Vaughn Company.

Stafford-Clark, D. (1966). *What Freud really said*. New York: Schocken Books.

Stone, I. (1937). *Dear Theo: The autobiography of Vincent Van Gogh*. New York: Signet.

Swensen, C. H. (1965). Empirical evaluations of human figure drawings. In B. I. Murstein (Ed.), *Handbook of projective techniques* (pp. 609–653). New York: Basic Books.

Tresidder, J. (2000). *Symbols and their meanings*. London: Duncan Baird.

Untermeyer, L., & Untermeyer, B. (Eds.). (1962). *Grimm's fairy tales* (Vols. 1–2). New York: Heritage Press.

Vass, Z. (01/18/2002). Perspectives on objective assessment of projective drawings. Retrieved January 18, 2002, from http://members.tripod.com/ZoltanVass/paper2000jcp.htm © 2001.

Wadeson, H. (1980). *Art psychotherapy*. New York: Wiley.

Whitmont, E. C. (1969). *The symbolic quest: Basic concepts of analytical psychology*. New York: G. P. Putnam's Sons.

Wittkower, E. D., & Rin, H. (1965). Transcultural psychology. *Archives of General Psychology, 13*(5), 387–394.

Wilson, B. (1985). The artistic tower of Babel: Sex traceable links between culture and graphic development. *Visual Arts Research, 11*(1), 90–103.

Yalom, I. D. (1983). *Inpatient group psychotherapy*. New York: Basic Books.

Yalom, I. D. (1985). *The theory and practice of group psychotherapy*. New York: Basic Books.

Yarish, S. S. (2002). URL: www.incrediblehulk.com/bannerhistory.html.

Index

About the CD-ROM

Introduction

This appendix provides you with information on the contents of the CD that accompanies this book. For the latest and greatest information, please refer to the ReadMe file located at the root of the CD.

System Requirements

- A computer with a processor running at 120 Mhz or faster
- At least 32 MB of total RAM installed on your computer; for best performance, we recommend at least 64 MB
- A CD-ROM drive

  NOTE: Many popular word processing programs are capable of reading Microsoft Word files. However, users should be aware that a slight amount of formatting might be lost when using a program other than Microsoft Word.

Using the CD with Windows

To install the items from the CD to your hard drive, follow these steps:

1. Insert the CD into your computer's CD-ROM drive.
2. The CD-ROM interface will appear. The interface provides a simple point-and-click way to explore the contents of the CD.

If the opening screen of the CD-ROM does not appear automatically, follow these steps to access the CD:

1. Click the Start button on the left end of the taskbar and then choose Run from the menu that pops up.
2. In the dialog box that appears, type **d:\setup.exe.** (If your CD-ROM drive is not drive d, fill in the appropriate letter in place of *d*.) This brings up the CD Interface described in the preceding set of steps.

What's on the CD

The following sections provide a summary of the software and other materials you'll find on the CD.

Figures

The CD-ROM includes full-color duplicates of some of the figures shown in the book in black and white. These figures are stored in the JPG image format, which should be viewable on any Windows or Macintosh computer.

eBook

Included on the CD-ROM is a bonus eBook that offers the mental health professional an improved understanding of the characteristics of children's art between the ages of 2 and 14. This eBook is stored in Adobe's PDF format. You will need to have software capable of viewing PDF files to view it. Many computers already have this software, however a copy of the free Adobe Reader has been included on the CD-ROM. You can download the latest version of it at **http://www.adobe.com**

Customer Care

If you have trouble with the CD-ROM, please call the Wiley Product Technical Support phone number at (800) 762-2974. Outside the United States, call 1(317) 572-3994. You can also contact Wiley Product Technical Support at **http://www.wiley.com/techsupport.** John Wiley & Sons will provide technical support only for installation and other general quality control items. For technical support on the applications themselves, consult the program's vendor or author.

To place additional orders or to request information about other Wiley products, please call (877) 762-2974.